FRONTIER INVESTOR

FRONTIER INVESTOR

HOW TO PROSPER IN THE NEXT EMERGING MARKETS

MARKO DIMITRIJEVIĆ

with TIMOTHY MISTELE

Columbia University Press
Publishers Since 1893
New York   Chichester, West Sussex
cup.columbia.edu

Library of Congress Cataloging-in-Publication Data
Names: Dimitrijević, Marko, author. | Mistele, Timothy, author.
Title: Frontier investor : how to prosper in the next emerging markets /
Marko Dimitrijević with Timothy Mistele.
Description: New York : Columbia University Press, 2017. | Series: Columbia
Business School publishing | Includes bibliographical references and index.
Identifiers: LCCN 2016000994 | ISBN 9780231170444 (cloth : alk. paper)
Subjects: LCSH: Investments—Developing countries. | Developing
countries—Investments, Foreign. | Portfolio management. | Risk management.
Classification: LCC HG5993 .D56 2016 | DDC 332.609172/4—dc23
LC record available at http://lccn.loc.gov/2016000994

Columbia University Press books are printed on permanent
and durable acid-free paper.

c 10 9 8 7 6 5 4 3 2 1

COVER DESIGN: NOAH ARLOW

CONTENTS

FRONTIER INVESTOR

Introduction

Imagine you are evaluating a new investment opportunity in a faraway country roiled by civil war and border disputes and considered by most to be rugged and lawless. Most people have heard of this country but have never actually been there, and most of the investment community sees this opportunity as far too risky and unorthodox. But you've traveled there, and you've seen for yourself that—despite the stories in the media—the infrastructure is sound and growing stronger, and many of the cities are stable and thriving. The investment opportunity offers mouth-watering upside, so long as the country truly is on a path toward growth and greater stability.

What do you do? Do you pursue the investment shunned by so many of your peers? Or do you look elsewhere, in more established markets, for an investment with more modest potential returns but considered a safer bet?

If I tell you the opportunity in question is in Rwanda, you'd likely choose the safer bet. But if I told you the opportunity was in the United States at end of the nineteenth century, suddenly the investment sounds more appealing. Just as it would if I said the opportunity was in South Korea in the 1960s. If you are one of the billion or so people in the world who own a Samsung phone, consider that as recently as 1966 its birthplace had an economy smaller than the Democratic Republic of the Congo. South Korea's economy is now forty times larger than DR Congo's and ranks as the thirteenth-largest economy in the world, ahead of Spain and just behind Australia.

Frontier markets, if governed properly, become emerging markets and, eventually, developed markets. Investors who understand and can take advantage of the investment opportunities in today's frontier markets can potentially bolster their portfolio returns and reduce portfolio risk.

How I Started Investing in Frontier Markets

Before we jump into the opportunity that frontier markets offer today, I want to briefly mention my first experiences with frontier countries, what led me to investment management, and how the difference between perception and reality molded my approach to investing.

Although I was born and raised in Switzerland, one of the most developed of developed markets, I come from a frontier market ancestry. My father was a refugee from Yugoslavia, leaving his birthplace and parents in 1954 to seek a better life in the West, first in Italy and then in Switzerland. As a child during the 1960s and 1970s, I traveled to Yugoslavia each summer to live with my grandparents. The summers of my early childhood were wonderful—what kid wouldn't want to spend the summer in a sunny seaside village being doted on by his grandparents?—but by my teenage years it began to dawn on me just how much the Yugoslavia I knew differed from its depiction in the Western media.

The Western press seemed enamored with the dictatorship of Marshal Tito and its "third way" between capitalism and Communism. Spending time in Yugoslavia, however, it was clear to me that the supposed third way was actually very close to the Soviet way. Even as a kid, I knew that phones were routinely tapped and that companies—in theory owned by the worker councils—were actually run by Communist Party heavyweights selected by the regime. But because Tito stood up to the Soviets, the Western press ignored his repression at home.

So I came to understand at an early age that the reality on the ground can be very different from the image projected by the media. I learned to believe my own eyes and to check the "facts" with on-the-ground research. This lesson has stayed with me during my travels beyond Europe while in college and throughout my career. On trips to Latin America in the late 1970s and early 1980s, to the People's Republic of the Congo in 1982, and to China in 1990, I noticed a similar gap between what I saw in the news and what I saw for myself. Some trips taught me that the on-the-ground reality can be significantly better than the perception from a distance; some trips, like those in the summers of my youth, taught me just the opposite.

My interest in investments began when I was an undergraduate at the University of Lausanne. I had saved a few hundred dollars, which were earning very little interest in my bank account. So I asked an advisor at the bank how my savings might earn a higher return, and he recommended a very safe REIT (real estate investment trust), whose shares traded like a stock and represented ownership in an income-producing real estate portfolio. This idea of owning a share of a company's future earnings stoked my curiosity, so I began reading about stocks and stock markets, and soon made a second investment—in Astra, an Argentine oil company (my first frontier market investment).

Astra's stock price was volatile and doubled soon after I bought it. I felt like a genius—until the stock plummeted a few weeks later. In the end, I did not make money on my Astra shares, but I did become intrigued by why stocks fluctuate, and this experience helped inform my decision to major in economics and business administration. I avidly consumed all the books and magazines on investing that I could find at my college's library, and I even suggested to the librarians several titles they ought to add to their collection. I was in the library devouring the latest issue of *Institutional Investor* magazine in the spring of my senior year in 1981 when I fell upon an article titled, "The World's Greatest Money Manager." This manager was a little-known (at the time) genius named George Soros. I was intrigued because he was Hungarian, and if an Eastern European was now the world's best money manager maybe I, too, had a shot at being a successful money manager. A decade later, I would meet him and have the honor of managing money for his fund.

Still fascinated by investing, after graduation I went to work for a small Swiss private bank. Switzerland is very small, and the Swiss tend to invest most of their money abroad; so my bank, like most in the country, practiced global investment management. This made the bank a fascinating training ground. And, being new, I got to ask a lot of questions. For example, every single portfolio in the bank held 5 to 10 percent—or more—in gold. When I asked why, I was told, "Well, because that's what you do—you always have to have some gold in the portfolio." That didn't make sense to me, as gold yielded nothing at a time of high single-digit yields in safe government bonds. I didn't understand why every client would need to hold the same asset, and why it must be held at all times.

One of the things I've come to appreciate most about investing is that you always find out if you're right or wrong. Sometimes you may be right for the wrong reasons, or you may be wrong for the right reasons, but the market always gives you a scorecard. There can be 999 people thinking one way and one person thinking another way, and that lone person could be right.

This idea was reinforced during one of my earliest adventures as a banker, a journey to Africa and the impoverished Communist state then known as the People's Republic of the Congo (now just the Republic of the Congo, Congo-Brazzaville, or Congo). Congo was an exotic place in the early 1980s. My employer (the Swiss bank) was involved in arranging a loan to a Congolese government agency, and as the junior banker I was designated my bank's representative. It was not a plum assignment, since no one else really wanted to travel there, but I'd never been to Africa and was very excited to go.

Even before setting foot in the country, though, I began to see red flags. I needed a visa to get into Congo, which I had to stop in Paris to pick up. Entering the fancy Parisian townhouse that housed the Congolese embassy, what immediately struck me was that, behind the façade, the embassy had very few employees and almost no furniture. I joined the dozens of other people forced to stand in the waiting area for hours to get our visas.

Finally arriving in the capital city of Brazzaville, there I was, twenty-three years old, with two forty-something senior bankers from the large French and Belgian commercial banks that were the lead lenders in the deal. Given my experience in Communist Yugoslavia and reports of Congo's widespread corruption, I had real doubts that any money lent to this country would ever be repaid. Spending time in Brazzaville only confirmed my suspicions. The ministry buildings that we visited had no electricity, the streets were riddled with potholes, and everything was disorganized. I was surprised that the bankers weren't concerned by this, and so I asked them, "Why would anyone lend money to this country in the first place? And why would you charge only LIBOR plus 2 percent to make such a risky loan?" (LIBOR is the interest rate that the highest-quality borrowers pay, so the banks were charging only 2 percent for the added Congo risk.) They told me that that was the market; that is what banks do. I thought it made no sense, but fortunately my bank was just arranging the loan for a fee—it was not putting its balance sheet at risk. These two senior bankers, on the other hand, represented the institutions that were providing the money and risking their shareholders' capital by making this loan. In fact, by 1986—just four years later—the debt of the People's Republic of the Congo was in default.

So that was my introduction to frontier markets credit. Since then, I have invested many times in the debt of developing markets, but I have always required high, equity-like potential returns. It makes no sense to settle for U.S. bond–type returns in environments that are hostile to bondholders, and I am amazed to see people still making the same mistake today: Lenders are extending thirty-year loans to countries like Honduras at inexplicably low rates. Déjà vu. I am interested in finding the flip side—times when lending money is a good idea, but no one will do it. I enjoy finding opportunities that few people—or sometimes nobody else—have really focused on, and that was one of the reasons I focused my career on mainstream emerging markets and the smaller emerging, or frontier, markets.

After working at the Swiss bank for two years, I went to America to pursue an MBA degree at Stanford. A lot of what I had done in Switzerland was macro focused—looking at whether we should invest in this country or that country, whether our investments should be in equities or bonds, whether currencies would appreciate or depreciate—and it was very good preparation for later investing in emerging markets. But one dimension I felt I hadn't learned at my previous job was microeconomic analysis, and that's where my Stanford Business School education was most rewarding.

I took many classes in investments, but one in particular still stays with me. It was taught by Professor Jack McDonald—who is still a dear friend, thirty years later—and it covered the bottom-up work needed to analyze companies. This whetted my appetite not only for looking at the macro side but also for finding the rare gems on the micro, or bottom-up, side. I came to realize that both the macro and the micro are very important in investing. Many people invest just in stocks. They analyze companies and say it doesn't matter what the market does, or what the country does, or what the currency does. Other people do macro investing, focusing just on currencies or fixed-income trends. I felt that the sweet spot was really where you combine the bottom-up micro and the top-down macro.

After Stanford I headed to Wall Street and worked briefly as an investment banker in high-yield debt and mergers and acquisitions, but my real passion was still investing. I was fortunate to then land a position working for two very smart investors, Nelson Peltz and Peter May, at Triangle Industries. There we looked at buying individual stocks, but also at buying whole companies. The four years I spent with them gave me great exposure to looking at companies, and because we were sometimes looking at buying entire businesses, I was encouraged to consider not only the company, but also the macro environment it was operating in and the possible changes to that environment over the next five, ten, or fifteen years. I once again learned the importance of this combination of top-down and bottom-up analysis.

Triangle moved to Palm Beach, Florida in 1988, where I launched my first investment management firm, Everest Capital, in 1990 with my own money plus additional capital from outside investors. I chose the name "Everest Capital" to convey a sense of strength and stability (and "Dimitrijević Capital," after all, would have been a mouthful for most investors to pronounce!), and I hoped to eventually build a strong team and not be just a one-man shop. My first outside investors were my two bosses at Triangle, which was a tremendous vote of confidence; my first boss out of university, at the Swiss bank, later became an investor as well.

When I started Everest Capital, I wanted to take an unconstrained approach to investing—to look at opportunities across all six continents. In the late 1980s and early 1990s, there were many promising opportunities in the United States and Europe, particularly in distressed debt. But much of the lowest-hanging fruit in the garden of global investments could be found in the certainly underresearched, mostly misunderstood, and oftentimes distressed emerging and frontier markets. Other hedge funds were focusing mainly on long/short U.S. equities, although a few were investing in western Europe, and a very few were focusing on emerging markets in Asia or Latin America. The lack of competition made emerging markets very attractive, and so my small team and I started focusing on countries in emerging Europe, Asia, and Latin America.[1]

Some of these countries were just becoming markets. Russia, for example, did not have a stock market; at first, it just had vouchers. China had only one class of stock that foreign investors could access (the B shares). Other countries had embryonic stock markets, even with already quite large economies. Although I looked at equities and debt in a variety of countries globally, by the mid-1990s I was focusing most of my time in emerging markets.

People think of emerging markets as very risky, when they are often less risky than one might perceive. Over the past two decades, the distinction between developed and emerging markets has eroded, as many of the emerging countries have come to dominate the developed ones in the size of their economies, the capitalization and liquidity of their stock markets, and the consistency of their economic policies and corporate governance. This is not only because emerging markets are improving in these areas; in recent years, many developed market governments have implemented erratic economic policies that rival those of a banana republic. In fact, since becoming a professional investor over thirty-five years ago I have experienced gains and losses—including some steep losses—in emerging markets, but it was a developed market, my home country of Switzerland, that hurt me the most (more on this in chapter 1). So while emerging markets have their share of ups and downs, developed markets do as well, which is why it is important to have exposure to both.

As a professional investor, I have invested in over 150 countries, including over 120 emerging and frontier markets, for my clients or myself. I have traveled to more than 100 countries, although I have not invested in all of them—some countries are still available only to browse, not to buy. Just as mainstream emerging markets have become a significant part of global investors' portfolios, I have no doubt that in the next fifteen years smaller emerging and frontier markets will become an important component as well. My goal in writing this book is to provide a guide for those who want to be in the forefront of this next wave of emerging markets investing.

What Is a Frontier Market?

Study any globe, and you will see that the world consists mainly of emerging and frontier markets—and most of these are frontier. The term "frontier market" was coined in 1992 by the World Bank's International Finance Corporation (IFC) to designate smaller, less liquid "emerging" emerging markets. Of the 195 "countries" in the world (the 193 members of the United Nations plus Hong Kong and Taiwan), thirty are developed markets and fourteen are what I call mainstream emerging markets; the remaining 151 I consider frontier.

I define *developed markets* as the twenty-three countries in the MSCI World Index plus seven smaller developed countries (Andorra, Iceland, Liechtenstein, Luxembourg, Malta, Monaco, and San Marino). I define *mainstream emerging markets* as the fourteen countries in the MSCI Emerging Markets Index with weightings of 1 percent or more at time of inclusion (Brazil, Chile, China, India, Indonesia, Korea, Malaysia, Mexico, Poland, Russia, South Africa, Taiwan, Thailand, and Turkey; these fourteen countries constitute 96 percent of the capitalization of the MSCI Emerging Markets Index). I define *frontier markets* as the nine smaller members of the MSCI Emerging Markets Index (Colombia, Czech Republic, Egypt, Greece, Hungary, Peru, Philippines, Qatar, and UAE) plus the other 142 countries in the world.

Many of these 151 countries are not even represented in any stock market indices, including so-called frontier market indices. Indeed, some frontier countries do not yet have any tradable securities at all. Although most frontier markets are low-income economies, some are actually quite rich. Many Middle Eastern countries are wealthy but considered frontier due to their small size or trading restrictions, such as bans on foreign ownership of shares. Saudi Arabia, for example, is one of the largest and richest frontier markets, but has been kept out of the MSCI Frontier and Emerging Markets indices because of its foreign ownership restrictions. Once this ban is lifted, Saudi Arabia, due to the size of its market, may skip inclusion in frontier market indices and move directly into emerging markets indices.

According to Google Trends, the popularity of the search term "frontier markets" is a small fraction of the popularity of "emerging markets." This could lead one to conclude—incorrectly, as I will argue— that frontier markets are just a marginal niche of the emerging markets universe. Granted, frontier markets are currently extremely underrepresented in most investment portfolios. Only a fraction of 1 percent of the assets of U.S. equity mutual funds are invested in frontier markets, even though these countries represent nearly 19 percent of global GDP when adjusted for purchasing power parity (more on this in chapter 1). Nineteen percent of the world's economy may not sound like that much, but it is bigger than the United States or China and over four times the size of Japan. As a group, frontier markets are an economy larger than the United States, but unless they suffer a natural or man-made tragedy like a tsunami or military coup, you hardly ever hear about them. Yet many of today's frontier markets are poised to make the journey from frontier to mainstream emerging market status, just as many of today's mainstream emerging markets have emerged and should soon join the ranks of developed markets. Today's frontier markets will be propelled to the mainstream by the tailwinds of fast economic growth, strong macroeconomic fundamentals, favorable demographics, and accelerated integration with the global economy.

And their transition to mainstream is a golden opportunity for the global investor. From an investment perspective, these markets are cheap; and if the history of mainstream emerging markets is any indication, their strong economic growth and improving fundamentals can drive earnings growth that could lead to attractive long-term returns. Frontier markets' low correlations with developed and emerging markets (as well as low correlations between individual frontier markets) also offer investors the risk-reducing benefit of portfolio diversification. Some frontier markets will languish, but many others will thrive. For these reasons, I think of frontier markets as the new emerging markets.

* * *

Here is the road map for the remainder of the book:

Part One—Why Invest in Frontier Markets?—explains why frontier market investments should be in every global investor's portfolio. Chapter 1 argues that emerging markets have emerged; the traditional distinctions between emerging and developed markets—the size of their economies, the size of their financial markets, corporate governance, government policies, even growth—have blurred or disappeared; the one surviving distinction between them is the price you pay for growth. Chapter 2 traces the path of evolution of yesterday's frontier markets into today's mainstream emerging markets and describes how today's frontier markets are on a similar track. Chapter 3 describes frontier markets' fast growth and argues that the strong macroeconomic fundamentals of today's frontier markets, including shrinking or well-financed current account deficits, lower debt levels, moderate inflation, and increased foreign direct investment, will help these markets mimic and accelerate the path to emergence taken by today's mainstream emerging markets. Chapter 4 highlights frontier markets' favorable demographics—large, young populations—and the one-time demographic dividend of modernization. Chapter 5 discusses the integration of today's frontier markets into the global economy and how technology and education in particular will accelerate this integration. Chapter 6 makes the case for frontier market equities on a valuation basis: They're cheap, they trade in inefficient markets, and they provide portfolio diversification.

Part Two—How to Invest in Frontier Markets—is a primer on frontier markets investing. It looks at how and where to invest in frontier markets today—directly, if possible, or indirectly, for investors who are unable to invest in frontier markets but still want to profit from their growth. Chapter 7 addresses the pitfalls of passive management of frontier market investments and makes the argument for active, and sometimes activist, frontier markets investing. Chapter 8 discusses do-it-yourself frontier markets equity investing for self-directed investors. Chapter 9 addresses investing in special situations in frontier distressed debt. Chapter 10 explores investments in privatizations, from the eastern European voucher programs of the 1990s to current efforts by many frontier markets to privatize state-owned assets.

In Part Three, I explore the Risks and Opportunities in Frontier Markets. Chapters 11 and 12 look at the political, macro- and microeconomic, and "headline" risks of investing in frontier markets, and which of these risks to avoid, which to mitigate, and which to embrace. Chapter 13 discusses megatrends that will inevitably drive major changes in frontier markets in the coming years and that may provide exciting investment opportunities. Chapter 14 ponders the possibility of future investment opportunities on the frontiers of frontier markets—those markets that are currently closed to outside investors—as well as in places beyond the frontier, such as Cuba, Iran, and North Korea. The appendix lists the 195 countries in the world today, 151 of which I categorize as frontier markets.

Many of the topics in this book came from ideas I originally wrote about in my quarterly investor letters and white papers as well other pieces I've published, and various past media articles and interviews.

* * *

For over thirty-five years, I have actively invested around the world across many market cycles in developed, emerging, and frontier markets. My experiences convince me that what mainstream emerging markets accomplished during this time can happen again in today's faster-growing frontier markets. Mainstream emerging markets are still a cheaper place than developed markets to invest for growth, but the even faster growth of frontier economies makes frontier markets an essential component of a globally diversified portfolio.

I

Why Invest in Frontier Markets?

1

Emerging Markets Have Emerged

On September 29, 2009, I wrote an article in the *Financial Times* announcing that the term "emerging markets" was obsolete. What traditionally distinguished developed from emerging markets, I argued, no longer applied. My assertion was bolstered by the Group of Twenty (G-20) meeting four days earlier in Pittsburgh, Pennsylvania, where the gathered finance ministers and central bank governors officially declared that the G-20 would replace the G-8 as "the premier forum for international economic cooperation" in recognition of the new reality of the global balance of power.[1] Of the nineteen countries in the G-20 (the European Union is the twentieth member), eleven are emerging or frontier markets.[2]

Emerging markets have emerged, and they are bigger and more integrated with the global economy than you might think.

- China now buys more cars than the United States, and in fact requires so many commodities to fuel its growth that in 2007 it bought a 15,000-foot mountain in Peru for the two billion tons of copper inside.
- The first non-American name on *Forbes*'s 2015 list of the world's most valuable brands is the Korean company Samsung, beating out Toyota, General Electric, Facebook, and Disney.[3]
- The countries with the most Facebook users after the United States are India, Brazil, Indonesia, and Mexico—all mainstream emerging markets.[4]

As emerging markets become more like developed markets, investors have the opportunity to enhance their portfolios by increasing their exposure to emerging markets. But there's a flip side: The characteristics that once made emerging markets so appealing to the adventurous investor (their potential for much greater growth at a much lower price, for instance) are also beginning to fade. Those investors will want to turn their attention to frontier markets, to which I devote the rest of the book. But I'd like to start with a look at the emergence of emerging markets, which will help put into context both the possibilities and the challenges that frontier markets present.

Although emerging markets are growing in importance, they are still underrepresented in existing global benchmarks. Index provider MSCI's All Country World Index (ACWI), comprising twenty-three developed and twenty-three emerging countries as of this writing, has given increasing weight to emerging markets over the last quarter century. Its weightings, however, would still seem to indicate that emerging markets are not very important—warranting some interest, but considerably less so than developed markets. In fact, nine of the twenty-three countries that MSCI considers emerging are given so little weight in its indices that I categorize them as frontier markets. In 1990, one year after the fall of the Berlin Wall and shortly after Deng Xiaoping liberalized China, emerging markets represented only 2 percent of the MSCI ACWI. Twenty-five years later, the emerging markets weighting in the ACWI had grown to only 9 percent—a grossly insufficient representation of their true importance in the global economy (figure 1.1).

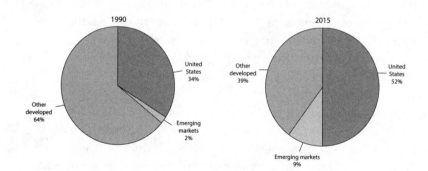

Figure 1.1
MSCI ACWI weightings, 1990 and 2015. *Source*: MSCI.

I have argued for many years that this underrepresentation of emerging markets in global benchmarks is a mistake. Because of this artificial classification—"emerging markets"—these markets are much smaller in investors' portfolios than their importance and the magnitude of their opportunity warrant, which could lead to the long-term underperformance of these portfolios. Given the lucrative opportunity of these markets, why are they so neglected? The historical arguments against emerging market investments usually fall into four broad categories: the size of their economies, the size and volatility of their markets, their government policies, and their corporate governance. I believe, however, that these differences are in the process of blurring or have disappeared completely.

The Size of Emerging Market Economies

Emerging market economies are no longer the insignificant players in the global economy that they once were. Eighty-seven percent of the world's population now lives in emerging markets, including over half in the fourteen mainstream emerging markets. And the economies of emerging markets are in aggregate bigger than developed markets. The rapid growth of emerging markets in the past two decades has made any distinction based on size largely obsolete.

In 1990, when emerging markets were just a sliver of the MSCI ACWI, they represented 21 percent of the world economy (figure 1.2). The four largest emerging market economies—Brazil, Russia, India, and China (the BRICs)—accounted for 8 percent. Although the United States and Europe were the dominant economies back then, and Japan was large as well, emerging markets were already a meaningful portion of the world's GDP. By 2014, emerging market economies had grown substantially, with almost a third of the world's GDP (measured in U.S. dollars) generated in the mainstream emerging markets. Taken together, the BRICs accounted for 21 percent, the majority of which was China. But while investor attention has focused on the BRICs, the remaining mainstream emerging and frontier market countries are just as large a share of the global economy. Based on U.S. dollar GDP, non-BRIC emerging market equity investments should nearly match the size of a typical global investor's investments in the United States.

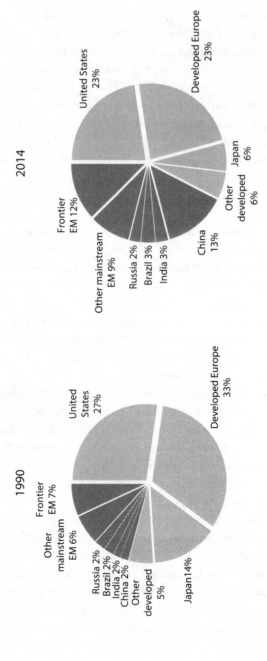

Figure 1.2
Share of world economy based on US$ GDP, 1990 and 2014. *Source:* IMF; World Bank.

The Power of Purchasing Power Parity

Although this measure of global GDP shows the growing importance of emerging markets, it actually still underrepresents these markets because it is calculated using current U.S. dollars. Depending on the local currency, this methodology may overvalue or undervalue a country's (or an entire region's) true percentage of world GDP. Those who consider the euro to be overvalued would see that as a reason why developed Europe's GDP in U.S. dollars is so large. Conversely, many Asian countries keep their currencies undervalued through government interventions, so their GDPs when measured in U.S. dollars understate their true contributions to the global economy.

Rather than using U.S. dollar GDP to measure the size of an economy, I find it more useful to look at economies adjusted for purchasing power parity (PPP), where one "international dollar" purchases the same quantity of goods and services in all countries. This is a more accurate way of looking at the world, because it accommodates not only exchange rate undervaluations and overvaluations, but also the fact that items in an emerging market may sell for a fraction of what they do in a developed market. If income in emerging country E is half the income in developed country D, but the cost of a phone call in E is only one-quarter the cost in D, then phone calls are twice as affordable in E as in D; the growth potential for a phone company in E is therefore much larger than for a phone company in D.

Figure 1.3 illustrates how PPP-adjusted GDP reflects what I consider the true size of emerging markets: Emerging and frontier markets now generate 60 percent of the world's PPP-adjusted GDP, including 41 percent by the mainstream emerging markets. In fact, the BRICs are together bigger than all the developed markets in the world combined excluding the United States. On a PPP basis, China is now larger than the United States; India is 50 percent larger than Japan; Russia, Brazil, and Indonesia are larger than France or the United Kingdom; and Mexico is larger than Italy (figure 1.4).

At nearly 30 percent of the global economy, the BRICs are obviously important. But what is more interesting to me is that the ten non-BRIC mainstream emerging markets (Mexico, Indonesia, and Korea, for example), while not large individually, are together 12 percent of global GDP. This makes their contribution, collectively, close to one-and-a-half times the combined economies of all the developed markets outside of Europe and the United States (Australia, Canada, Hong Kong, Israel, Japan, New Zealand, and Singapore).

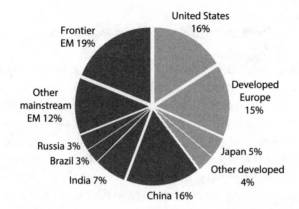

Figure 1.3
Emerging markets are now 60 percent of global PPP-adjusted GDP. *Source*: IMF;
Authors.

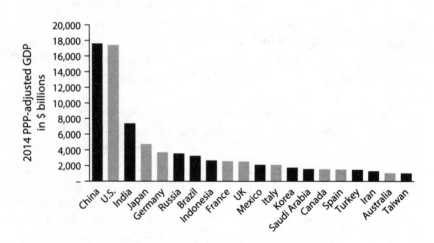

Figure 1.4
Emerging/frontier markets are eleven of the top twenty largest economies.
Source: IMF.

Distinguishing developed from emerging markets based on the size of their economies alone no longer makes sense. For investors, this is a very important point to keep in mind.

The Size of Emerging Market Financial Markets

Investors often think of emerging markets as having small, illiquid financial markets. But increasingly, emerging markets are larger and more liquid than many developed markets, with similar volatility.

Market Capitalization and Liquidity

The market capitalization of emerging markets has increased substantially over the last two decades, propelled by much faster economic growth than in developed economies. The listing of many private and government-owned companies during this period has also boosted the overall size of emerging equity markets. As a result, emerging markets are now larger and more liquid than ever before, making it easier for investors to increase their emerging markets exposure.

Mainstream emerging markets, in total, currently represent 22 percent of the world's equity market capitalization, up from 10 percent a decade ago. Mainstream emerging markets are truly "regular" markets with nearly $16 trillion of investable assets, and an investor can take advantage of this. Some of the larger emerging markets are viable alternatives to better-known developed markets. China's equity market, for instance, is now larger than Japan's; Korea and Taiwan, two emerging industrial powerhouses, are together larger than Germany; and Brazil is as large as Spain.

Liquidity in emerging markets has also increased dramatically. In 2014, Chinese markets traded more dollar volume than the NYSE (several times more during the first half of 2015, in fact), and Korea, India, Brazil, and Taiwan each traded more than Switzerland. Liquidity is clearly more than adequate in many of these markets.

Even for active investors who do not try to passively mimic a benchmark, I believe indices like the MSCI ACWI do influence the way they look at the world. The United States is by far the most overrepresented market, with a much larger weighting in the MSCI ACWI than its share of global

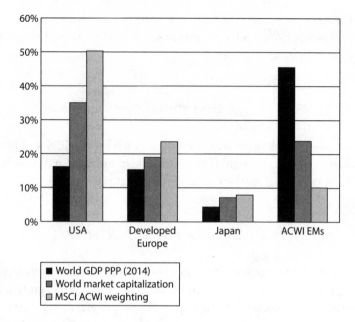

Figure 1.5
Benchmarks are not doing you a favor: weightings by GDP, market capitalization, and index. *Source*: IMF; World Bank; Bloomberg; MSCI.

market capitalization or GDP would warrant (figure 1.5). Europe and Japan are also overrepresented, but not as egregiously.

Meanwhile, the twenty-three emerging markets in the MSCI ACWI (the fourteen I consider mainstream emerging plus the nine smaller markets I consider frontier), which represent 45 percent of the world's GDP on a PPP-adjusted basis and 23 percent of world market capitalization, account for just 9 percent of the index. Benchmarks are therefore placing investors at a disadvantage as they underrepresent the current and future impact of emerging markets. Anyone investing based on benchmarks is looking in the rear-view mirror.

Volatility

In addition to market capitalization and liquidity, some investors cite volatility as an argument against investing in emerging markets. This common misperception is costing them money. Based on quantitative volatility measures, emerging markets and developed markets look much the same.

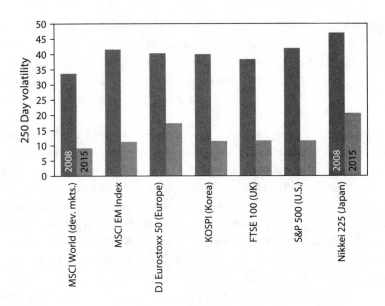

Figure 1.6
Emerging markets' volatility similar to developed markets during and after crisis.
Source: Bloomberg.

In 2015, emerging markets as a whole were less volatile than Europe, and volatility in individual markets such as Korea matched the volatility of the United Kingdom and the United States (figure 1.6).

Interestingly, in the extreme market environment of 2008, emerging markets were about as volatile as the S&P 500 and the major European indices, and less volatile than Japan; all of these markets' volatilities were in the high thirties to mid-forties. Even in the midst of a global financial crisis, emerging markets behaved similarly to developed markets.

Emerging markets are comparable to developed markets in size, liquidity, and volatility, and the prudent investor should not discriminate against them based on these criteria.

Government Policy

A third line of argument against emerging markets is that their economic policies are unpredictable. Many emerging markets in the past intervened to manage their currencies—weakening them to boost exports, for instance—and were criticized for this by the developed markets and the IMF. Similarly, several Asian countries in 1997–1998 suspended short selling and took other measures to support their stock exchanges. When countries in Latin America and Asia implemented such measures, the United States and Europe lectured them on government policy best practices, urging them to let the free market take care of itself.

Ironically, having criticized emerging government interventions in the 1990s, many developed countries resorted to similar interventions in the 2000s. During the financial crisis of 2008, the United States, Italy, and many others restricted the short selling of bank stocks or, in some cases, all stocks across their exchanges; these previously pilloried restrictions were now considered prudent efforts to stabilize the markets. The U.S. government's decision to engineer the rescue of Bear Stearns, for example, because it was "systematically important," only to decide to let the much larger Lehman Brothers fail a few months later, demonstrates an alarming lack of consistency in policy making. So too does the apparent favoritism toward certain constituencies—such as unions, in the nationalization and appropriation of GM and Chrysler from their existing bondholders— despite established legal precedent. Such policies seem more befiting a country like Venezuela, a pariah among emerging markets that MSCI kicked out of its emerging markets index in 2006. More recently, Japan has intervened aggressively to weaken its currency, and few voices outside of the U.S. automakers have complained; some even lauded its efforts to staunch its deflationary spiral.

Another example is the capricious actions of the Swiss government in early 2015, which caused losses for investors in my global fund (including myself and my family, the fund's largest investors). Faced with an overvalued currency that was hurting Swiss exporters, the Swiss National Bank (SNB) in September 2011 announced that it was "prepared to purchase foreign exchange in unlimited quantities" to keep the Swiss franc above 1.20 to the euro, a policy it upheld for three years.[5] I strongly believed that the SNB would continue to make it costly to hold Swiss francs, which would weaken the franc in the near and long term; many investors worldwide, I believe, felt the same way. On December 18, 2014, the SNB introduced negative interest rates to make it less attractive to hold the Swiss franc, at which time the Chairman of the SNB's governing board reiterated, "the SNB remains committed to purchasing unlimited quantities of foreign currency to enforce the minimum exchange rate with the utmost determination."[6] I expected that the SNB would introduce additional measures to weaken the franc, and public reports have suggested that many economists and forecasters expected the same.

Contrary to its own repeated public statements over a long period, however, the SNB decided suddenly and without notice on January 15, 2015, to remove the floor on the franc's exchange rate against the euro. Indeed, just days prior to this surprise action, the SNB had reiterated publicly that it would continue its policy. On, January 12, 2015, Jean-Pierre Danthine, vice-chairman of the SNB, stated, as part of an interview on Swiss television, "We are convinced that the minimum exchange rate must remain the pillar of our monetary policy."[7] Reports suggest that the consensus of analysts, economists, and currency strategists was that the SNB would retain the minimum exchange rate, and that the SNB's recent imposition of a negative interest rate on deposits was evidence of that commitment. In fact, none of the twenty-two economists surveyed by Bloomberg News between January 9 and January 14, 2015, expected the SNB would remove the peg in 2015. I believed the SNB would maintain the peg for many months and, if and when it removed the peg, it would do so in a managed and gradual way.

Immediately after the removal of the floor, the Swiss franc strengthened 30 percent, stunning the market. The euro plummeted from 1.20 to 0.78 francs, subsequently stabilizing that day at around 1.02. The rapid change in the Swiss franc's value in one day was unprecedented. Goldman Sachs's CFO Harvey Schwartz characterized the daily change in the euro–Swiss franc exchange rate as "something like a 20-plus standard deviation move."[8]

After the SNB removed the peg, the Swiss stock market plunged, Swiss ten-year bond yields dropped below zero, and economists drastically lowered their growth forecasts for the Swiss economy. The SNB was roundly criticized for reneging on its commitment to maintain its floor on the franc and forgoing an orderly revaluation. To me, it was as if Janet Yellen had publicly committed to maintain current rates, then three days later raised rates 5 percent. In this case, Switzerland—one of the world's most developed economies—mimicked the worst caricature of a banana republic's economic mismanagement. But the damage was done.

To this day, developed market central banks are keeping interest rates artificially low, while emerging markets are implementing more orthodox rate-setting policies. Uneven and erratic policy decisions like these across the developed world raise the question of whether developed markets are leading by example. Incidentally, this about-face in developed market policy making has not gone unnoticed in the emerging world. In July 2009,

Timothy Geithner, then the U.S. Treasury secretary, traveled to China to give a speech at Peking University. He was met with laughter when he lectured students on the soundness of U.S. Treasury bonds. This was a sign of the times—how the world's perspective has changed.

It no longer seems that developed market government policies are particularly astute or that they are necessarily good models for emerging markets to follow. I believe that the combination of starkly improved government policies in emerging markets and inconsistent policy making in developed markets has led to a blurring of the distinction between the historically prudent, responsible, and market-friendly policy making of the United States and Europe versus the rest of the world.

Corporate Governance

Finally, improved corporate governance practices in emerging markets have largely laid to rest the view that emerging market companies are run less professionally or ethically than businesses in developed markets.

Developed market managements can no longer claim to practice corporate stewardship superior to that of their counterparts in emerging markets. Not only has corporate governance in emerging markets risen to the standards of developed markets, but the developed markets' aura of quality has also diminished. A long list of publicly traded companies in the United States, Europe, and Japan either committed outright fraud, manipulated their books, or abused shareholders (Enron, WorldCom, Parmalat, Countrywide Credit, and most recently Toshiba and VW represent only a handful of examples in this regard). Some took advantage of loopholes that, even if they were technically legal, were certainly unethical (e.g., Porsche) or otherwise exhibited very poor judgment (rarely in emerging markets, for instance, do we see the bloated compensation packages and bonuses of the West). Outside of the well-publicized accounting scandals at some Chinese companies listed in the United States and Canada, I can think of only a very few cases—the Indian company Satyam, which committed outright Enron-type fraud, comes to mind—where shareholders in an emerging market company have had such problems.

The belief that companies in the United States, western Europe, or Japan are better managed than those in emerging markets is also no longer valid. In the midst of the Asian crisis in the mid-1990s, many emerging market companies succumbed due to poor management, but we see this less often today. During the global financial crisis, for example, emerging market banks were much better managed than banks in the United States and western Europe. In my travels, I have met hundreds of management teams of emerging market companies, and it is impressive to see how quickly they have adopted best practices in disclosure and governance, and a focus on enhancing return on capital and creating shareholder value. Many of these current managers graduated from U.S. or western European universities and business schools, and in meetings, I've noticed little that differentiates them from managers in developed markets. The distinction in quality of management between emerging and developed markets is largely gone.

Growth

Against the many opposing arguments, the main historical argument for investing in emerging markets was their superior growth. But this, too, is changing.

For the twenty years from 1994 to 2014, today's mainstream emerging market economies expanded at an annualized rate of over 9 percent in nominal U.S. dollar terms—more than twice the 3.6 percent average growth rate of developed markets over the same period. Businesses also grew their revenues and earnings faster in emerging markets than in developed markets during this time. This makes sense—starting from a lower basis, many of these countries' needs had not yet been met, so consumption and investment grew faster. From 2004 to 2010, emerging market companies (as measured by the MSCI Emerging Markets Index) grew revenues at 11 percent and net income at 10 percent annually, over twice as fast as developed market companies (as measured by the MSCI World Index).

Now, however, the differential in revenue and earnings growth between emerging and developed markets has narrowed. From 2010 to 2015, earnings growth turned negative in emerging markets and sputtered in developed markets, and consensus estimated earnings growth for 2017 and 2018 are in the 11 to 12 percent range for both groups.

But what still distinguishes mainstream emerging markets as of this writing is the price you pay for growth. Emerging markets in early 2016 traded at under ten times estimated 2017 earnings versus 13.5 times estimated 2017 earnings for developed markets. Thus an investor could buy the same growth rate in emerging markets at an almost 30 percent discount.

* * *

Emerging markets represent over half of the world's economy. Their equity markets are large and liquid with volatility similar to that of developed equity markets. Their government economic policies and corporate governance are at par with, or superior to, those of developed markets. The distinctions between developed and emerging markets have disappeared. Today's mainstream emerging markets have emerged, and while investors can usually pay less for growth in emerging markets, this too will likely change in the coming years.

It is thus time to focus on the frontier—"emerging" emerging—markets.

2

Frontier Markets Are the New Emerging Markets

The first time I traveled to Turkey was as a tourist in May 1981. Back then, Turkey was a rather exotic destination (recall the movie *Midnight Express*, and if you haven't seen it, rent it—it's thrilling). I had driven from Switzerland, crossing Italy and stopping in what was then Yugoslavia to visit relatives. I continued on to Bulgaria, where I was stopped for speeding, even though the roads there were so bad that speeding was impossible (the policeman just wanted a bribe), and then into Turkey. I finally arrived in Istanbul in the afternoon, not realizing that the military had imposed a curfew. (From 1978 until 1983, much—and sometimes all—of the country was under martial law.) I had to hurry to reach my hotel in Istanbul before the curfew, or I would face arrest. Turkey was a dicey place to visit, let alone invest. (Strict capital controls for foreigners would have prevented me from investing at the time anyway, and the Istanbul Stock Exchange only opened in 1986.) I certainly was not in Switzerland anymore.

Contrast my first visit in 1981 to today: Turkey's military is firmly under the rule of the executive branch, and thanks to the economic liberalization that came with the return to democracy in the 1980s, Turkey has a vibrant economy and has experienced strong growth that has lifted GDP per capita from $1,200 in 1984 to over $10,000 in 2014. By opening its capital markets to outsiders, Turkey now has some of the deepest and most liquid equity and debt markets in the emerging markets universe, attracting investors from around the world. Urbanization has increased from 44 percent of the population to 75 percent, and the country's infrastructure has kept pace. Turkey now has over 350,000 kilometers of paved roads and highways, up from 60,000 when I first visited there (which would have made my drive much more pleasant). Two of Turkey's airports now rank in the top twenty-five in the world in international passenger traffic, and Turkey is building a new Istanbul airport that when operational will have the second-largest passenger capacity in the world behind a new airport that is being planned for Beijing.[1] So there has been profound change during this period, as Turkey made its transition from frontier to mainstream emerging market. I would note that while Turkey is thriving economically, politically all is not well, which goes to show that economic growth is not necessarily incompatible with decreased democracy (or even a lack of democracy, as China has proven).

Countries like Turkey serve as historical precedents for the evolution from a frontier market to a mainstream emerging market and have laid a path for today's frontier markets to follow. This path includes:

- Increased economic freedom, leading to greater economic and political stability, and the development of domestic capital markets
- Increased urbanization, as higher employment in the industrial and service sectors brings jobs and workers to the cities
- Improved infrastructure
- Greater wealth, leading to a rising middle class and increased consumer demand
- Stronger corporate governance
- Strong stock market performance (largely due to stronger governance)

Frontier markets that follow this path will become the next mainstream emerging markets. Indeed, with the example of those that went before them and with access to modern technology, they may emerge even faster than their predecessors did.

Freer Economies

Freer economies lead to a virtuous cycle of economic growth and increased standards of living. Economic freedom is essentially the right to acquire, use, and sell private property. One of the pivotal changes that allowed many of today's mainstream emerging markets to rise from frontier market status was the introduction of free markets and the promotion of capitalism over centrally planned economies, including the privatization of formerly state-owned assets.

The Heritage Foundation's Index of Economic Freedom measures ten components of economic freedom related to rule of law, size of government, regulatory efficiency, and market openness. Its studies show that countries with higher levels of economic freedom have greater economic growth, higher per-capita incomes, better health care, and higher levels of education, among other advantages.[2] Of today's mainstream emerging markets, Poland, India, Chile, and Brazil showed the most improvement in economic freedom from the index's inception in 1995 to 2015. Only Thailand showed a significant decrease over that period. Today's frontier markets have, on average, levels of economic freedom near what today's mainstream emerging markets had twenty years ago (see figure 2.1).

Strong evidence also indicates that allowing foreigners to invest in equities has a positive effect, not only on emerging market equity returns but also on economic growth.[3] According to a paper by Columbia professor Geert Bekaert and colleagues, "Equity market liberalizations increase

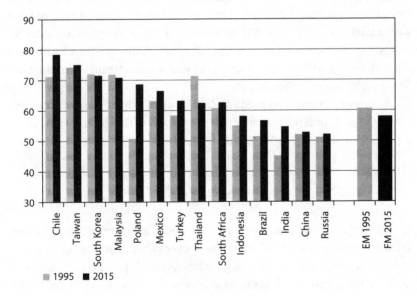

Figure 2.1
Index of Economic Freedom. *Source*: Heritage Foundation.

subsequent average annual real economic growth by about 1 percent, even after controlling for other variables that are commonly used in the economic growth literature."[4]

Freer economies also lead to greater economic stability (i.e., low inflation and full employment), in particular a reduction in unemployment for women and younger workers.[5] And economic stability in turn engenders political stability. Political stability and economic stability are in fact mutually reinforcing; as one increases, the other follows.[6]

Political stability, like economic freedom, usually—with notable exceptions—takes the form of more democracy over autocracy. The Center for Systemic Peace uses a measurement called a "polity score" to rate countries from complete autocracy (–10) to complete democracy (+10). It has given polity scores of ten to all of the twenty-three developed markets in its universe (it does not rank Hong Kong), with three exceptions: Belgium scores an 8, France a 9, and Singapore, the outlier, a –2. Four countries currently earn a polity score of –10: North Korea, Bahrain, Qatar, and Saudi Arabia. China's polity score has barely budged from –8 at the founding of the People's Republic in 1949 to –7 today, which shows that political stability and autocracy are not mutually exclusive.

Today's mainstream emerging markets have an average polity score of 6.4 (dragged down from 7.1 by Thailand's recent tumble from 7 to –3), up from 2.9 in 1990 and –1.2 in 1985. Chile, Poland, and Taiwan all evolved from autocracies in the early 1980s (polity scores of –7) to complete democracies by 2006 (polity scores of +10), where they remain. Today's frontier markets have an average polity score of 3.2, about where mainstream emerging markets were in 1990 (see figure 2.2).

Greater economic and political stability gives private owners of companies increased confidence to invest in the growth of their enterprises, creating jobs and boosting employment in the industrial and service sectors.

Urbanization

Over half the world's population now resides in urban areas, up from one-third in 1960. By 2050, it will increase to over two-thirds (see figure 2.3).

As demand for services and manufactured products grows—and as a further mechanized agrarian economy displaces excess rural laborers—factories and service centers replace farms as a developing country's major employers. These new employers are almost always in or near major

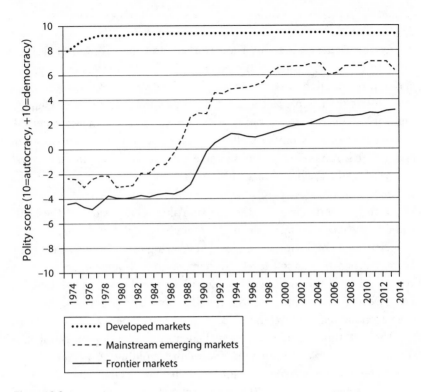

Figure 2.2
Increasing democracy over time. *Source*: Center for Systemic Peace.

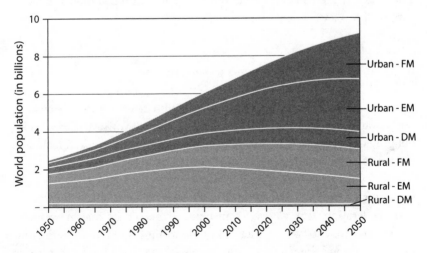

Figure 2.3
World population, urban and rural. *Source*: UN Department of Economic and Social Affairs, Population Division (2012); Authors.

population centers, attracting rural workers and increasing urbanization rates. In China, for instance, the percentage of total workers employed in agriculture shrank by half in the last thirty-five years, from 69 percent in 1980 to less than 35 percent today. Conversely, the percentage of Chinese living in urban areas grew from 19 percent to 55 percent in the same period. Korea experienced a similar shift; the percentage of workers employed in agriculture shrank sharply from 34 percent of the workforce in 1980 to just 5 percent, while the percentage of Koreans living in urban areas grew during that period from 57 percent of the population to 84 percent.

Today's frontier markets will see similar migrations out of the fields and into the cities. Bangladesh and Vietnam have high but shrinking levels of agricultural employment, and low but growing urbanization rates. Their current urban population levels, 34 percent and 33 percent, respectively, are very close to the 30 percent average urban population level of the UN's Least Developed Countries (LDC) classification. By comparison, the average urban population level in OECD countries is 80 percent.

Urbanization provides a host of benefits to a developing country: it promotes economic development (600 cities, holding 20 percent of the world's population, generate 60 percent of the world's GDP),[7] better education, and better healthcare.[8] The challenge to frontier urban planners is to get the infrastructure right. Because the speed of urbanization has accelerated with improvements in technology and transportation, improperly planned cities are vulnerable to everything from noise pollution and traffic jams to slums and violent crime.

Improved Infrastructure

Increased urbanization requires improved infrastructure: roads, railways, ports, water and sewer systems, and electrical grids. Infrastructure build-out provides immediate improvements in standards of living and facilitates economic growth to improve future living standards.

Today's mainstream emerging markets paved their way out of frontier status with millions of kilometers of roads. According to International Road Federation data, Korea, for instance, increased its road network by 85 percent, from 56,700 kilometers in 1990 to 105,000 kilometers in 2009, including 4,000 kilometers of expressways. These roads were necessary to support Korea's fivefold increase in passenger and other motor vehicles over that time. That hallmark of frontier travel—the proverbial rutted dirt road clinging to the side of a mountain with no guard rail—is being replaced by pristine, multilane expressways. Outside of San José, Costa Rica's digital road signs even promote its traffic department's Twitter feed.

Water systems are also improving rapidly. Access to "improved" drinking water sources (defined as those likely to be protected from contamination, like piped water, public taps, and protected wells) and sanitation facilities (like flush toilets, piped sewer systems, and septic tanks) are a given in the developed world, with availability of over 99 percent in every country. Improved drinking water is a near given in mainstream emerging markets as well, available to 95 percent of a country's population on average. Those with access to improved water sources in China grew from 70 percent in 1992 to 92 percent in 2012 and in India from 72 percent to 93 percent over the same period. By contrast, on average only 65 percent of Sub-Saharan African populations had improved water access in 2012. As Figure 2.4 shows, the biggest percentage gains in access to improved infrastructure have come in rural areas, but large gains in access for the overall population are also due to the migration from rural to urban areas, where infrastructure build-out is much more efficient on a per capita basis.

Infrastructure also includes telecommunications, and the explosion in teledensity growth (teledensity, or telephone density, is measured by the number of phone lines per 100 people) in emerging and frontier markets over the past decade has been astounding, due almost exclusively to the proliferation of mobile phones. The cost of installing mobile phone infrastructure is a small fraction of the cost of building equivalent fixed- or land-line capacity, particularly in rural areas, which is why most emerging

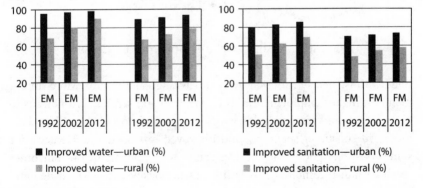

Figure 2.4
Access to improved water and sanitation. *Source*: World Health Organization; Authors.

markets (other than Korea) have very low fixed-line teledensity; India, for example, has fewer than three fixed phone lines per 100 people. Mobile technology has allowed frontier markets to increase teledensity from an average of less than eight phone lines per 100 people in 1993, to nearly 100 by 2013. More on this in chapter 5.

Investors can profit from these infrastructure build-outs. In the 1990s, I invested in a number of emerging market infrastructure opportunities including several electric utility and telecom company privatizations in Latin America. In the mid-2000s, we profited from several Emerging Asian infrastructure companies such as Korea's Doosan Heavy Industries & Construction, the world leader in desalination plant construction and a builder of power plants, as this company helped fast-growing Middle East countries build out their power and water infrastructure. Today, with infrastructure build-out accelerating across Africa, investors can look to a number of recently listed frontier market infrastructure plays. Dangote Cement, Nigeria's largest cement manufacturer, is expanding operations into fourteen other African nations. It went public in October 2010 and is now the largest company on the Nigerian Stock Exchange. Shares in the much smaller Ugandan electricity distribution company Umeme have compounded at over 38 percent per year (29 percent in U.S. dollars) including reinvested dividends since its IPO on the Uganda Securities Exchange in November 2012 through 2015. Umeme's earnings are forecast to grow at over 25 percent per year for the next several years, yet the company trades at only six times estimated 2016 earnings. And in 2014 the Portuguese engineering and construction firm Mota-Engil, builder of ports, railways, and roadways, listed its African subsidiary, a pure play on infrastructure build-out in a dozen African countries.

Greater Wealth and a Rising Middle Class

Better infrastructure is driven by, and drives, greater wealth. More fundamentally, higher employment in the industrial and service sectors leads to higher wages and greater wealth, which in turn leads to a rising middle class, increased consumer spending, and improved infrastructure. Demand for some consumer goods and services can grow exponentially once incomes reach certain thresholds. This is the classic hockey-stick-shaped demand curve, where demand for a product (e.g., automobiles) gradually rises to an inflection point at a certain income level and then spikes dramatically.

Such was the case for Korea in the 1980s and China in the 2000s. Once their PPP-adjusted per capita GDPs approached $4,000 (a generally accepted, but by no means universal, threshold for the "middle class" in developing markets), they saw annual vehicle sales accelerate sharply, rising over fivefold in the following decade. China's vehicles per thousand people doubled from eighteen in 2003 to thirty-eight in 2008, and doubled again to seventy-nine by 2012 (although these numbers vary greatly by province; in general, China's eastern provinces have many more cars per capita than the western provinces). In India, PPP-adjusted GDP per capita reached $3,900 in 2012, when the number of vehicles per thousand people was about twenty (see Figure 2.5). India could see a sharp upturn in vehicle penetration in the coming years, as could frontier markets like Vietnam, Pakistan, and Nigeria, whose per capita GDPs are at or approaching the $4,000 level and whose current vehicle penetration rates are in the low to mid–double digits per thousand people. Most mainstream emerging and frontier markets have a long way to go to reach the per capita car ownership levels in developed markets: the average number of passenger cars per thousand people in developed markets in 2010 was 460 versus 166 in mainstream emerging markets.

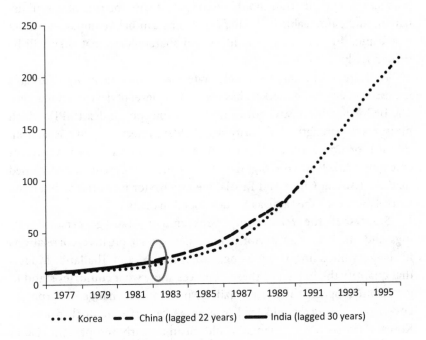

Figure 2.5
Vehicle penetration (vehicles per 1,000 people). *Source*: CLSA; Authors.

Growing consumption raises standards of living and, through the multiplier effect, gross domestic product. In addition, a rise in the size of a country's middle class leads to increases in public health and education expenditures as a percentage of GDP, trade and credit market liberalization, an increase in democracy, and a reduction in corruption.[9]

Stronger Corporate Governance

A hallmark of a country's ascension to mainstream emerging market recognition is a culture of strong corporate governance, what economist Rafael La Porta calls "a set of mechanisms through which outside investors protect themselves against expropriation by the insiders."[10] Emerging market companies often bring in Western-educated managements trained in corporate governance, and this knowledge-sharing helps bring emerging markets in line with best practices. One way a country can show its dedication to a culture of strong corporate governance is by implementing the OECD's Principles for Corporate Governance, which state that "the legal and regulatory requirements that affect corporate governance practices in a jurisdiction should be consistent with the rule of law, transparent, and enforceable."[11] Taking such steps can help companies attract new capital by convincing creditors and shareholders that they will be treated fairly.

As I argued in chapter 1, corporate governance in many of today's mainstream emerging markets has reached the level of developed markets. The IFC maintains a Strength of Investor Protection Index (SIPI), which measures the strength of minority shareholder protections (on a scale from 0 to 10) for 187 countries. In 2015, the average SIPI score for mainstream emerging markets was 6.3, slightly below the 6.5 average score for developed markets. (Absent China and Russia, the average for mainstream emerging markets was 6.5—the same as for developed markets.)

Studies of the relationship between corporate governance ratings and stock market performance have shown positive correlations in markets including Hong Kong, India, Russia, and Thailand. Models that quantify the impact of these practices show what countries stand to gain from adopting them. In Brazil, a worst-to-best change in corporate governance ratings would lead to a 95 percent rise in stock prices; in Korea, a worst-to-best change would mean a nearly 160 percent rise in stock prices.[12]

Strong Stock Market Performance

In general, there is a strong link between economic growth and stock market returns in emerging markets. This link is of particular importance when studying the long-term potential of frontier markets, because frontier markets are expected to account for seventy-one of the seventy-five fastest-growing countries from 2016 to 2021 (according to IMF economic forecasts). I expect this faster growth to drive market returns in these countries and to underpin the long-term attractiveness of frontier markets relative to emerging and developed markets.

Some contention surrounds this assertion. Many studies by academics as well as by Wall Street economists have attracted the attention of the financial press by claiming to have found either no correlation, or even a negative correlation, between countries' economic growth and their stock market returns. I see two reasons why these studies miss the mark on the link between economic growth and market performance.

The first reason is that it makes sense intuitively that something that grows over time will be more valuable than something that stagnates or grows slowly, and investors (including me) are drawn to fast-growing companies. Of course, if everybody else recognizes this growth before you do and bids up the price of the company's stock, you will invest too late to profit from that growth. For me, the sweet spot is to find growth at a reasonable price (GARP) or to find countries, sectors, or companies not yet recognized by the market as fast growing.

The second reason that these studies miss the mark is that they rely on real growth (i.e., growth after adjusting for inflation). And while the subject of real growth may be of academic interest, I invest in companies, and companies don't generate real growth—they generate nominal growth (i.e., growth measured in current dollars, unadjusted for inflation). So I look instead at the relationship between nominal GDP growth and market performance. (The caveat here is that if one invests in a currency other than the U.S. dollar, and if nominal growth is high because of inflation, then the inflation differential may cause that currency to depreciate against the dollar over time.) As an investor, I care about how growth translates into U.S. dollar returns. So I look for high nominal growth in U.S. dollars, and very strong studies show that nominal growth in U.S. dollars does indeed correlate with market performance over long periods of time. One such study by Emerging Advisors Group (EAG) found that "global investors don't care per se about inflation-adjusted local stock market returns, nor do they particularly care about the real growth rate of GDP or earnings. What they care about, rather, are currency-adjusted (e.g., U.S. dollar) returns, currency-adjusted earnings and currency-adjusted growth."[13]

The two charts below show the relationship between GDP growth and market returns for all fourteen mainstream emerging markets from 2000 to 2012. Real GDP growth shows virtually no correlation at all to market returns (see Figure 2.6a), just as many other studies have concluded. There is, however, a very tight relationship between equity returns and nominal U.S. dollar GDP growth (see Figure 2.6b), with a few outliers (notably Mexico and China).

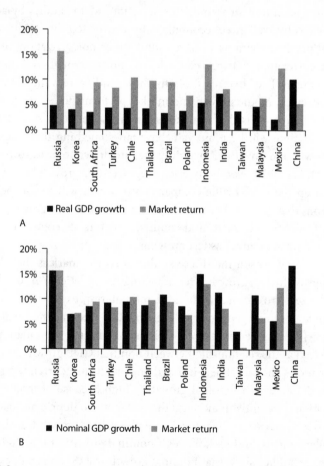

Figure 2.6
Annual GDP growth and market returns in mainstream emerging markets. *a*: real GDP growth/return, 2000–2012; *b*: nominal GDP growth/return, 2000–2012.
Source: Emerging Advisors Group.

The same relationship holds true for frontier markets with real GDP growth between 3.5 and 4.5 percent from 2000 to 2012, as Figure 2.7 shows.

Looking even further back, for those eleven emerging markets with long-term data available,[14] this relationship (with the exception of Mexico) is effectively as close as it was for the 2000–2012 data (see Figures 2.8 and 2.9). The Mexican aberration—equities strongly outperforming nominal GDP growth—is caused in part by Mexico's entrenched and protected monopolies growing earnings amidst a dearth of new publicly traded companies, a recipe for stagnant domestic investment and economic growth.[15]

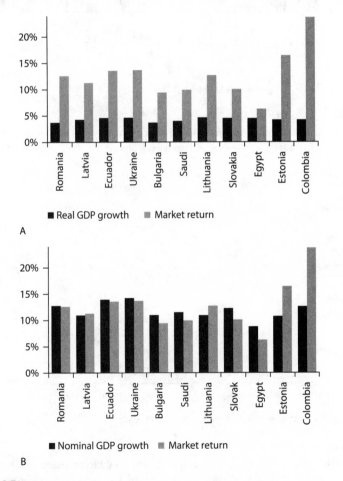

Figure 2.7
GDP growth and market returns in select frontier markets. *a*: real GDP growth/return, 2000–2012; *b*: nominal GDP growth/return, 2000–2012. *Source*: Emerging Advisors Group.

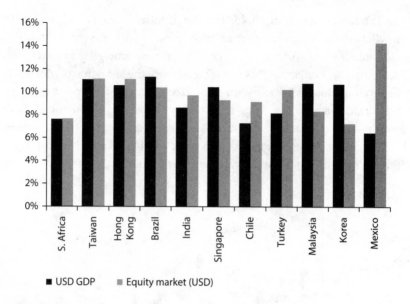

Figure 2.8
Long-term correlation of nominal GDP growth and equity returns. Annual rate of growth/return, 1970–2012 (or earliest available). *Source*: Emerging Advisors Group.

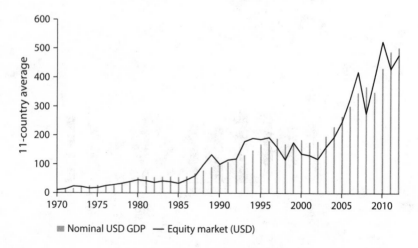

Figure 2.9
Equity performance versus U.S. dollar GDP, 1970–2012. Eleven-country emerging market average; indexed so that 1990 = 100. *Source*: Emerging Advisors Group.

Case Study: Get the Macro Right

One of the swiftest and most impressive transitions from developing to developed market took place in Singapore over the last half century. The transformation of this small city-state illustrates many of the shifts discussed above. It also demonstrates how crucial a macro outlook is.

The island of Singapore was mostly swampland when Sir Thomas Stamford Raffles ventured there in 1819 looking to establish a trading post and eventual naval base for the British. Ideally situated at the tip of the Malay Peninsula, Singapore saw tremendous population growth over the following century. From just a few hundred inhabitants in 1819, the population grew to over 100,000 by the 1870s and half a million by the 1930s, as Singapore's status as a free port attracted Chinese, Indian, and Malay immigrants. The island suffered heavy damage after the British surrendered it to the Japanese during World War II, so it is no surprise the locals were less than enthusiastic about a return to British rule following the war. After declaring independence from Britain in 1963 and ending a brief merger with Malaysia in 1965, Singapore started in earnest on its path from a frontier, to an emerging, to a developed market.

By 1965, Singapore's population had reached nearly two million, but it was still a poor country with a GDP per capita of $540 (in line with Jamaica and about one-seventh that of the United States at the time). Its people suffered from high unemployment and low literacy rates, and an estimated 70 percent of the population lived in overcrowded conditions and one-third in slums. To address these challenges, the new government set a number of priorities: strong adherence to free markets, education of citizens to create a highly skilled labor force, and prudent budget policy. It succeeded on all fronts. During the next two decades, Singapore attracted tremendous outside capital that created manufacturing jobs, spent upwards of a fourth of its budget on education (emphasizing math and science), and still balanced its budget every year from 1968 to 1986.

When I first visited Singapore in 1979, its investment in infrastructure—including highways and mass-transit systems—was already apparent. By then, per capita GDP had risen to $3,990, three times that of Jamaica and one-third that of the United States.

Unemployment had fallen from double digits in 1965 to 3.3 percent, manufacturing's share of GDP had grown from 14 percent to 24 percent, and GDP growth averaged 10 percent per year. Because labor was no longer cheap relative to other Asian markets, the country focused on attracting high-value industries that required Singapore's skilled labor. I was so impressed with Singapore, on my initial visit as well as in subsequent visits in the 1980s, 1990s, and through the early 2000s, that I decided to locate my Asian operations there. We opened an office in 2004 with the assistance of a government and a central bank that were keen to bring new businesses to the city-state.

By 2014, Singapore's GDP had grown to over $56,000 per capita, eleven times that of Jamaica and greater than that of the United States. Singapore's PPP-adjusted GDP per capita topped $82,000, ahead of all other countries in the world except Qatar and Luxembourg. The right macroeconomic policies brought the country, in two generations, from frontier market status to one of the richest and most developed countries in the world.

"In short," EAG concludes, "if you got the dollar growth call right you got the equity call right."[16] I could not agree more.

Round Trip: From Emerging Market to Frontier Market

Although most of today's frontier markets are poised to become mainstream emerging markets, some emerging markets have made the reverse trip, at least in the eyes of the index providers. Several companies are in the business of creating equity market indices (e.g., Dow Jones, Standard & Poor's, Nikkei), but the best-known producer of global and international indices is MSCI. MSCI's classifications are a standard in the investment community, so when it reclassifies a country, regardless of the rationale, the shift is generally adopted by the asset management industry. Many reclassifications (promotions and demotions) are triggered by a market's size or liquidity, which governments have some ability to influence by promoting more market participation. But the surest path to demotion from emerging to frontier index status (or worse—exclusion from any index) is for a government to meddle with the market's free flow of capital. The ramifications of previous such actions provide clear warning signs to those countries still navigating the path to development.

Two countries in the original 1988 MSCI emerging markets classification have been demoted to frontier: Jordan in 2008 and Argentina in 2009. The Jordanian stocks could no longer meet the index's size and liquidity requirements, but it was Argentina's repatriation constraints and other restrictions on capital flow that got that country demoted. Interestingly, Colombia—so small a member of the MSCI Emerging Markets Index that I classify it as frontier—was nearly booted by MSCI to frontier status along with Argentina in 2009 due to its capital flow restrictions. Morocco, added to the emerging markets index in 2001, was demoted to frontier status in 2013 after several years of insufficient liquidity.

Three other countries have made the round trip from frontier to emerging and back. MSCI promoted Sri Lanka, Pakistan, and Venezuela from frontier to emerging status in 1994. Sri Lanka was removed from the emerging markets index in 2001 due to the decline in the size of its equity market and was added to the frontier markets index in 2007. MSCI removed Pakistan from the emerging markets index in late 2008 after the country initiated a price floor on stocks; Pakistan abandoned this ill-conceived and ill-received effort even before the MSCI removal went into effect, but the damage was done. When MSCI reinstituted Pakistan in 2009, it was into the frontier markets index, where Pakistan has remained. MSCI removed Venezuela from its emerging market classification in 2006, opting not to include the country even in its frontier bucket, after Venezuela's 2003 foreign exchange controls reduced its market's investability and liquidity (more on Venezuela's politics in chapter 11).

One country—Malaysia—has made it back to emerging status after being demoted. MSCI removed Malaysia from the emerging markets index in December 1998 after the country imposed capital repatriation restrictions, but reinstated it eighteen months later once it lifted those restrictions. Finally, I would note that Greece actually made the round trip from emerging market in 1988 to developed market in 2001, back to emerging market in 2013 (I categorize Greece, like Colombia, as a frontier market due to its miniscule size in the emerging markets index). Besides failing the size criterion, Greece also lacked sufficiently developed stock lending and short selling practices to be deemed a developed market by MSCI.

* * *

Today's frontier markets will be the next wave of emerging markets if they follow the example of mainstream emerging markets to increase economic freedom, urbanization, infrastructure, wealth, corporate governance, and ultimately market performance. And these markets will get a boost not just from mimicking their predecessors. Several exciting factors, which I discuss in the following chapters, will accelerate frontier markets' ascension to emerging status.

3

Frontier's Bright Economic Outlook

One factor that will accelerate today's frontier markets to emerging market status is their bright economic outlook. Many frontier markets are experiencing improved macroeconomic fundamentals, including shrinking or well-financed current account deficits (and, in some cases, surpluses); less debt (government and private) than developed markets; moderate inflation under control; and growing foreign direct investment. These factors all help promote economic stability and growth, and contribute to a virtuous cycle of improving macroeconomic fundamentals.

Improving or Well-Financed Current Account Deficits

The biggest determinant of a country's current account balance is its balance of trade—its exports minus its imports. Early in its economic development, a country will run a current account deficit as it borrows against future exports (e.g., commodities) to pay for current imports (e.g., equipment and infrastructure to extract and deliver those commodities). Once an economy is producing and exporting goods, its current account may turn to parity or even surplus. We see this phenomenon now in many commodity-producing frontier markets.

We also see this pattern in historical current account data for several of today's mainstream emerging markets. Current accounts for these countries on average moved from deficits in the early 1990s to surpluses in the 2000s. They are projected to move back into deficit territory in the next ten years as these economies mature and as higher incomes increase the demand for imported goods.

Weak trade balances do not inevitably lead to current account deficits. Although the balance of trade is generally the largest component of a country's current account, remittances are also a current account item, and for many frontier markets—Pakistan and Bangladesh come to mind—remittances play an important macroeconomic role. The Philippines is the best example of a country that has benefited from exporting labor for the last twenty years, where large remittances from overseas workers help balance that country's current account.

It is not critical that a country's current account stay out of deficit, as long as that deficit is financed and is not going entirely toward consumption but, ideally, into investment in exportables and the infrastructure to deliver them. Many countries such as Kenya can run large current account deficits because they have been able to finance those deficits through foreign direct investment inflows. So I look for investment opportunities in countries that have either current account surpluses or well-funded deficits, and I try to avoid countries dependent on hot money.

Lower Debt Levels

Frontier markets are not burdened with the large debt levels of developed markets. Debt levels in developed countries exploded following the 2008 financial crisis, much more so than in mainstream emerging or frontier markets. As a group, frontier markets' average public and external debt burdens in 2014 were both about 50 percent of GDP, versus 80 and 180 percent, respectively, in developed markets (figure 3.1). Under the IMF and World Bank's Heavily Indebted Poor Countries Initiative begun in 1996, over thirty countries (mostly in Africa) have seen tens of billions of dollars of their external debt forgiven or reduced to sustainable levels. Mainstream emerging markets enjoy even lower public and external debt burdens than frontier markets, although these debt ratios should converge as strong GDP growth in frontier markets and exports by prospective frontier commodity producers improve current accounts and reduce the need for external financing.

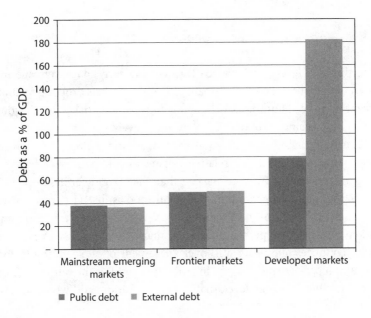

Figure 3.1
Average debt to GDP, 2014. *Source*: CIA World Factbook; World Bank; Authors.

In terms of consumer debt, frontier markets' domestic credit penetration levels are also much lower than are those in developed and mainstream emerging markets, signaling the potential for tremendous growth in frontier markets' consumption (figure 3.2).

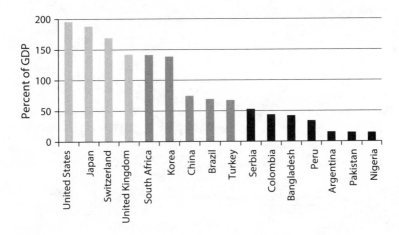

Figure 3.2
Domestic credit to private sector as a percent of GDP. *Source*: World Bank.

Controlled Inflation

From the high levels of the 1970s through the early 1990s, average inflation in both frontier and mainstream emerging markets dropped to about 5 percent by 2009 (figure 3.3). Although it subsequently ticked up in frontier markets, it has since dropped to below 2009 levels.

The bulk of inflation in 2008 stemmed from spiking oil and grain prices, which have a larger relative impact on the consumer baskets of goods and services in frontier markets than in emerging or developed markets. While the average amount spent on food is just 12 percent of total consumer expenditures in developed markets, it is 22 percent in emerging markets and nearly 30 percent in frontier markets, with consumers in many poorer countries allocating well over 50 percent of all spending to food.[1] Food and oil prices spiked again in 2010–2011, but it is the rate of change in prices, not their absolute level, that impacts inflation, and when oil settled

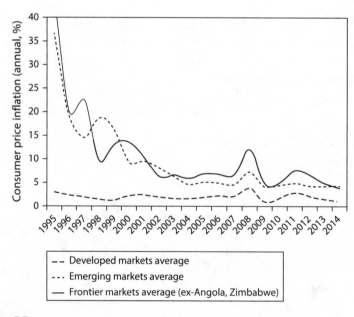

Figure 3.3
Inflation in frontier markets is moderate now. *Source*: World Bank.

at about $110 per barrel, inflation began to ease. By the end of 2015, oil prices had dropped by two-thirds from their 2011–2013 average, which further dampened inflation.

Once central banks gain independence from governments, they use monetary policy less to stimulate growth and more to promote price stability, particularly in democracies. So as frontier markets make improvements toward greater political stability and savvier monetary policy, they have a good shot at bringing inflation levels down even further, perhaps even to those of developed markets.

Increased Foreign Direct Investment

In the early years of a country's economic development, when public stock exchanges may not yet exist, foreign investment takes the form of capital invested directly into private companies, called foreign direct investment (FDI). The low levels of debt in frontier markets and their resulting low interest burdens result in cleaner government balance sheets, bringing increased economic stability and attracting increased FDI. The attractiveness of a country's political, institutional, and legal environments also influences FDI inflows, particularly for developing economies.[2]

FDI activity is monitored closely by organizations such as the United Nations Conference on Trade and Development (UNCTAD). Parsing the UNCTAD data, we see that frontier markets attracted in total a little over half the FDI of mainstream emerging markets in 2014 (figure 3.4). From 1994 to 2014, however, annual FDI inflows into mainstream emerging markets increased by six times, as foreigners sought to invest in, and profit from, the growth of these markets. If frontier markets follow this path, they could attract over $1.2 trillion in FDI inflows annually by 2034.

Foreigners invest in developed markets as well, but UNCTAD estimated that in 2014 almost 60 percent of global FDI went to developing or transition economies (UNCTAD's classifications). And foreign direct investment into frontier markets is coming not just from developed markets; mainstream emerging markets are also getting into the game. Brazil, India, Korea, and Thailand, for example, are investing in Mozambique's mineral and hydrocarbon industries (see chapter 13). Similarly, Indorama

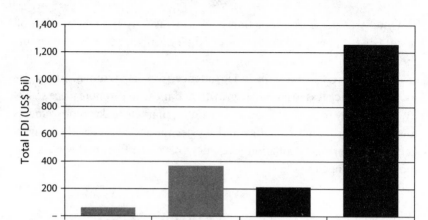

Figure 3.4
Foreign direct investment inflows. *Source*: UNCTAD; Authors.

Ventures, a Thai chemical company with global operations, is expanding into Nigeria, where it sees both robust demand for its products and a cheap source of natural gas feedstock.

Lesson Learned: "The Macro Matters"—São Tomé and Príncipe

The importance of macroeconomic improvement, including good government policies and political will, is obvious in countries where it is absent. Take São Tomé and Príncipe, a small country of less than 200,000 people made up of two main islands just off the western coast of central Africa. The country should be a bustling frontier market with prosperous agriculture and thriving tourism. Instead, what I saw when I went there were abandoned Portuguese cocoa plantations.

I visited São Tomé and Príncipe on a return trip from Nigeria in 2006. Nigeria is a very crowded, active, and relatively dangerous country. São Tomé and Príncipe is the reverse: it's extremely quiet, languid, and safe. I went there to discuss the country's oil prospects, but even in the oil sector, I sensed a paralyzing reluctance to move forward with development projects. This was partially due to an overcautious political attitude; São Tomé and Príncipe is a democracy, and every time someone is about to do something in the oil sector, accusations fly that it might involve corruption. To avoid the accusations, no one does anything.

While on São Tomé, the larger of the two islands, I drove from the coast toward the interior to see a bit more of the country and to visit some of the old plantations. São Tomé and Príncipe was colonized by Portugal in the late 1400s and quickly became one of the richest Portuguese colonies. Its fertile land made it Africa's largest exporter of sugar in the 1500s and the world's largest producer of cocoa as recently as the early 1900s. The country still produces what is arguably some of the best, if not the best, cocoa in the world.

São Tomé and Príncipe had very active plantations before gaining independence from Portugal. Following the downfall of Portugal's dictatorship in April 1974 in a bloodless military coup known as the Carnation Revolution—and after being nearly bankrupted by fifteen years of a costly and unpopular Portuguese colonial war—the Portuguese abruptly abandoned their African colonies (Angola, Cape Verde, Guinea-Bissau, Mozambique, and São Tomé and Príncipe) and left the continent. São Tomé and Príncipe avoided falling into civil war, the fate of Angola and Mozambique, but ever since independence its plantations, and its economy, have slowly but surely decayed. The plantations that I saw were a striking illustration of the country's plight. They were like their own little towns, with their own hospitals, railways, and schools, but after languishing for the past forty years they looked like some of the mining ghost towns in the American West (figures 3.5 and 3.6). The difference is that in São Tomé and Príncipe the wealth is still potentially there, but the drive and political will to rekindle the country is not. Per capita GDP at the time of independence in 1975 was under $700 in current US dollars; it was at about the same level in 2003, prior to a joint venture agreement with Nigeria to develop its offshore oil reserves.

São Tomé and Príncipe is still a very poor country—not the poorest of the poor, but close. With a 2014 GDP per capita of about $1,800, two-thirds of its population lives under the poverty line. São Tomé and Príncipe exemplifies the trap that frontier countries can fall into in the absence of clear macroeconomic guidance, and it highlights the importance of looking for growth when investing in frontier markets. A country will not grow just because it is poor.

Figure 3.5
Deserted plantations. *Source*: Author.

Figure 3.6
Friendly children, a lost generation? *Source*: Author.

The good news for São Tomé and Príncipe is that GDP growth has finally begun to accelerate, averaging over 4 percent annually over the past decade, and is forecast to grow even faster in the next five years. In December 2012, the country was finally connected to the vast global submarine fiber optic cable network when the ACE (Africa Coast to Europe) cable system went live. If it can shepherd its oil resources responsibly, São Tomé and Príncipe may join some of its mainland African neighbors on the path to development.

Fast Growth

The most important thing frontier market countries as a group have in their favor is that they are growing fast—projected to expand at a 6 percent average compounded annual growth rate (CAGR) through 2021. Of the seventy-five markets the IMF expects to grow fastest from 2016 to 2021, seventy-one are frontier markets (figure 3.7).

Over time, this faster growth will increase frontier markets' share of the global economy, as we saw with today's mainstream emerging markets over the past two decades. In 1994, although wielding relatively insignificant global purchasing power, China had one of the world's highest projected growth rates. By 2014, China's economy had grown at a compounded annual rate of 11 percent for twenty years and raised its per capita PPP-adjusted GDP to $13,200, an increase of 700 percent. In those twenty years, China's share of the world's GDP tripled, from 5.7 percent to 16.6 percent. India, Turkey, and Chile also saw their shares of global GDP grow over this time, by 60 percent on average, albeit from smaller bases.

These and many other emerging markets saw the same result: economic growth and greater accumulation of wealth over time. In 2014, emerging markets had an average per capita GDP equal to 43 percent of the developed markets' average, up from 32 percent in 1994. Frontier markets had an average per capita GDP in 2014 that was just 27 percent of the developed markets' average—and when you leave out the richer countries of the Gulf Cooperation Council (GCC) comprising Bahrain, Kuwait, Oman, Qatar, Saudi Arabia, and the United Arab Emirates, per capita GDPs in frontier markets are at only 22 percent of the developed markets' average (figure 3.8).

As I describe in chapter 2, today's frontier markets largely mimic the development path of mainstream emerging markets where, when certain

Estimated GDP (PPP) CAGR 2016-2021

8%+	6-8%	5-6%	4-5%	Less than 4%
Bangladesh	Albania	Afghanistan	Antigua and Barbuda	Austria
Bhutan	Benin	Algeria	Argentina	Azerbaijan
Brunei Darussalam	Botswana	Angola	Australia	Belarus
Burkina Faso	Burundi	Armenia	Bahrain	Belgium
Cambodia	Cabo Verde	Bolivia	Barbados	Brazil
China	Cameroon	Bosnia and Herzegovina	Belize	Ecuador
Côte d'Ivoire	Central African Republic	Colombia	Bulgaria	Equatorial Guinea
Djibouti	Chad	Comoros	Canada	Finland
Ethiopia	Costa Rica	Eritrea	Chile	France
Ghana	Dominican Republic	Estonia	Croatia	Germany
Guinea	DR Congo	Fiji	Cyprus	Italy
India	Egypt	Guatemala	Czech Republic	Japan
Kenya	Gabon	Guyana	Denmark	Marshall Islands
Laos	Georgia	Haiti	Dominica	Micronesia
Liberia	Guinea-Bissau	Honduras	El Salvador	Netherlands
Libya	Indonesia	Ireland	Greece	Norway
Mongolia	Iran	Korea	Grenada	Oman
Mozambique	Iraq	Latvia	Hong Kong	Portugal
Myanmar	Jordan	Lithuania	Hungary	Russia
Niger	Kyrgyz Republic	Luxembourg	Iceland	Samoa
Panama	Lesotho	Macedonia	Israel	San Marino
Philippines	Madagascar	Mauritania	Jamaica	Slovenia
Rwanda	Malawi	Moldova	Kazakhstan	Spain

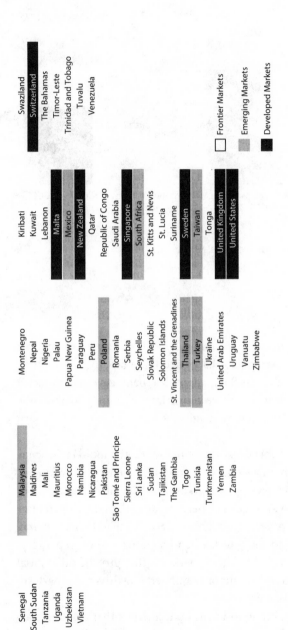

Figure 3.7

Seventy-one of the seventy-five fastest-growing economies through 2021 are frontier markets. *Source:* IMF estimates.

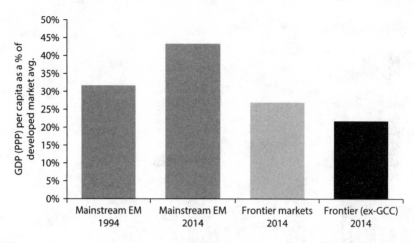

Figure 3.8
Economic growth produces wealth over time. *Source*: IMF.

factors aligned, the shift from an economically insignificant economy to a significant global market participant happened quite rapidly. From meetings with government leaders in Bangladesh, Vietnam, and many eastern European countries, it's clear that these countries are looking to apply the lessons learned from their successful neighbors India, China, and western Europe, respectively.

For at least the rest of this decade, frontier markets should experience significantly faster growth on average than most of the mainstream emerging markets and all of the developed markets. Frontier market economies are expected to expand an average of 50 percent faster than developed market economies over the five years through 2021, according to IMF economic forecasts. This compares to the 1990s, when emerging market economies grew 65 percent faster than developed markets. That growth differential versus developed markets was an important underlying driver of long-term returns for emerging market equities.

Investors are just beginning to warm up to the fact that frontier markets have long, sustainable growth ahead of them, and that this growth is structural. With many frontier markets, investors can purchase a Turkey, Indonesia, or Brazil—not of today, but of twenty years ago, when policy and structural changes drove growth.

Case Study: Why Mongolia's Economy Will Quadruple (Again) in the Next Ten Years

If São Tomé and Príncipe's abandoned plantations illustrate how some frontier markets can languish, Mongolia's thriving capital city demonstrates how they can grow. You may not yet be familiar with Ulaanbaatar, but it is already a boomtown. It is home to luxury brand shops like Louis Vuitton and Cartier, and Apple opened a store in 2011. Luxury hotelier Shangri-La built a five-star property there in June 2015 with financing from the IFC. There were even press reports of a proposed 120-story, $1 billion Trump Tower offering $9 million condominiums. Apartment rents in Ulaanbaatar nearly doubled from 2010 to 2013 and are projected to quadruple from 2013 to 2018. Mongolia possesses some of the largest copper and coal reserves in the world, and as it mines these resources, its GDP should likewise quadruple.

Mongolia was for centuries a land of nomadic tribesmen. It broke from China in 1911, and became the Soviet-allied People's Republic of Mongolia from 1924 until its first free elections in 1990. By the time I visited modern-day Mongolia in 2004, the only vestige of its Soviet past was Ulaanbaatar's architecture—a distinctly Eastern European circa 1960 style, somewhere between nondescript and truly ugly. Even the presidential palace was unremarkable (figure 3.9). Mongolia is vast (six times the size of the United Kingdom and larger than Texas, California, and Montana combined) but has only three million people, making it the most sparsely populated country in the world. You can see that flying over. I traveled south to the Gobi desert to inspect Oyu Tolgoi, a prospective copper mining investment that was literally in the middle of nowhere. The land was barren, with almost no vegetation, and the mining camp was dotted with the traditional yurts used throughout the Mongolian countryside (figure 3.10).

While on my visit, I could see the potential for Mongolia's resource discoveries to reshape its economy, as was the case with some of the smaller countries in the Middle East whose oil discoveries transformed their economies and to some extent their social structures. This was my investment thesis for Mongolia back in 2004, and it turned out to be accurate. Mongolia's PPP-adjusted GDP in 2004 was $12.3 billion. By 2014 it had reached $34.7 billion, a compounded growth rate of 11 percent per annum (its nominal U.S. dollar GDP compounded at 19.7 percent per annum).

Figure 3.9
Reception at the presidential palace in Ulaanbaatar in 2004. *Source*: Author.

We ultimately invested in the Oyu Tolgoi mine. The stock did well for a while, but later was affected by delays and risks associated with the Mongolian government's renegotiating the terms of its license, and so by the summer of 2011 we had sold the bulk of our shares. Mongolia was experiencing one of the problems that occur when a

Figure 3.10
Traditional yurts still used by nomads. *Source*: Author.

country discovers natural resources—infighting over how to divvy up the riches—a challenge that many frontier and emerging markets, even well-managed ones, have faced.

The Oyu Tolgoi mine, now owned by global mining giant Rio Tinto, completed infrastructure construction and began producing copper in 2013. But Rio Tinto has delayed planned mine expansions as the company fights the government's demands for higher tax receipts and greater ownership of the mine. With the mine's output well below forecasts, the government's spending of revenues it has yet to collect has wreaked havoc on the country's budget and fueled a nearly 40 percent depreciation of Mongolia's currency, the tögrög, from 2011 to early 2016.

Once the mine eventually reaches full capacity, though, its output will multiply Mongolia's GDP. Ironically, at that point Mongolia may be prone to so-called Dutch disease, the paradoxically harmful effects on a country from a sudden influx of wealth, coined after the discovery by the Dutch of massive natural gas reserves in the North Sea in the 1960s. Large export revenues can push up the value of your currency, making everything else you produce uncompetitive. Because Mongolia produces little else, however, it would welcome a stronger currency.

* * *

As a group, frontier markets exhibit the elements that create an auspicious economic outlook: manageable current account deficits (and sometimes surpluses); low levels of government and private debt; moderate inflation; and growing foreign direct investment. It helps if a country has exportable natural resources, such as São Tomé and Príncipe's oil or Mongolia's copper. (São Tomé and Príncipe also needs macroeconomic direction; what Mongolia needs is its government to stop tripping over its own feet.) All of these macroeconomic fundamentals contribute to fast economic growth, one of frontier markets' most attractive attributes. Another fundamental contributor to frontier markets' fast growth is its people, which I discuss next.

4

The Young and the Restless
Frontier's Favorable Demographics

Demographics—the statistical characteristics of a population—play a major role in the economic success of a country. Large and youthful countries, for example, have economically attractive labor forces to lure foreign investment, and their young populations grow up to be consumers in subsequent years. Such countries are well positioned, demographically, for growth.

Frontier markets have large, and growing, populations. Of the twenty most populous nations in the world today, nine are frontier markets, and only three are developed markets (figure 4.1). A large population implies a large base of potential consumers, and a growing population means a larger labor force (working at home and abroad) and a growing demand for basic products and services.

Frontier markets also have young populations. Forty-one percent of the world's fifteen-to-twenty-four-year-olds and 36 percent of the world's twenty-five-to-thirty-four-year-olds lived in frontier markets in 2015—a larger number of young adults than in China and India combined (figure 4.2).

Today's youth and young adults will be tomorrow's producers and consumers, which for the coming decades will drive economic growth faster in frontier markets than in the more aged developed markets. A closer look at how demographics affect future growth can help investors spot countries with promising opportunities.

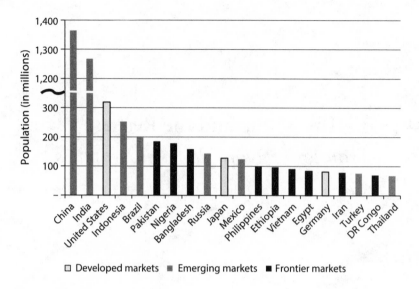

Figure 4.1
Nine of the twenty most populous countries are frontier. *Source*: World Bank; Authors.

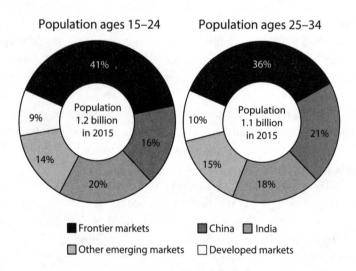

Figure 4.2
The world's young people live in frontier markets. *Source*: UN Population Division; Authors.

Demographic Transition and the Demographic Dividend

Countries, as they modernize, see infant mortality rates decrease and life spans increase. This ultimately leads to lower fertility rates, as parents become more confident in the survival of their children. This is generally a one-time demographic transition, and since infant mortality rates decline before fertility rates, this transition can produce one final large cohort of children (an "age wave"). When this youth bulge reaches working age, and fewer children are born to replace it, the country sees a decline in its dependency ratio—the ratio of the nonworking population (dependents) to the total workforce (providers). Research shows that declining dependency ratios and larger working populations add significantly to GDP growth. This is the so-called demographic dividend a country earns when it makes a demographic transition; it is amplified as the country focuses fewer resources on child rearing and more on economic development, and it can last for several decades.

Ultimately, however, these age-wave workers reach retirement age, and they become the dependents of a smaller workforce. As dependency ratios rise, therefore, the demographic dividend turns negative, especially as retirees live longer. So the demographic transition to lower birth rates and longer lives is a two-edged sword. Countries have a finite period to get rich before they get old.

Looking at graphs of a country's age-sex distribution—so-called population pyramids—illustrates the ephemeral nature of demographic dividends. Once a youth bulge reaches working age, the clock starts ticking: unless young populations replenish through biology or immigration, youth bulges become elderly bulges.

Before considering the demographics of particular countries, it's helpful to consider what's happening on a global scale—namely, a transition from high fertility and mortality to low fertility and mortality, which will stretch the world's population pyramid into a pillar top-heavy with aging developed and emerging populations and buttressed by younger frontier populations (figure 4.3).

The age wave in developed markets as a group is beginning to reach retirement age (see figure 4.4); in mainstream emerging markets, the biggest wave is in its prime working years; and in frontier markets, it may still be literally in its infancy. Empirically, while "children are not immediately helpful to GDP. . . . [Y]oung adults are the driving force in GDP growth."[1]

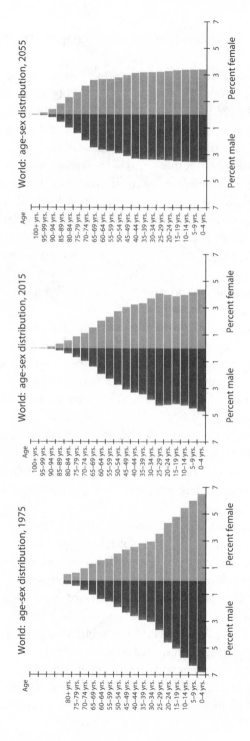

Figure 4.3
World population pyramids 1975, 2015, 2055. *Source:* UN.

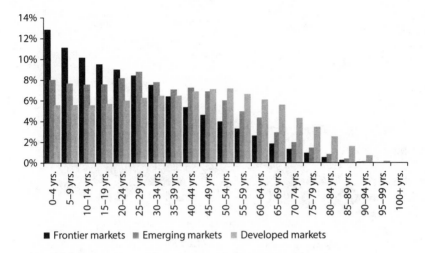

Figure 4.4
Percent of population by age group. *Source*: UN; Authors.

Within the same development status, some countries have a better demographic composition than others. As figure 4.5 illustrates, the United States, with a fertility rate of 1.9 total births per woman (slightly lower than the 2.1 "replacement rate" necessary to sustain a stable population), is in a much better position going forward than Germany, which has a fertility rate of only 1.4 and a large age wave heading toward retirement.

Emerging markets exhibit demographic heterogeneity as well. China's sharp drop in fertility—from 2.5 births per woman in 1990 to 1.5 in 2000—created an age wave entering its early working years in 2015 (figure 4.6, top). An earlier wave, just reaching its forties, resulted from China's overly successful population control campaign in the 1970s that reduced fertility rates by nearly half. India's gradual drop in fertility from 3.9 in 1990 to 2.5 today (still above the replacement rate) created no apparent age wave at all (figure 4.6, bottom).

Although lower mortality and longer lives will stretch a country's population pyramid, continued high fertility rates, such as those currently found in Nigeria and much of Sub-Saharan Africa, delay the demographic dividend that usually results from reduced dependency ratios (figure 4.7).

Looking at how the demographics of an emerging country compare to those of a developed country twenty years earlier (figure 4.8) can offer

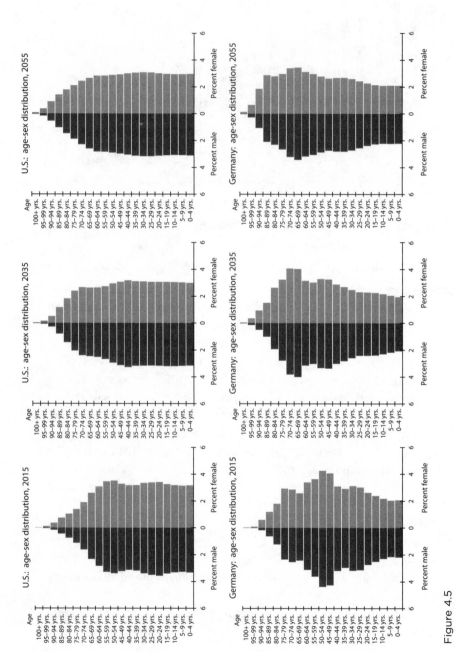

Figure 4.5
U.S. and German population pyramids. *Source:* UN.

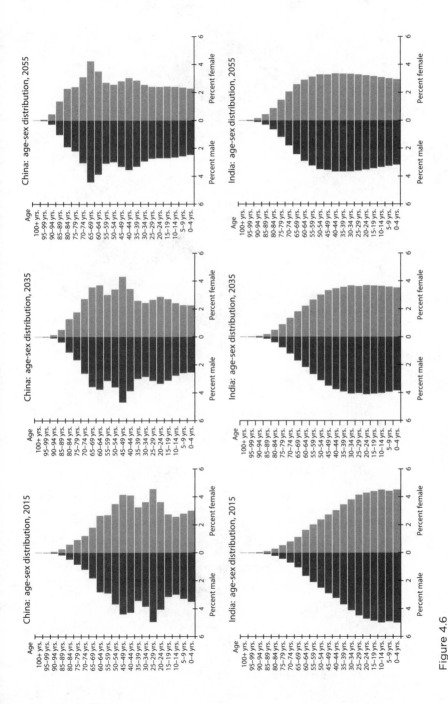

Figure 4.6
Chinese and Indian population pyramids. *Source:* UN.

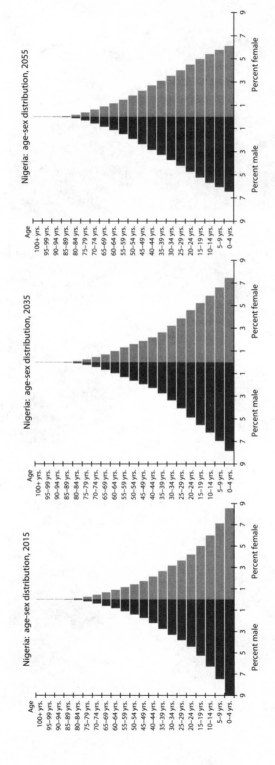

Figure 4.7

Nigerian population pyramids. *Source:* UN.

a glimpse into the future. Korea's wave of young workers in the 1990s, like Japan's in the 1970s, helped fuel the enormous growth of its economy for the next two decades; but once this wave of workers enters retirement, the country will face steep negative demographic dividends, as there will be too few workers to support the retirees. Longer lives and lower fertility rates only exacerbate the aging problem. In Japan, because this aging happened so rapidly, the government had little time to implement pension and social security reforms, and Japan is now one of the world's most heavily indebted nations due in part to the cost of its retirees' pensions. But Japan faces an even direr future—virtual extinction—if it does not ease its tight immigration restrictions and/or somehow boost its extremely low fertility rate. Korea—with an even lower fertility rate—be warned.

Next to Nigeria's broad pyramid and Korea's spinning top, Bangladesh's population pyramid (figure 4.9) is a strong pillar, neither too young nor too old, showing only a modest bulge in the teen years—a gentle age wave that will provide a tailwind to economic growth in the coming decades.

Indeed, Bangladesh is a good example of ideal demographics: a large, young population (160 million people, overtaking Russia as the eighth-largest population in the world, 32 percent of whom are below the age of fifteen), and positive population growth that until recently was well above the world average. This may earn Bangladesh an attractive demographic dividend—and may in turn offer investors a solid financial dividend as well. A closer look at the situation in Bangladesh (see page 72) shows the opportunities that good demographics can proffer—from the expanding consumer demands of a larger domestic workforce, to the burgeoning demand for banking services by the growing ranks of young, mobile workers heading abroad and sending money back home.

Frontier markets' young, growing populations are as valuable an asset as their natural resources. Entering the workforce at home, frontier youth will generate wealth and increase consumer demand. Young frontier workers will also migrate to those more-developed countries with stagnant, aging populations and insufficient native labor forces, raising remittances. This migration, made cheaper and more attractive by advances in information and communications technologies (Skype, for example), is one example of how frontier markets benefit from, and contribute to, global integration, the topic of the next chapter.

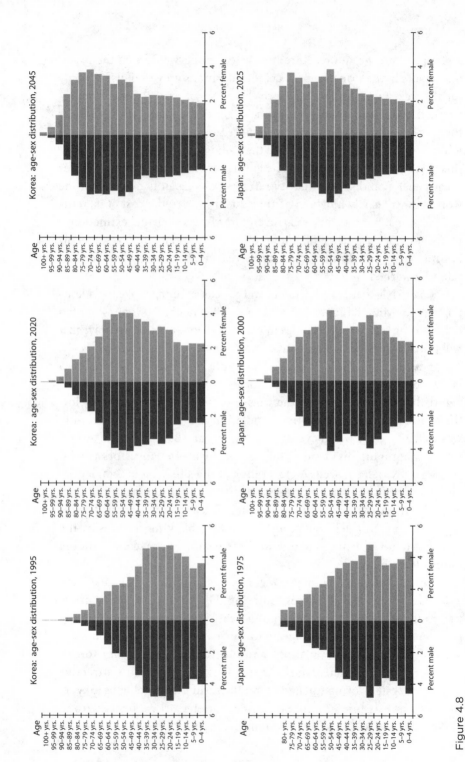

Figure 4.8
Korean population pyramids mirror Japan's twenty years earlier. *Source:* UN.

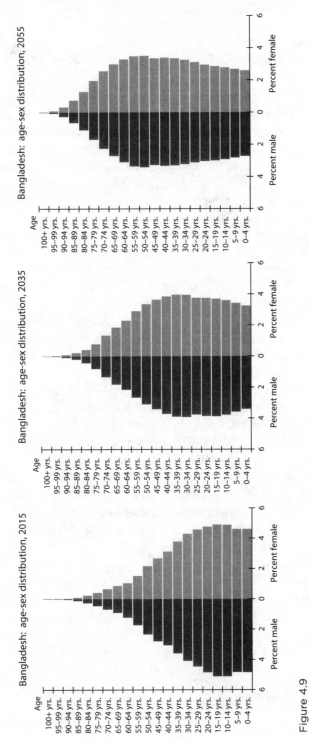

Figure 4.9

Bangladeshi population pyramids. *Source:* UN.

Case Study: Bangladesh

Bangladesh is in many ways an archetypal frontier market. Its economy expanded at a 7.8 percent compounded annual growth rate (CAGR) over the five years through 2014, nearly as fast as India's 9 percent CAGR and faster than Pakistan (5.2 percent) and Vietnam (7.6 percent).[2] This robust economic growth is expected to accelerate to 9 percent by 2020 driven by flourishing service and manufacturing industries, large remittances from nonresident Bangladeshis, and private investment. Agriculture, while still employing half the population, is increasingly mechanized and is no longer the central stimulus for growth, and its contribution to total GDP had fallen to under 16 percent by 2014. Workers have shifted instead into manufacturing and services jobs; the services sector accounts for over 56 percent of GDP, and the garment industry accounts for 80 percent of total exports. From 2009 to 2014, Bangladesh's manufacturing sector grew at an 11 percent CAGR, and I forecast that the manufacturing and service sectors collectively will grow at an even faster rate over the next ten years.

I started looking at investing in the Bangladeshi equity market in 2006. Our team analyzed valuations and the usual macroeconomic indicators (inflation, GDP growth, current account balances, tax receipts, etc.) that we look at in other countries, and what we saw in Bangladesh looked good—valuations were cheap, and the market was undiscovered. Although the Dhaka Stock Exchange's roots go back to the early 1950s, locals were doing the bulk of trading, with very little foreign participation. After we decided that Bangladesh looked like a good opportunity on paper, one of my partners from my Singapore office got on a plane and went to visit.

Landing at Dhaka International Airport, he was greeted by a two-lane highway jammed with trucks, buses, and cars. His first impression was that the people in Dhaka, the capital city, seemed a lot busier than the people in some other financial capitals. In Mumbai, for instance, you see many people sitting around doing nothing. But Dhaka was very busy, and the people were all doing something. This kind of observation is hard to input into a spreadsheet, but it helps form an overall view of a market and speaks to the importance of doing on-the-ground research when investigating frontier markets.

My partner was quickly reminded of Bangladesh's frontier status when he encountered another strain on its underinvested infrastructure: the lack of investment in power, which leads to frequent blackouts. His first meeting in Dhaka was with the country's largest private electric power company, and ironically, a blackout occurred halfway through the meeting. But with signs of strain came signs of promise, like the dozens of Korean and Chinese textile buyers in the lobby of his hotel. Low labor costs lead to strong growth in textiles, which leads foreign multinationals to invest in the country. This growth creates a virtuous cycle of rising employment, consumer spending, and infrastructure development.

Once we did the work—visiting the country several times to perform on-the-ground research and meet with company managements, and crunching the numbers back in the office—I concluded that the banks were the best way to express our positive view. The large, young, and growing population entering the workforce and the fast-growing corporate sector presented a significant opportunity for the banking industry, analogous to what I had seen in Indonesia and Brazil ten years before. So—consistent with my experience in those two countries, where domestic banks consolidated, foreign banks entered the market through mergers or joint ventures, and the sector as a whole took advantage of robust domestic growth—we bought what we thought were the five best Bangladeshi banks based on their branch networks, how well they were run, and whether we thought they might be taken over by another bank:

• BRAC Bank Ltd., the fastest-growing bank in the country and rated one of the four most successful and sustainable SME (small and medium-sized enterprise) banks in the world by the Council for Microfinance Equity Funds. With a network at the time of 36 branches, 392 small and medium enterprise (SME) offices, and 1,900 remittance delivery points, BRAC Bank hoped to grow its client base by focusing on the SME sector of the economy, which it believed would contribute the most to rapid-generation job creation in Bangladesh.

• National Bank Ltd., founded as the first private sector bank in 1983. With 101 branches, it had one of the largest branch networks in the country. After restructuring its operations and significantly improving its asset quality in the early 2000s, the bank saw marked improvement in its core financial ratios. Management planned to more fully utilize its branch network to tap the growing corporate and retail market, and it already had one of the best remittance channels for expatriate Bangladeshi workers to send money back to Bangladesh. I believed it was a candidate for foreign partnership in the medium term.

• Prime Bank Ltd., which consistently outperformed its peers in the Bangladeshi banking sector in earnings growth and profitability through its network of sixty branches. Founded in 1995, its low level of nonperforming assets gave it one of the highest levels of asset quality in the industry. With very experienced and talented management, I expected Prime Bank to retain its leadership position in the industry.

• Pubali Bank Ltd., the largest private commercial bank in Bangladesh. With over 370 branches, it had the largest branch network of any bank in the country. If the bank could operate its branch network more effectively, both by increasing sales volumes and increasing efficiency, I believed there could be significant upside—and its branch network would also be of interest to foreign banks that sought to solidify their presence in the country.

• Southeast Bank Ltd., a provider of a substantial portion of credit to firms involved in Bangladesh's export industries, essentially financed the country's trade and commerce. It also achieved high growth in remittances as one of the top banks in that business. Key shareholders owned only 37 percent of the bank, a low figure relative to its peers, making it more attractive to other banks in terms of possible M&A activity.

We began buying the banks in late 2006 and continued through mid-2007. Although I was concerned with the political instability and the state of emergency imposed in January 2007 by the military-backed interim government, I was optimistic that the Bangladeshis would ultimately settle on a government and remove much of the political uncertainty. I felt the country traded on strong fundamentals and would be minimally affected by the credit issues troubling U.S. financials at the time, and so I remained positive on Bangladesh in general and its financial sector in particular.

As global economies stumbled in 2008, however, market liquidity in Bangladesh dried up completely—one of the real risks of investing in frontier markets. But coming out of 2008 and into 2009, it was clear that Bangladesh's economy wasn't significantly affected. There was a slowdown in textile exports, especially to the United States and

Europe, but Bangladesh's large population kept domestic consumption high enough to support the economy.

Another key factor keeping the economy healthy were remittances, which grew from $8.9 billion in 2008 to $10.5 billion in 2009 through official channels (they would grow to $15 billion by 2014) plus an estimated two-thirds of that amount through unofficial channels. At over 12 percent of GDP, Bangladesh's (official) remittance level is one of the highest in the world and contributes to the wealth effect and to consumption growth. The bulk of these remittances come from neighboring India, but a significant share originates in Saudi Arabia, Kuwait, and the United Kingdom. Consider that as many as 90 percent of the 10,000 "Indian" restaurants in the United Kingdom are actually owned and operated by Bangladeshis, doing £3 billion in business per year, much of which is sent home.

International migration spurs economic growth and reduces poverty, because workers who relocate to where they are more productive increase output and incomes. The United Nations estimates that in 2013 more than 230 million people around the world lived away from their home countries; that year, remittances to developing countries (through official channels) reached an estimated $404 billion and were expected to grow to $436 billion in 2014.[3] Indeed, seven of the ten developing countries receiving the most remittances are frontier markets (table 4.1).

Table 4.1
Top Ten Developing Country Remittance Recipients, 2013

Country	Remittances (US$ billions)	Remittances (% of GDP)
India	70.0	3.7%
China	60.0	0.7%
Philippines	25.4	9.8%
Mexico	22.3	2.0%
Nigeria	21.0	7.9%
Egypt	17.5	7.5%
Pakistan	14.6	6.1%
Bangladesh	13.8	12.2%
Vietnam	11.0	7.1%
Ukraine	9.6	4.8%

Source: World Bank.

Table 4.2
Recipients of Remittances over 20 Percent of GDP, 2013

Country	Remittances (% of GDP)	Remittances (US$ billions)
Tajikistan	51.9%	4.0
Kyrgyz Republic	31.4%	2.3
Nepal	24.7%	5.2
Moldova	24.6%	2.0
Samoa	23.5%	0.2
Lesotho	22.6%	0.5
Armenia	21.4%	2.4
Haiti	20.6%	1.7
Liberia	20.4%	0.4

Source: World Bank.

Remittances are even more crucial to poorer countries; the top fifty remittance recipients as a percent of GDP are all frontier markets (table 4.2). Remittances to developing countries in aggregate outpace official development assistance by a factor of three.

The World Bank has found that, in addition to lowering poverty, remittances produce a host of benefits, including "higher human capital accumulation; greater health and education expenditures; better access to information and communication technologies; improved access to formal financial sector services; enhanced small business investment; more entrepreneurship; better preparedness for adverse shocks such as droughts, earthquakes, and cyclones; and reduced child labor."[4] But while advances in technology and increased competition are reducing the cost of sending money home, the price still remains high—8.4 percent of the amount sent on average. Reducing the cost to 5 percent would save migrant workers $14 billion annually.

On the strength of domestic consumption and remittance growth, markets in Bangladesh started to recover fairly strongly, and our basket of banks performed extremely well. Through 2009 and 2010, a confluence of strong growth, good earnings (banks were making money from domestic customers as well as through the remittance business), and cheap initial valuations led the stocks up sharply—some up five times from their 2009 lows and up two to three times from where we bought them in 2006 and 2007. During this period, Bangladeshi trading volumes also increased dramatically: Daily volume on the Dhaka stock exchange soared from a low of $10 million in 2008 to over $450 million in 2010.

I traveled to Dhaka in October 2010, and while I was very positive about the country and by then had been invested in it for several years, it was clear from my visit that things were getting frothy. Dhaka property prices were booming—in some cases, they were higher than in Manhattan. Hotel rooms, at $240 per night, were all full. Traffic was still a nightmare; the strong economy meant many more people had bought cars, but Bangladesh had made very little progress on the infrastructure side. The main topic of conversation among the local friends I visited was how so-and-so had made money flipping land and how various industrial companies were getting into real estate development. Even in the banks there was a speculative feeling; many banks (including some we had invested in) were generating a significant portion of their earnings from proprietary stock trading. I met with the chairman of the Bangladesh Securities and Exchange Commission, and even he was alarmed by the level that the stock market had reached. The final red flags came in my meetings with CEOs and other officials of the banks that I owned, where many were more excited talking about profits from their stock trading than from their actual lending business. While my frontier markets' investment thesis is based on growth, growth by itself is not enough. It is crucial to consider valuations, and the banks were no longer trading at reasonable valuations; in fact, they had become quite expensive. I decided to sell.

By coincidence or luck, the market peaked a few weeks later, then rolled over, and spent the next three years in the doldrums. Trading volumes on the Dhaka Stock Exchange, which peaked in late 2010 at over $450 million per day, dropped to lows of under $20 million per day through 2013. Property prices slumped. A big asset bubble had burst and is only now starting to recover; in 2015, market volumes had improved but only to about $55 million per day, one-eighth of their peak in 2010.

With their stock prices down 50 percent or more from their 2010 highs, and with their fundamentals improving, we gradually began repurchasing some of the banks beginning in the third quarter of 2011. After all, my original interest in Bangladesh stemmed from its demographics, and that macro factor wasn't changing. So when valuations again became more reasonable, I was happy to reenter the market.

Bangladesh remains a very interesting story. As Chinese incomes keep growing (wages in the Pearl River Delta increased over 15 percent per year for the last few years) and as the Chinese currency appreciates, the cost of producing garments in China keeps rising—which has pushed apparel companies to go to frontier markets such as Vietnam, Pakistan, and Bangladesh. That's essentially the bull case for light manufacturing in Bangladesh, which employs four million people, mostly women, and has provided opportunities for many of them to find jobs and improve their standards of living. Of course we all saw in the news the tragic Rana Plaza factory collapse in April 2013 that killed 1,100 workers and the Tazreen Fashion factory fire that killed 117 workers five months earlier, and unsafe factories cannot be tolerated (more on this in chapter 12). But they're not the whole story. Many of Bangladesh's garment factories are very high quality—as I've seen with my own eyes.

It's hard to come by tours that show the inner workings of a garment factory, since most of Bangladesh's garment factories are privately owned by locals. Luckily, the son of a director that I met at the National Bank managed several different businesses, one of which was a midtier, mid-size garment factory, and he was kind enough to show me around. I toured all five levels and saw the entire production process, from washing the denim, to sewing, to packaging (I could clearly see the packaging for the U.S. retailer The Gap). The factory did everything but attach the price tag. It had a fair amount of automation, and so while there were factory workers there, the conditions and the standards of safety and comfort were quite modern (figure 4.10).

Foreign direct investment into Bangladesh has picked up in recent years, particularly in the manufacturing sector. As production costs rise in China and India, I believe that Bangladesh, with its young, growing, low-cost labor force, is ideally positioned to capture a larger share of the next round of outsourcing. Following a 75 percent increase in the minimum wage in December 2013, the average hourly wage of a Bangladeshi garment worker rose to $0.62 in 2014, on par with Pakistani and Vietnamese garment workers but only 25 percent that of a garment worker in China. In large part due to its growth in ready-made garment exports, Bangladesh's total trade (exports plus imports) grew from 27 percent of GDP in 2004 to 45 percent in 2014.

The success and growth of its garment industry notwithstanding, in the longer term Bangladesh must expand beyond its narrow

Figure 4.10
Many of Bangladesh's garment factories are modern and safe. *Source*: Author.

manufacturing base. It must also upgrade its transportation, communications, and power supply infrastructure to help offset the inflationary pressures that accompany rising energy and commodity prices, and years of rapid economic growth. Due to its dependence on imported crude oil, Bangladesh has suffered trade deficits every year for the past forty years, and faces an inflation rate of slightly over 6 percent (down from 7.5 percent in 2014—the retreat from $100 oil has helped). Given the government's limited financial resources, a high proportion of Bangladesh's much-needed capital investment will have to be funded by foreign equity participation, something we have recently seen signs of.

5

"Can You Hear Me Now?"
Frontier's Integration with the Global Economy

While the macroeconomic and demographic advantages of frontier markets spur economic growth, the integration of these economies into the global marketplace will accelerate this growth. Global integration, marked by a country's participation in international markets, can be measured in several ways, such as by trade volumes and foreign direct investment (FDI). Such integration is a virtuous cycle; the more integrated a country becomes, the better able it is to attract foreign investors.

You can find examples of this global integration everywhere. Take the case of the clothes on our backs. The United States is the world's largest consumer of garments, yet it imports 97 percent of them—a higher percentage than any other country. And they're not just MADE IN CHINA or MADE IN MEXICO; if you look through the clothes in your closet, you may find a polo shirt made in Lesotho alongside almost identical polo shirts made in Jordan and Vietnam. While China still accounts for 36 percent of all U.S. garment imports, Vietnam and Bangladesh are now in second and third place, respectively, and countries like Kenya, Sri Lanka, and Haiti are growing their apparel production at 20 percent or more per year. I expect that in the near future we will see garments made in Ethiopia, Bolivia, and Mauritius in our wardrobes.

Another example of frontier's global integration: In Norway, known for its potato crop, you might drive past several potato farms on your way to the local grocery store to buy a bag of potatoes. Imagine your surprise when you discover the potatoes you just bought came from Saudi Arabia! Saudi farmers grow these potatoes (which I am told are delicious) and transport them over 6,000 kilometers to grocery stores in Norway—just down the road from hectares of homegrown Norwegian potatoes.

Frontier markets, which have suffered from historical underdevelopment, are poised to benefit from this kind of integration with the global economy, and frontier market governments have been keen to embrace free enterprise in an effort to attract foreign development capital. As a result, these countries are constructing modern technology and communication infrastructures at an accelerated pace. Increasingly powerful technology allows today's frontier economies to integrate into the global economy more rapidly than did yesterday's frontier markets (which, of course, are today's mainstream emerging markets); access to education at home and abroad and transfers of knowledge and capital by expatriates further this integration.

Technology Accelerates Global Integration

Adopting new technologies has benefited humankind for millennia— think, for instance, of the invention of the wheel—and technological advancements in areas as diverse as health care (anesthesia, pasteurization, penicillin), travel (on land, sea, and air), and communications (printing press, telegraph, television) have improved standards of living vastly and spurred economic growth. Adoption rates for new technologies accelerated so quickly during the past 200 years that, rather than needing centuries to take hold, new technologies are now adopted globally in a matter of decades. It took only twenty-five years for the spread of agricultural technologies like fertilizers, irrigation systems, and pesticides to produce the Green Revolution that doubled cereal production in Asia from 1970 to 1995 on only 4 percent more land area.[1] And some recent technologies, such as the smartphone and the tablet, have taken only a few years to catch on. This acceleration in the adoption and diffusion of technology means that frontier markets with amenable political environments can accelerate their integration into the global economy.

To this end, frontier markets have, and will, benefit tremendously from new information and communications technologies (ICTs). ICTs like mobile phone and Internet technology offer frontier market businesses and consumers an entrée into the global marketplace, and enable countries to improve logistics systems and communications networks to become globally competitive in order to attract foreign direct investment. More broadly, ICTs also give frontier populations access to local, national, and world events, turning local citizens into global citizens.

One clear measure of the uptake of technology in frontier markets is their teledensity rates (the number of phone lines in a country per 100 people). Prior to the early 1990s, telephone lines were almost exclusively land-based. These copper phone lines were very expensive to install, especially in rural areas, and so while the average teledensity rate in developed markets reached over fifty lines per 100 people by 1992, the majority of frontier markets had fewer than five. Because of the high cost of fixed phone lines, poorer countries had to depend on GDP growth or foreign aid to finance teledensity growth—but the ability to grow GDP and attract aid depended in part on higher teledensity levels, and only at a certain critical-mass teledensity rate (40 per 100) does additional teledensity itself drive further economic growth.[2]

How, then, did all but twelve frontier markets raise their teledensity levels above forty, and all but seven raise their levels above thirty, by 2013? The answer: cellular technology. Fixed-line teledensity in frontier and mainstream emerging markets plateaued starting in 2000 at about twelve and twenty, respectively; in developed markets, fixed-line teledensity peaked in 2000 at about fifty-seven and has declined since. Meanwhile, frontier markets' average mobile phone subscription rates are nearing 100 per 100 people and catching up to emerging and developed markets (figure 5.1).

This boom in frontier markets' mobile teledensity levels stemmed from the tremendous cost advantage of cellular over fixed lines. Frontier markets leapfrogged the landline technology they lacked the wealth to install and instead implemented much cheaper and more efficient cellular technology, allowing them to integrate into the global economy at a pace much faster than history would have predicted. The explosion of mobile phone access has made a phone line available to nearly everyone, and unlike land lines—which were always utilized more by service sectors (commerce and transport) than by agriculture—cellular technology is available to rural as well as urban dwellers.

Every frontier market has been touched by this change. In 1996, Nigeria had only 120,000 phone lines. Fixed-line capacity build-out was expensive and controlled by the government, and waiting times for a new phone

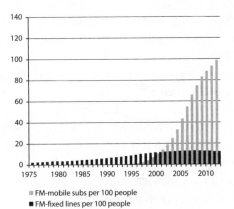

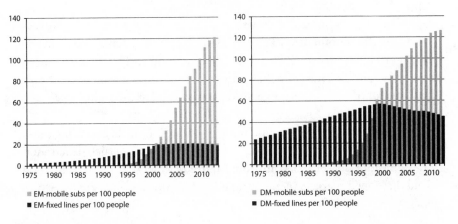

Figure 5.1
Fixed and mobile teledensity levels. *Source*: World Bank.

line exceeded three years. All that changed in 2001, when the government awarded the first mobile licenses—by that year's end, Nigeria had 600,000 fixed lines and 266,000 mobile lines. By the end of 2013, the country had over 125 million phone lines, 99.7 percent of which are cellular. This adoption of mobile technology has benefited Nigeria's economy enormously. Take, for example, the case of the Nigerian cashew farmer.

Nigeria is the second-largest grower of cashew nuts in the world (behind Vietnam), and almost all of its cashews are grown on small farms across the country. For decades, these cashew farmers had no choice but to deal with intermediaries—local buying agents who would arrive with their trucks and offer farmers a price for their cashew crops. Far from the market and with no access to a phone, farmers had no idea what prices intermediaries were getting for cashews at the port. So a middleman might pay a farmer $200 for a metric ton of cashews and then resell those cashews at the port for $500.

Today, however, Nigerian farmers need only text a friend at the port or check the Internet to learn the going rate for cashews; after that, they can negotiate a price in line with the true market value of their crop. Instantly available pricing information is clearly good for the farmer, pushing margins upstream, but is not so good for the intermediary. Publicly listed commodity traders that thrived as intermediaries in markets with incomplete or asymmetrical information are now seeing their profits squeezed by this new pricing transparency, available thanks to the spread of technology.

The other winners, of course, are the technology firms. For investors, owning companies like Russia's Mobile Telesystems and Vimpel-Com or South Africa's MTN in the late 1990s and early 2000s, and more recently Kenya's Safaricom, has proven that getting into mobile technology in frontier and emerging markets early—and at the right price—can be very profitable.

Frontier market penetration rates for other ICTs are also nearing those of mainstream emerging markets. Average frontier Internet penetration rates in 2014, for instance, mirrored those of emerging markets in 2009 and developed markets in 2000 (figure 5.2). I expect even faster growth in

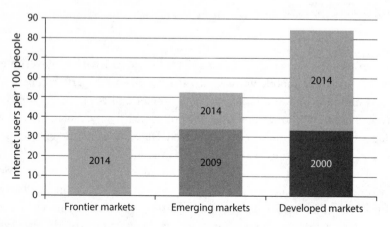

Figure 5.2
Internet penetration in frontier markets only five years behind emerging markets.
Source: World Bank; Authors.

frontier markets' Internet penetration as the Internet becomes more available on mobile phones.

As ICTs get cheaper, they become more accessible to poorer countries. These technologies are helping many frontier market economies grow at a much faster pace than did their predecessors. Instead of building on legacy technologies, frontier markets are able to skip ahead and use today's most efficient technologies, which were already underwritten by decades of research and development by developed economies. Frontier markets recently have been able to leapfrog 2G cellular technology and install even newer systems. When traveling through several frontier markets in the past few years, I have noticed that the locals rely completely on their cellular phones for personal and business calls, but most are also able to check emails and connect to the Internet via their low-cost smart phones. A growing awareness of the importance of technology has led to a global push to bring the latest ICTs to frontier markets. The United Nations Conference on Trade and Development (UNCTAD) recently focused its efforts on how low- and middle-income countries should utilize the cloud.[3]

Technology has been a major player not only in the economics of frontier markets but also in their politics, especially with the growing availability and popularity of social media. As we saw during the Arab Spring uprisings in 2011, mobile devices can now bring news of world events to a user's fingertips almost instantaneously. This real-time access to information can also have real political repercussions. Following the death of President Bingu wa Mutharika of Malawi in 2012, Peter Mutharika, the brother of the deceased, tried to install himself as the country's next president—much to the consternation of then–vice president Joyce Banda. Prior to the omnipresence of Facebook, this coup might have succeeded. Banda's million-plus followers on Facebook, however, persuaded frère Peter otherwise. In fact, far from moving into the presidential palace, Peter Mutharika was briefly jailed on charges of treason.

With increasingly fast and ubiquitous ICTs, the world is now more interconnected than ever. High-speed data makes its way between far-flung parts of the world on over 300 undersea fiber optic cables (see figure 5.3) that stretch from Argentina to Senegal and from Morocco to Vietnam. Frontier markets have taken advantage of the vast advances in technology to narrow the global digital divide with developed economies and create a robust communications infrastructure to integrate with the rest of the world and to support their future growth.

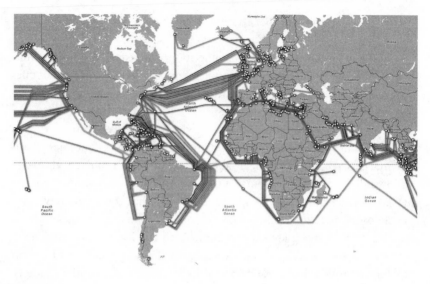

Figure 5.3
Undersea fiber optic cables connect the world. *Source*: Submarinecablemap.com.

Global Integration and Education

Education helps countries integrate their populations with the rest of the world, stay competitive and innovative in the global marketplace, and sustain growth and development over the long term. Higher educational attainment not only helps attract foreign investment but also drives domestic technological innovation and the creation of new industries and businesses. And as countries shift from agricultural economies to manufacturing and service-based economies, employers require a more highly skilled and more literate labor force.

Literacy (the percentage of a population age fifteen and older that can read and write) is essential to completing a high school or higher education, and increasing enrollment in primary education is a crucial first step to raising literacy rates. Successful government policies have resulted in significant upticks in school enrollment in frontier markets. Primary and secondary school total enrollment has improved markedly since 2000, and average primary enrollment is nearing 90 percent of children of primary age. Secondary enrollment in 2010 (the latest year with sufficient data for comparison) reached 67 percent, broadly in line with secondary enrollment in emerging markets a decade earlier (figure 5.4). Within this overall picture of improvement lie some overwhelming success stories—such as Mozambique, which nearly doubled primary enrollment and more than tripled secondary and tertiary enrollment (albeit from a very low base) over this same period.

Of course, these improvements in frontier enrollment rates need to be followed by improvements in the quality of education, as well as equal access. Equality of literacy rates for women and men in frontier markets has a strong positive correlation with higher per capita GDP, especially at lower income levels (figure 5.5). The obvious outlier is Lesotho, a poor country where until recently most young boys dropped out of school to become herders, then miners.

The interplay between technology and education is also vital to frontier markets' global integration. Students in the twenty-first century must have the technological literacy to operate the ICTs required to compete in a global marketplace. To this end, Rwanda worked with organizations including the Massachusetts Institute of Technology's One Laptop per Child (OLPC) initiative to bring hundreds of thousands of computers into its primary schools. Prices for technology have plummeted, even since the launch of OLPC, and more recently the

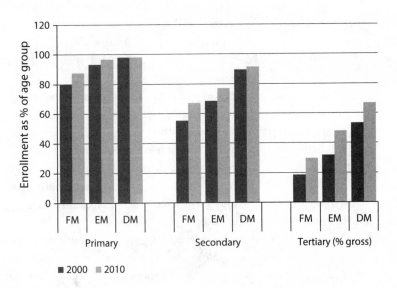

Figure 5.4
School enrollment rates, 2000 and 2010. *Source*: World Bank; Authors.

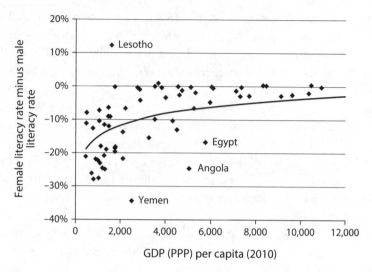

Figure 5.5
Literacy rate differentials and GDP. *Source*: World Bank.

focus has been on even cheaper devices like tablets and even mobile phones to help teach the three Rs (writing, reading, and arithmetic) while increasing technological literacy. E-learning expert Duncan Clark has predicted that mobile phones will be "the single most important factor in increasing literacy on the planet," noting that children in developing countries "become obsessive readers and writers through mobile devices."[4]

The pursuit of higher education also leads to greater global integration. As students complete increasingly higher grade levels, many look to continue their educations at overseas institutions. Frontier market students who travel to mainstream emerging and developed markets for their higher education learn advanced economic and business management skills—among many others—and then bring these skills back to their native countries. This trend can have two positive effects. First, students often apply the skills learned overseas when they return home and start businesses of their own. These new business leaders add significant economic value as they create local jobs and accelerate economic development in their home markets. Second, students who take jobs in more developed markets send remittances back to their home countries. These remittances become a source of capital for their home economies.

Frontier to Frontier

Increased global integration not only means that frontier markets are connecting to the emerging and developed world; frontier markets increasingly are connecting to one another. Pakistan's Lucky Cement Limited, already exporting cement to East Africa by sea from Karachi Port, is building plants in the Democratic Republic of Congo and Iraq. Or take Agriterra, a Mozambican company listed in London that began as an agricultural firm growing crops such as barley, sorghum, and wheat. The company was selling its by-product—husks—to local cattle farmers for feed when it decided, instead of selling the husks, to start its own cattle farms. Agriterra was selling its cows to the local slaughterhouses when it began to wonder why it didn't operate its own slaughterhouses. So the company started its own slaughterhouses and began selling its meat locally. Agriterra calls this its "field to fork" strategy. And friends who have eaten Mozambican steaks say they are the best steaks they have ever tasted.

Agriterra's management then met with billionaire Saudi prince Sultan bin Mohammed bin Saud Al Kabeer—founder and largest individual shareholder of Almarai, the world's biggest integrated dairy company—while he was visiting Mozambique. Apparently, the prince too must have eaten one of these Mozambican steaks, because he decided they needed these steaks in Saudi Arabia. So Agriterra had its newest slaughterhouse Halal certified (that is, compliant with Islamic Sharia law, which requires among other things that animals must be facing Mecca when slaughtered), and Agriterra now exports beef from one frontier market—Mozambique—to another— Saudi Arabia.

Saudi Arabia also leases farmland across Sub-Saharan Africa to grow its own wheat. The Middle East is very dependent on imported wheat, so if a country can grow its own, even on land leased on another continent, it is still cheaper and safer than trying to buy wheat on the open market. This is especially vital for those governments whose people are prone to riot when they are hungry.

* * *

Global integration increases trade and investment between frontier markets and the rest of the world, accelerating their growth. This integration, in turn, is accelerated by advances in technology, especially information and communications technology, and is supported by increased education levels. Improved technology will also drive frontier markets to trade more among themselves directly, without the need for an emerging or developed market intermediary.

So far, I have discussed why frontier markets are attractive from a macroeconomic and demographic perspective. But their fast growth and integration with the global economy do not alone make frontier markets attractive from an investment perspective. As we will see in the next chapter, frontier markets are also cheap, and they can diversify your investment portfolio.

6

Frontier Equity Markets Offer Value and Diversification

In addition to the top-down macroeconomic and demographic advantages of frontier markets, their equity markets are attractive from a bottom-up perspective as well. Even with run-ups in 2013 and early 2014, frontier market equities are still cheap on an absolute and relative basis, especially given their expected growth. And most frontier equity markets are inefficient, which means they may hold undiscovered bargains that the frontier market investor can take advantage of. This market inefficiency also helps explain the low correlation of frontier equities as a whole with other asset classes, as well as the low correlations between individual frontier markets, making frontier markets an attractive portfolio diversification tool.

Frontier Equities Are Cheap

Frontier markets, as a group, have not participated in the post–financial crisis market gains to the same extent as mainstream emerging and developed markets.[1] From January 2009 through 2015, they underperformed emerging markets by over 25 percent despite their strong outperformance in 2013 and the first half of 2014. Their multiyear underperformance, plus their strong balance sheets and excellent growth potential, mean that these diverse, fast-growing markets are trading at attractive valuations on both an absolute basis and relative to either emerging or developed markets.

At a multiple of only 9.1 times forward estimated earnings, frontier market equities at the start of 2016 were trading at a discount to both emerging markets (11.1 times earnings) and developed markets (16.0 times earnings) despite higher dividend yields and returns on equity (see figure 6.1), and superior overall growth prospects. If these ratios remain constant, frontier market equity prices will rise as earnings grow. Over time, however, I expect frontier market P/E ratios to expand, further boosting prices.

Frontier markets are as attractive today as their predecessors were in the 1990s. In the six years 1992 through 1997, emerging markets traded at an average discount to developed markets of 22 percent in terms of growth-adjusted P/E ratios (PEG, or price/earnings to earnings growth); frontier markets traded at a nearly identical PEG ratio discount to developed markets at the start of 2016 (table 6.1). This means that, when adjusted for earnings growth, frontier market equities are trading at valuations as compelling as those of emerging market equities in the 1990s. Looking ahead, from a bottom-up perspective, frontier markets could deliver accelerated earnings growth for the next five years, which is going to be very challenging to do in mainstream emerging and developed markets.

If the MSCI Frontier Markets Index was a single company—call it Frontier Markets Inc.—it would be truly multinational, invested in twenty-four different countries over a well-diversified group of industries with double-digit earnings growth forecast for the next several years. Yet, it could be bought for about nine times forward earnings. If Frontier Markets Inc. were a conglomerate, you would say, "This is a great story." And while it's not a story everyone has caught onto, savvy corporate buyers from developed and mainstream emerging markets have begun to take note. This can in itself create further opportunities—as was the case with the Slovenian pharmaceutical company Lek (see Case Study below).

Frontier Markets Are Inefficient

One reason why frontier markets are cheap relative to their more developed market peers is that they are inefficient, particularly with respect to information flow. If you call any major international brokerage firm

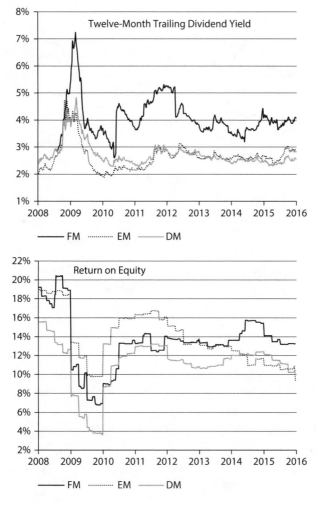

Figure 6.1
Frontier markets offer attractive valuation metrics. *Source*: Bloomberg; Authors.

and ask what its office in such-and-such frontier market thinks, you'll quickly run into a problem: It doesn't have an office there. That is a barrier to market efficiency. But to me, this market inefficiency is an investment opportunity.

Despite frontier markets' large share of global GDP, strong top-down economic foundations, and attractive fundamentals, their equity markets are underowned by institutional investors (who are still too heavily weighted toward developed markets) and underfollowed by the

Table 6.1
Price/Earnings to Growth Multiples: Then and Now

EM versus DM	1992–1997
Emerging Markets	
P/E	16.7
EPS Growth	17.9
EM PEG	**1.0**
Developed Markets	
P/E	23.5
EPS Growth	19.4
DM PEG	**1.2**
EM Discount to DM	**−22%**

FM versus DM	2016
Frontier Markets	
P/E (last twelve months)	10.2
EPS Growth*	10.6
FM PEG	**1.0**
Developed Markets	
P/E (last twelve months)	18.9
EPS Growth*	15.3
DM PEG	**1.2**
FM Discount to DM	**−22%**

*Average of 2015–2017 EPS growth estimates.

Case Study: Lek

Lek came onto the radar as part of a growing trend in global mergers and acquisitions starting in the early 2000s, which involved large multinational companies gaining entry into new geographic markets by acquiring regional market leaders. This trend was particularly strong in emerging and frontier markets as large, global players looked for opportunities in fast-growing markets. These transactions were often ignored by traditional merger arbitrage managers due to their complexity or to the managers' lack of local expertise. In the United States and western Europe, so many smart investment managers focus on merger arbitrage that returns have been squeezed to single digits.

In emerging and frontier markets, fewer investors focus on event-driven strategies, and the expected returns are much higher.

We had previously profited from similar opportunities in the banking and beverage industries, such as when the Italian bank Unicredito purchased Croatia's Zagrebačka Banka (see chapter 9); when U.S. banking giant Citigroup acquired Mexico's Grupo Financiero Banamex Accival; when U.S. soft drink bottler Pepsi Bottling Group bought Mexico's Pepsi-Gemex; and when the Netherlands's Heineken acquired Egypt's Al-Ahram Beverages Company. But the potential purchase by the Swiss-based pharmaceutical giant Novartis of Slovenia's Lek Pharmaceuticals was the first deal of this type that I saw in the pharmaceutical sector.

Lek Pharmaceutical and Chemical Company d.d. (Lek), based in Ljubljana, Slovenia, was a market leader in the generic pharmaceutical business in central and eastern Europe in the early 2000s, with particular strength in anti-infective, cardiovascular, and gastrointestinal tract drugs. Lek employed approximately 3,600 people and had 2001 sales of $335 million, net income of $35 million, a pre-bid market capitalization of $482 million, and a historical P/E ratio of 13.8.

What caught the attention of Novartis's generic business unit was Lek's ability to manufacture a generic version of the antibiotic Augmentin (amoxicillin) suitable for U.S. distribution. Augmentin was one of the largest sources of revenue for Novartis competitor GlaxoSmithKline, generating $2.25 billion in sales in 2001. But Glaxo's U.S. patent protection was set to expire in December 2002, paving the way for generic manufacturers to enter this profitable U.S. market. Novartis was developing its own U.S. version of Augmentin and would most likely face competition not only from Lek, but also from Israel's Teva Pharmaceuticals and India's Ranbaxy Laboratories.

Clearly, Lek would be a key strategic fit for Novartis. By acquiring Lek, Novartis would eliminate a competitor in the U.S. market for Augmentin and bolster its global generic operations by gaining access to the pharmaceutical market in eastern Europe, estimated to be growing at over 12 percent per year.

Shares of Lek traded up sharply to 88,000 Slovenian tolars (approximately $379 per share) from a prior level of 62,000 tolars in the last few days of August 2002 as reports surfaced that Novartis and Lek were in talks regarding either an outright acquisition or a joint venture to manufacture a generic Augmentin. While this represented a share price increase of over 40 percent, Lek was still trading at only 19.3 times historical earnings, versus Novartis's 21 times.

On August 29, 2002, Novartis announced its intent to purchase all outstanding shares of Lek for a total of $730 million (95,000 tolars per share) in cash. This bid had the backing of Lek management but was subject to a number of conditions, including approval by the Slovenian Securities Market Agency (government approval, essentially), acceptance by at least 51 percent of outstanding share capital, the waiver of certain voting restrictions, and changes to the composition of the board that would give Novartis control.

I believed that Novartis's bid for Lek had the support of the Slovenian government and would not encounter any regulatory snags or delays, as Novartis pledged to maintain Lek's headquarters in Slovenia and to run Lek as a separate company in order to maintain Lek's strong national identity. The last two conditions (lifting of voting restrictions and changes to the board) would be subject to a vote at an Extraordinary General Meeting (EGM) on September 27. Slovenian takeover law was remarkably shareholder friendly and on par with, or better than, those found in developed European markets, and there was a good chance that the two large government pension funds controlling almost 30 percent of Lek's shares outstanding, which had announced they wanted a price of at least 100,000 tolars per share, would use their blocking position at the EGM as leverage to negotiate a higher price.

After this and other due diligence, we began acquiring shares in mid-September at an average cost of 89,200 tolars per share, which would provide an excellent return if the bid was successful at 95,000 tolars, and an even better return if the ultimate price was equal to or greater than 100,000 tolars. I was confident that Novartis would not walk away from the deal; it had excellent strategic rationale; and even at 100,000 tolars per share, Lek would be valued at historical multiples just on par with Novartis (before factoring in growth prospects and synergies). Furthermore, I felt that other pharmaceutical companies would also look to acquire Lek should the Novartis deal fall through, which would provide downside protection.

The EGM meeting was as eventful as anticipated. Despite Novartis raising its offer to 98,000 tolars per share in an eleventh-hour attempt to secure an affirmative vote, the pension funds held firm their demand for at least 100,000 tolars per share. Rather than let the acquisition fall through (as it had previously threatened), Novartis left the original 95,000 tolar offer on the table and continued to negotiate. This gave us further encouragement that Novartis would see the deal through—if it was going to walk away from Lek, surely it would have made a clean break once shareholders rejected its improved 98,000 tolar offer, rather than leave the initial offer outstanding.

We continued to accumulate Lek as the shares traded down on disappointment over the lack of an immediate resolution to the standoff. I believed the two large holders of Lek shares were negotiating with Novartis in earnest from a position of strength, emphasizing the compelling strategic rationale and the potential of other interested parties. Finally, on October 21, the companies announced a deal struck at 105,000 tolars in cash per share, a multiple of 22.8 times Lek's historical earnings. Novartis extended the offer period to early November in accordance with Slovenian takeover law, and we tendered our shares, realizing a return of over 15 percent in less than two months. Returns of this magnitude for announced mergers and acquisitions are rarely available in more developed markets, where many more investors focus on arbitrage opportunities.

I always like to discover undervalued equities before a corporate buyer does; but even after a deal is announced, an acquisition target in frontier markets can still trade at cheap valuations because of the extra work and expertise needed to appraise the deal.

equity analyst community. Hundreds of frontier market listed equities are ignored by global sell-side investment research firms, leaving investors without on-the-ground research capabilities at a distinct disadvantage. This is a major blind spot, given the strength and potential within these markets.

One measure of market inefficiency is the market capitalization-to-GDP ratio—the size of a country's equity market in relation to the size of its economic activity. As economic output increases, typically so too does market size and liquidity. In countries like Indonesia and Turkey, for example, market capitalization-to-GDP ratios increased from under 10 percent in 1992 to 40 percent by 2012, about the average ratio for developed

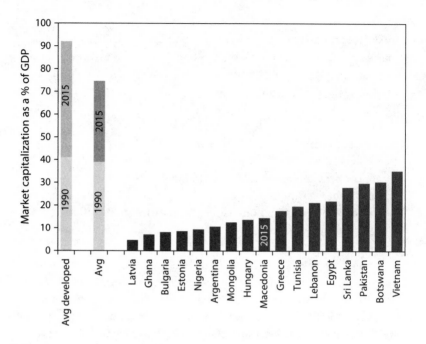

Figure 6.2
Many frontier markets are at similar market capitalization-to-gdp starting points as mainstream emerging markets over two decades ago. *Source*: World Bank; Bloomberg; Authors.

markets in 1990. Today, market capitalization-to-GDP ratios are at low starting points in many frontier markets, similar to those of mainstream emerging markets over two decades ago (figure 6.2). As these countries' economies grow, more of their companies will also list shares on publicly traded equity markets, and their market capitalizations as a percent of GDP should expand, increasing liquidity and producing a multiplier effect on their equity markets.

Given the long-term growth story, market inefficiencies offer an attractive entry point for investors with research capabilities and with the infrastructure and relationships in place to access these markets. This can allow you to see opportunities where others aren't even bothering to look—such as in Rwanda. Rwanda's U.S. dollar GDP per capita in 2014 was only $652 ($1,557 PPP adjusted), less than half the average of Sub-Saharan Africa. But Rwanda is one of Africa's recent significant success stories, and it is taking itself public.

Case Study: Rwandan IPOs

Rwanda is a small country—roughly the same size as Burundi, its neighbor to the south, and dwarfed by the Democratic Republic of the Congo, its neighbor to the west ninety times its size. Patricia Crisafulli and Andrea Redmond in their excellent book *Rwanda, Inc.* note that Rwanda is so tiny, the name "Rwanda" overlaps the country's borders on most maps. The only map I've seen where this isn't true is the six-foot map of Africa hanging in my office, where the name "RWANDA" just fits inside the country's borders. Rwanda's small size and population of 11.5 million makes it the most densely populated country in Africa.

When I first visited Rwanda in 1991, the country looked as rural as one might expect—small farms spread across the countryside, with the occasional town (figure 6.3). I was heading out of the capital city of Kigali to the Virunga Mountains, a range of volcanoes covered by rainforest and bamboo that is home to the elusive and critically endangered silverback mountain gorillas. (These are an amazing sight, and the high price of tourist permits to see the mountain gorillas helps fund the expansive protection and veterinarian programs that

Figure 6.3
Marko with Rwandan villagers in 1991. *Source*: Author.

Rwanda has established to ensure the gorillas' survival.) It was about a hundred miles to Gisenyi, a small city on Rwanda's northwestern border with the DR Congo and the gateway to the Virunga Mountains. Although the road was in decent shape, the drive took six hours. Every ten or fifteen miles we came across a checkpoint, often manned by teenagers who looked as young as thirteen or fourteen armed with machine guns.

These checkpoints were just one aspect of Rwanda's militarization at the time. There were also soldiers patrolling in and around the hotels, and you could feel the tension on the ground. Three years later, this tension erupted into massive human tragedy, with the genocide that killed one million Rwandans. But from this misery, Rwandans were able to rebuild their country.

On a macro basis, Rwanda is a very good example of the renaissance of the African continent over the last decade. Indeed, the World Bank recognized Rwanda as the second-most-active reformer globally between 2006 and 2011, and it is now possible to incorporate a new business in Rwanda in twenty-four hours.[2] Exports are still dominated by coffee, tea, and minerals, but the country has also had recent success in attracting multinationals such as IBM and Visa International to set up shop in Kigali.

Rwanda came back on my radar when Rwandan companies began the process of going public. Over the last twenty-five years, I have participated in many initial public offerings (IPOs) across frontier and emerging markets, providing equity capital to companies in these fast-growing economies. The development of the capital markets in Africa is one of the most exciting opportunities in the coming decade, and Rwanda is a great illustration of this. As of early 2016, Rwanda had seven market listings: four dual-listed companies from Kenya's Nairobi Stock Exchange; and three local listings, Bralirwa Breweries and Bank of Kigali, which both held IPOs in 2011, and Crystal Telecom, which went public in 2015.

Bralirwa, or Brasseries et Limonaderies du Rwanda, is a beer brewer and soda manufacturer. Its initial product, Primus beer, debuted in Gisenyi in 1959 and was the only beer available in Rwanda for the next twenty-eight years. In the 1970s, Bralirwa sold a 70 percent stake to Heineken and began producing Coca-Cola products under license. Bralirwa is still part of the Heineken Group, but its publicly available shares have traded on the Rwanda Stock Exchange since it became that exchange's first listing in January 2011. Bralirwa currently controls 94 percent of the Rwandan beer market and 99 percent of the carbonated beverage market. Beer consumption in Rwanda is growing but is still only about ten liters per capita per year. By comparison, annual South African beer consumption is fifty-five liters per capita—the United States is eighty liters and Germany is 100 liters—so I see a multiyear, possibly a multidecade opportunity ahead for Bralirwa.

As I discuss in chapter 8, to capture opportunities in frontier markets, you cannot just invest in blue-chip developed market companies that happen to have some frontier market operations. The stock of Heineken, the parent company of Bralirwa, did well for the four years from Bralirwa's IPO in January 2011 through January 2015; it was up about 80 percent including reinvested dividends. But you capture very little of the opportunity of consumer growth in Rwanda by investing in Heineken. You capture it by investing in Bralirwa, which was up 250 percent in euros four years after its IPO (figure 6.4).

If Bralirwa exemplifies the frontier consumer theme, Bank of Kigali exemplifies another theme: the development of a financial services industry. Eighty percent of Rwanda's population is engaged in subsistence farming. As this population moves from an agrarian subsistence

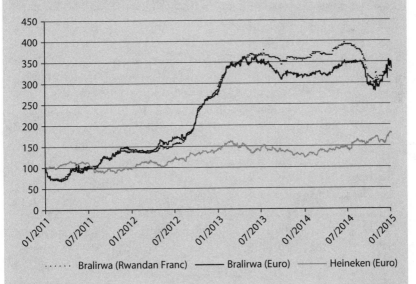

Figure 6.4
Performance of Bralirwa vs. Heineken. *Source*: Bloomberg.

economy into a more urban manufacturing and services economy, it will experience a significant increase in disposable income. This, along with the Rwanda central bank's accommodative monetary policy, will spur the development and growth of credit as these former farmers take out loans to buy middle-income goods—appliances, a motor-cycle, someday a car—and ultimately take out a mortgage to buy a house. This all requires a robust and well-managed banking system.

Banks in developed markets are very cyclical businesses—but in frontier markets at the early stage of development, banks are growth businesses (more on this in chapter 13). Bank of Kigali is very well positioned to take advantage of the strong economic growth in Rwanda, with a dominant market share of 33 percent of total assets, strong management capabilities, and a very robust balance sheet to fund 20 percent annual loan growth. Shareholders invest alongside the government of Rwanda, which remains a 30 percent shareholder for now.

I believe in the concept of hubs, or centers of activity for a region. I am located in Miami, which is a Latin American hub, and for ten years I had an office in Singapore, which is a big Asian hub. We have invested in Dubai and Panama, which are regional hubs. Kigali, the capital of Rwanda, is striving to become an East African hub—for financial services as well as logistics (including air travel). So Rwanda has invested in the kinds of infrastructure that can make this ambition possible, including 4,000 kilometers of fiber to provide broadband across the country, connecting rural areas, schools, and health centers. IBM and Visa have invested heavily in operations in Rwanda, and Carnegie Mellon University opened a campus there in 2012.

Only twenty years after the 1994 genocide, Rwanda still has hurdles to overcome. Dependence on foreign aid, which was 86 percent of the national budget in 2000, has dropped but is still significant at 40 percent—and this decline in aid has slowed GDP growth. And while corruption is low and ease of doing business is high in Rwanda (by African standards), the government has faced accusations by its opponents of authoritarian rule, political repression, and other suppressions of freedoms. But overall Rwanda has made a lot of progress and remains a very interesting opportunity in Africa. Investors who take the time to research new or overlooked opportunities like those in Rwanda will be able to take advantage of market inefficiencies and capture returns that may not be available in more efficient developed and emerging markets.

Frontier Markets Can Diversify Your Portfolio

Not only are frontier markets cheap and inefficient; they are also a great way to diversify a portfolio. The chief benefit of portfolio diversification is risk reduction, and portfolio diversification is often considered the only free lunch in the investment world. Diversification reduces risk, however, only to the extent that your portfolio consists of assets that are not correlated with one another. Investing in two perfectly correlated assets (i.e., with a correlation of 1.0) provides no diversification benefit.

One of the most frequent criticisms of investing in mainstream emerging markets is that these markets are too highly correlated with developed markets and with one another. When one market goes up (or, more ominously, down), so too do the others. Thus, the critics would argue, diversifying from developed into emerging markets does not reduce portfolio volatility sufficiently to compensate for taking on the other risks (real and perceived) of investing in emerging markets.

This criticism is not without merit. During the period from 2002 (when the first frontier markets index was introduced) through 2015, mainstream emerging market equities as a whole (as measured by the MSCI Emerging Markets Index) had a high correlation with developed markets (as measured by the MSCI World Index), with a correlation coefficient of 0.82 and an R^2 of 0.67,[3] and had a meaningful average correlation coefficient among themselves of 0.46.

But contrast the high correlation of emerging with developed equity markets and the low correlation of frontier equity markets as a whole with either developed markets (0.36) or emerging markets (0.36) over this period. Only about 13 percent (0.36 squared) of frontier market returns are explained by emerging or developed market returns. And less than 3 percent of the returns of individual frontier markets, on average, are explained by the returns of other individual frontier markets; the average correlation of individual frontier markets with one another is very low (see figure 6.5). Hence investing in a basket of frontier equity markets can reduce portfolio risk by providing the valuable diversification benefits inherent in lowly correlated investments.

The diversification benefit of investing in frontier markets today mirrors the diversification benefit of emerging markets twenty years ago (figure 6.6). The five-year correlation between emerging and developed markets in 1995 (0.44) was slightly higher than the correlation between frontier and developed

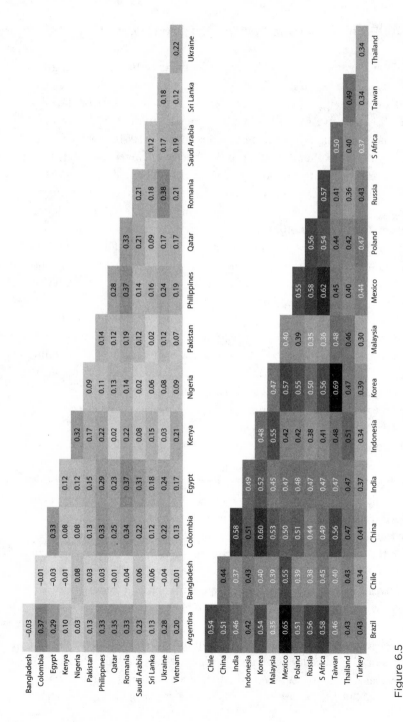

Figure 6.5

Individual frontier markets are less correlated with one another (0.16 on average) than are individual emerging markets (0.46 on average).

Source: Bloomberg.

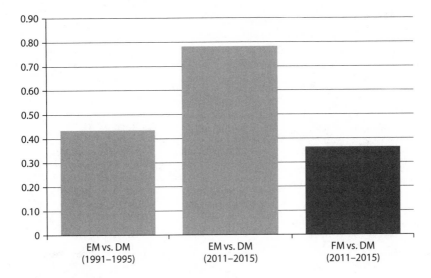

Figure 6.6
Five-year correlations of EM vs. DM (1995 and 2015) and FM vs. DM (2015).
Source: Bloomberg.

markets in 2015 (0.38). For emerging market investors interested in allocating to frontier markets, the diversification opportunity is also attractive, as the most recent five-year correlation between frontier and emerging markets is at a similarly low level of 0.37.

Investors willing to put in the research time will likely find that frontier markets offer an array of rapidly growing businesses at very attractive valuations, and these markets are less correlated with developed markets than are mainstream emerging markets. On valuation and diversification metrics, frontier equity markets are reminiscent of today's mainstream emerging markets twenty years ago.

How to Invest in Frontier Markets

7

The Pitfalls of Passive Management and Advantages of Active Management in Frontier Markets

Passive investment management is investing on autopilot. You buy either the underlying stocks that compose a market index or a fund that mirrors the index. The argument for passive investing is that markets are efficient, and trying to select individual stocks to beat the market's return is a waste of time and money. Proponents of passive investing point to numerous studies that show (mainly for U.S. equity managers) that the average active manager underperforms the market after fees. This may be true, but outside the heavily researched and very liquid developed markets, passive investing encounters two major pitfalls: indices do not accurately reflect the composition of the universe they purport to represent; and they completely miss many attractive investments in underresearched, misunderstood, and hard-to-access countries and companies. Such opportunities can be uncovered only through active management. This has been true in mainstream emerging markets for the past two decades, and it is even truer in frontier markets today.

The Pitfalls of Passive Management

Let's look at the granddaddy of emerging market indices: The MSCI Emerging Markets Index. This index has changed dramatically since its inception in 1988, growing from ten countries—three of which are no longer in the index—to twenty-three at this writing. The left side of table 7.1 shows the original ten countries in the index and the evolution of their weightings over the twenty-eight years from inception on January 1, 1988, to January 1, 2001, to January 1, 2016. Of the original ten countries, Portugal graduated to developed status, and Argentina and Jordan moved to frontier status. Greece moved to developed in 2001 but was brought back to emerging in 2013. The remaining original seven countries today constitute less than one-fifth of the total index; the sixteen new countries, which include Korea and three of the four BRICs, account for the other 80+ percent. Most of these new countries joined the index before 2001 as their markets matured and became more generally investable.

The right side of table 7.1 ranks the top ten largest country weightings in the MSCI Emerging Markets Index as of January 1, 2016. Note that seven of the top ten, including the top five, were not even members of the index at its inception. Note also that while the index was relatively balanced in 2001 (thus more accurately representing the emerging universe), it was quite imbalanced at inception (with 43 percent in Malaysia and Thailand) and is imbalanced again today (with 54 percent in China, Korea, and Taiwan).

Clearly, this index undergoes frequent change; but even with continual updates, it cannot always capture the emerging universe in a timely manner, and it mostly looks through a rearview mirror. Index investing can therefore force you to buy past winners regardless of their future prospects.

Table 7.1

MSCI Emerging Markets Index Top Weightings over Time

	1988	2001	2016		1988	2001	2016
Malaysia	**33.8%**	6.5%	3.3%	China	—	6.6%	**26.6%**
Brazil	**18.9%**	10.6%	5.5%	Korea	—	9.3%	**15.5%**
Thailand	**9.1%**	1.4%	2.0%	Taiwan	—	11.7%	**12.1%**
Chile	**8.9%**	3.1%	1.2%	India	—	7.5%	**8.7%**
Portugal	**8.5%**	—	—	South Africa	—	9.7%	**6.8%**
Mexico	**7.7%**	9.6%	4.5%	Brazil	18.9%	10.6%	**5.5%**
Greece	**5.3%**	5.5%	0.5%	Mexico	7.7%	9.6%	**4.5%**
Philippines	**3.1%**	0.9%	1.4%	Russia	—	2.0%	**3.5%**
Jordan	**2.9%**	0.1%	—	Malaysia	33.8%	6.5%	**3.3%**
Argentina	**1.8%**	1.4%	—	Indonesia	—	0.8%	**2.6%**

Note: The columns with bold figures are sorted in descending order.
Source: MSCI; Bloomberg.

Of the twenty countries added to the MSCI Emerging Markets Index since 1994, thirteen performed better than the index in the year prior to their inclusion; ten of these thirteen then did worse than the index in the following twelve months.

Take Russia: In the twelve months from December 1, 1996 to November 28, 1997, MSCI's Russia index outperformed the emerging markets index by nearly 127 percent (after outperforming by over 150 percent the prior year). Russia debuted in the MSCI Emerging Markets Index the following Monday, December 1, 1997, with a healthy 5.7 percent weighting. One year later, the Russia index had dropped 74 percent, while the emerging markets index slid by only 23 percent.

Or Greece: It debuted in the emerging markets index on November 26, 2013, after having risen over 58 percent the prior year; the following year, it dropped by 24 percent. In both periods, the emerging markets index rose a little over 3 percent. Most recently, Qatar and the UAE outperformed the emerging markets index by 51 and 93 percent, respectively, for the twelve months prior to their June 2, 2014, inclusion, only to underperform by over 20 percent each the following year. Investing passively by buying an index is momentum investing at its worst: You buy more of what has run up in the past and is generally expensive, and less of what is selling at cheap valuations with good growth prospects.

Frontier benchmarks face similar limitations. MSCI launched its Frontier Markets Index in late 2007 with nineteen countries. In a little over six years, two countries representing a combined 30 percent of the index were dropped (Qatar and UAE were designated as emerging market countries by MSCI and removed from the frontier index in June 2014) and seven new countries added. These seven (Argentina, Bangladesh, Jordan, Morocco, Pakistan, Serbia, and Sri Lanka) accounted for nearly one-third of the index at the start of 2016. Table 7.2 lists the ten largest country weightings in the index as of that date. Note that three of the top five countries in 2016 are new to the index—clearly, as with the emerging markets index, weightings can change significantly from period to period. The frontier markets index is still unbalanced, with 34 percent in Kuwait and Nigeria alone, and even if the index becomes more aligned with the actual frontier markets universe over time (as the emerging markets index did in the 2000s), it could also move back out of balance again (as the emerging markets index has done).

This flux in the composition of indices underscores the first pitfall of passive investing in developing markets: Indices do not reflect the reality of the universes they purport to represent. This is one reason I advocate an

Table 7.2

MSCI Frontier Markets Index Top Weightings over Time

	2007	2016
Kuwait	32.2%	20.7%
Nigeria	12.1%	13.7%
Argentina	—	12.1%
Pakistan	—	8.5%
Morocco	—	6.7%
Kenya	1.1%	5.3%
Oman	2.3%	4.6%
Vietnam	1.5%	3.9%
Lebanon	3.4%	3.6%
Romania	3.3%	3.4%

Source: MSCI; Bloomberg.

index-agnostic investment approach (agnostic in the sense that I doubt the existence of a truly representative benchmark), given the added potential returns from investing in the abundance of companies excluded from the benchmarks. Such an approach is especially promising in frontier markets today. The number of companies in the MSCI Frontier Markets Index has actually declined from 183 in 2009 to 122 in 2016. (With Qatar and the UAE dropping from the index in June 2014, the total market capitalization of the index constituents has fallen over 50 percent from $614 billion to under $300 billion.) My universe for potential investments in frontier markets is significantly broader than the index both in number of countries and companies and in total market capitalization (see table 7.3).

Table 7.3

MSCI Frontier Markets Index Versus My Expanded Universe

	Index	Frontier Markets Expanded Universe
Management	Passive	Active
Countries in Opportunity Set	24	102
Companies in Opportunity Set	122	930*
Market Capitalization of Opportunity Set	$265 billion	$2+ trillion

*Companies with a minimum $400 million market capitalization or $2 million average daily volume traded.

Of course, there are other frontier indices to choose from. However, the performance of indices can vary so widely as to raise the question of whether they are trying to measure the same thing. While the 2013 returns for some frontier indices were roughly similar—the MSCI FM Index gained 25.9 percent while four lesser-known frontier market indices were up from 21 percent to 28 percent—the Bank of New York Mellon New Frontier DR Index (which comprises ADRs and GDRs of frontier market companies)[1] fell 12.8 percent. This is a 38 percent spread in the one-year returns of two indices that purportedly measure the same asset class. This demonstrates a particular hazard of investing passively in frontier markets: Because of the low correlation between frontier markets (described in chapter 6), indices following different markets can have such divergent returns that the benchmark you choose can mean the difference between double-digit losses and double-digit gains.

The second pitfall of passive investing is that it gives investors no freedom of choice. While passive investors are stuck with the index constituents, active investors can use a combined top-down and bottom-up approach not only to pick better companies from those countries already in an index but also to expand their universe to encompass countries with strong and improving fundamentals that are implementing structural reforms. (Ultimately, such reforms may lead to inclusion of these countries into indices and thus greater interest and flows from foreign investors more bound to benchmarks.) Actively managing away from benchmarks by investing in countries and companies before their inclusion in frontier indices offers significant sources for additional investment returns. For example, one of the largest country exposures in our frontier market funds in 2014 was Saudi Arabia, which is not even part of the benchmark frontier index. It is, however, one of the deepest and most liquid markets in my frontier universe.

The Problem with Frontier ETFs

Passive investors were given a powerful new investment tool with the invention of the exchange-traded fund ("ETF") in 1993. An ETF looks like an index fund but trades like a stock. The first ETF, the Standard & Poor's Depositary Receipt (ticker: SPY, nicknamed "Spider"), mimics the S&P 500 Index, and in 2015 SPY traded on average $25 billion per day (Apple, the world's largest corporation by market value, traded about $6.1 billion per day).

ETFs offer investors better liquidity, better tax efficiency, and oftentimes lower commissions and fees than index mutual funds.

Like frontier indices, though, not all frontier market ETFs are created equal. Take the iShares MSCI Frontier 100 ETF (ticker: FM) and the Guggenheim Frontier Markets ETF (ticker: FRN). The iShares ETF tries to match the performance of the MSCI Frontier 100 Index,[2] while Guggenheim's ETF mimics the BNY Mellon New Frontier DR Index. Just as with their corresponding indices, the 2013 returns varied wildly. The iShares ETF was up 23.7 percent (the MSCI FM 100 Index was up 25.8 percent in 2013), while the Guggenheim ETF fell 14.6 percent. These same companies' emerging market ETFs, however—the iShares MSCI Emerging Markets ETF (ticker: EEM) and the Guggenheim MSCI Emerging Markets Equal Weight ETF (ticker: EWEM)—were both down a little under 6 percent in 2013, in line with their more highly correlated underlying emerging market benchmarks. This highlights the problem with frontier ETFs: Not only can they have trouble replicating their benchmark indices due to market liquidity, but their benchmarks do not accurately represent the investable frontier universe. So even benchmark-hugging ETFs do not necessarily give you adequate exposure to the asset class. At the start of 2016, the iShares MSCI Frontier 100 ETF was invested 24 percent in Kuwait, a country that represents less than 2 percent of the frontier universe's GDP, so investing in an ETF or any other passive investment gets you a very warped frontier portfolio composition.

Active Management

Given these pitfalls in passive investing—be it in ETFs or other indexed products—an active approach to frontier markets is often much more desirable. This is not to say, though, that active investing is without its own downsides.

The first is that, if done correctly, active investing takes more work—research, analysis, decision making, and decision monitoring—than does passive investing. I have included examples of this type of work throughout the book in the form of case studies of some of our past investments; as those discussions show, active investing is a time-consuming and resource-intensive process.

The second disadvantage of active investing is that it is more expensive. Trading costs are higher because turnover is usually higher, and active investors often buy less-liquid securities with higher commissions or wider bid/ask spreads. Active managers also charge higher management fees than passive managers. Funds and ETFs that track developed market indices charge less than ten basis points (0.1 percent) per year, and emerging markets ETFs can be had for fifteen basis points (although the popular iShares MSCI Emerging Markets ETF charges sixty-seven basis points per year). Active managers typically charge seventy basis points or more for mainstream emerging market portfolios and upwards of 1.25 percent for frontier portfolios. These higher fees handicap active managers' performance every reporting period. But frontier market indices' irrational construction make them relatively easy to beat by active managers over long periods of time despite the managers' higher fees.

Active management can also involve higher risk. Actively managed portfolios typically hold fewer positions than passive portfolios, so they derive less benefit from diversification, and a poorly performing position in a more concentrated portfolio will have a greater negative impact on overall returns. An actively managed portfolio might perform too far out of line with its benchmark—called tracking error. (Of course, you may prefer that your manager create tracking error by avoiding overpriced stocks that happen to be part of the benchmark.) And there is also the risk that the manager may not know what he or she is doing; this risk can be mitigated by studying the manager's track record and (more importantly) how it was achieved, and by making sure that the manager has skin in the game in the form of a meaningful personal investment in the strategy. Having a substantial chunk of your manager's net worth invested alongside you is a great way to ensure your manager keeps his or her eye on the ball.

So despite the possible downsides—more work, higher fees, and greater risk—I still believe that active investing is the right approach to frontier markets. Once you have decided to take this approach, the next step is to hire an investment manager, or invest in a mutual fund, specializing in frontier markets. (Chapter 8 discusses another option: do-it-yourself investing in frontier markets.)

What do frontier market active managers bring to the table? In addition to the financial analysis demanded of all active managers, they conduct extensive research and due diligence, traveling around the world to meet with frontier market company managements and government officials, consultants, IMF and World Bank personnel, and bankers. I have traveled to over 100 countries, and my team and I regularly conducted over a thousand meetings per year around the globe. Active managers then construct portfolios of securities based on their outlook for countries, industries, and companies, within the constraints of the portfolio's mandate.

In addition to the work involved in security selection, managing a frontier market portfolio takes a great deal of time, effort, and resources—more than many self-directed investors are willing to commit. It takes a lot of time, for instance, to open brokerage accounts in frontier markets. And given the onerous compliance requirements and potential penalties under the U.S. Foreign Account Tax Compliance Act, many foreign banks and brokers no longer want to open new accounts for U.S. investors. Many other logistical details make it very difficult for individual investors to get into the markets—take, as just one instance, the complications surrounding settlement.

Settlement is the process of completing securities trades through the simultaneous delivery of securities and receipt of payment (known as Delivery Versus Payment) by the two parties to the trade. For centuries, this was done through physical settlement—paper checks paying for paper stock certificates. The physical settlement process could take several days or longer, and in the time between trade and settlement, the buyer of the security was at risk of default by the seller. Physical settlements can be fraught with other mishaps. Egypt did not open its Misr Clearing and Settlement Department until October 1996, and so prior to this, an investor had to possess a physical stock certificate to prove ownership of shares of a company. Whenever we purchased or sold Egyptian shares, the local brokerage firm dispatched a messenger on scooter to collect or deliver the certificates. Once, the messenger was mugged, and the stock certificates he carried were lost. We were still able to collect dividends on the stock, but because we did not physically hold the certificates, we could not sell the shares until a replacement certificate was issued.

Markets can reduce settlement risk by shortening the settlement period and by using a clearinghouse to assume the risks of the trade from the two parties. Both of these advances became increasingly necessary as the number of stocks and the volume of trades on markets have grown, and fortunately, both have been possible with advances in technology. Today most markets use an indirect holding system (where the shareholder of record is not you but your broker or a central securities depository) and an electronic settlement system. On exchanges in the United States and many other developed markets, securities transactions are settled three days after the trade, or T+3. Three days between trade and settlement can still leave investors exposed to counterparty default risk, as happened with the collapse of Lehman Brothers in 2008.

So markets are moving to reduce T+3 to T+2. In October 2014, twenty-nine European markets migrated to T+2. India, an early adopter of T+2, is now studying the logistical challenges of moving to T+1, with the Securities and Exchange Board of India calculating that a one-day settlement cycle would reduce value at risk by 30 percent.[3] Interestingly, several frontier markets, such as Bulgaria and Panama, already use T+2, so custody and settlement is another area where frontier markets have benefited from advances in technology. An understanding of these nuances of settlement is just one example of the knowledge that active investors need but that individual investors may not possess.

Case Study: Activist Investing in Croatia

Investors' interests are often best served when their manager takes not just an active approach but an activist approach to maximize shareholder value, especially in nascent public equity markets. In some circumstances, such as with the Polish privatization funds that I discuss in chapter 10, the investment manager may need to take over day-to-day management of a portfolio company to realize an investment's full potential. Activist investing can also mean agitating for the brokerage community to change its policies, as with our investment in the Romanian property restitution fund Fondul Proprietatea, which I also discuss in chapter 10. In any case, such an activist approach can lead to a significantly improved outcome for shareholders—as was my experience with Unicredito's purchase of Zagrebačka Banka.

I began purchasing shares in Zagrebačka Banka, the leading Croatian bank, in early 1997. I have often invested in holding companies that were not properly priced by the market, especially if some of their holdings were publicly traded and thus easy to value. Most often, this happened in developed markets such as the United States or France. But because of the turmoil in emerging markets at the turn of this century, a similar opportunity existed in Zagrebačka Banka, the largest and best-quality bank in Croatia.

Our team did a lot of work on Croatia in 1995 and 1996, when I invested in the restructuring of the former Yugoslav debt (see chapter 9). Croatia was doing well, with GDP growth of 5 percent, low inflation of 4 percent, and an economy free of large amounts of government debt. In contrast to Asia, which was overleveraged and overbanked, the banking market in Croatia was undeveloped, and Zagrebačka dominated a growing market for financial services. Zagrebačka was well run and had been upgrading its systems and benchmarking procedures to the best international standards. Its loan book was overprovisioned, and the bank was able to start releasing provisions in 1997.

In addition to its core banking business, Zagrebačka had substantial equity stakes in a wide range of Croatian business. Many of these stakes were acquired following the breakup of the former Yugoslavia when companies were unable to service their debts as a result of the war. The value of these stakes was substantial, but the bank's stock price didn't reflect this. On a reported basis Zagrebačka's stock traded on a P/E ratio of 8.4 times 1998 earnings; in fact, the bank was much cheaper because of its large nonbanking investment portfolio.

Zagrebačka's investment portfolio was dominated by a 12 percent ownership stake in Pliva, the successful Croatian pharmaceutical company. Pliva was the only eastern European drug company that had been able to develop and sell its own branded, proprietary drug in the United States (the antibiotic Azithromycin marketed by Pfizer). The company was listed in Croatia and in London. Pliva's stock had also declined and was itself an attractive investment, but even at its depressed current price, it represented over a third of Zagrebačka's market capitalization. Other listed and unlisted holdings, conservatively valued, represented another 40 percent of Zagrebačka's market capitalization. The management of Zagrebačka had stated clearly that it intended to sell this portfolio in the next eighteen months and to reorient the proceeds into the development of its core banking business. The bank would not have to pay any tax on the proceeds of these sales, making its divestment plan even more attractive. In total, these noncore assets represented close to 75 percent of Zagrebačka's market capitalization. After subtracting them, the bank was trading on a P/E ratio of two times 1998 earnings and a price-to-book ratio of 0.4 times. Zagrebačka's core banking business was almost being given to investors for free.

A P/E of two times is an absurdly low valuation for a conservative bank that is growing and that dominates its local market. Even after recent declines, most of the emerging Europe banking sector was selling on a 1998 P/E ratio of over ten times. If Zagrebačka's core banking business were valued at ten times earnings, then the implied value of the bank plus the portfolio holdings would be $40 per share compared to the then current $20 share price, an upside of 100 percent.

Zagrebačka's stock dropped 33 percent during the second quarter of 1998 and was more attractive than ever. Following the Russian crisis that summer, I re-examined the strategic position of Zagrebačka and was still impressed. Emerging markets were hit hard in the second half of 1998; but Zagrebačka continued to be well run, enjoyed a great franchise, still contained significant hidden value, and after its stock price fell in response to the worldwide emerging market crisis represented exceptional value. Zagrebačka was also the only high-quality eastern European bank that had not been effectively taken over by a western European or U.S. banking group (the exception was OTP in Hungary, where the government had a "golden share" that effectively prevented a takeover).

We continued to own shares in Zagrebačka throughout the emerging market crisis. After the worst of the crisis had passed, I re-examined our analytical work on both the current condition of Zagrebačka and the Croatian economy. I then met the management of Zagrebačka at the end of 1999 and determined that the bank was financially sound and management appeared to have developed a more flexible approach to the bank's strategic options. As a result, we began to steadily increase our holdings of Zagrebačka throughout 2000, buying the bulk of our position at an average price of $15.40 per global depositary receipt (GDR).

At that point, Zagrebačka still held extensive investments in non-banking assets: its strategic holding in Pliva and other assets including hotels and holiday resorts on the Dalmatian coast. By the first half of 2000, these "hidden" assets were worth at least $11.50 per Zagrebačka GDR (split roughly between the listed Pliva holding and the tourism and other assets). Therefore out of the $15.40 Zagrebačka GDR price, only $3.90 was directly "attributable" to the banking business, which I conservatively expected to earn $1.69 per share in 2000. This effectively valued the banking business on a P/E ratio of just over two times (as it had been in 1998); its underlying price-to-book valuation had increased only slightly, to 0.65. The potential for unlocking value at Zagrebačka was enormous. I believed that this could be achieved through unbundling or selling the noncore assets, which would then highlight how inexpensive the underlying banking franchise was. While this had once been part of management's plan, they now appeared less sanguine on the idea of unbundling. But I thought that the value was so extreme, and the quality of the underlying franchise so strong, that it would not be long before another bank would consider bidding for Zagrebačka.

As we increased our position, we also decided that we needed to take a more active role to extract the fullest possible value from our

Zagrebačka holdings. I started discussions with the senior management of the bank. In my first strategic meeting with them in October 2000, I expressed my strongly held belief that if the management wanted to realize shareholder value, they should quickly sell the many noncore investments that Zagrebačka held. In addition, they should then return the proceeds to shareholders, through either a special dividend or a share buyback. I let them know that in the absence of a total unbundling and return of cash to shareholders, I would be in favor of a takeover.

Although they were initially resistant, by March 2001 they realized the seriousness of the situation and retained Credit Suisse First Boston to maximize shareholder value and look for potential buyers of the bank. In May 2001, Unicredito of Italy and Allianz of Germany announced that they had jointly purchased 20 percent of Zagrebačka and that they were making an offer for up to another 55 percent of the company. This would give them a 75 percent position in Zagrebačka. While I was pleased that an offer had arrived, I didn't like the terms. We decided to fight for our own and other minority shareholders' rights.

I objected strongly to the terms of the proposed Unicredito offer for a number of reasons. I did not believe that the $23.80 per GDR that Unicredito was offering represented a sufficient takeover premium. More important, I believed Unicredito should offer to take out 100 percent of the free float. A common takeover practice in eastern and central Europe was for the acquiring company to purchase 75 percent of the shares of the target company and then leave the totally powerless 25 percent minority as a still-listed "orphan" stock. Many independent analysts at the time believed that the remaining shares (i.e., the minority shares left after the deal) could trade at a price as low as $15 per GDR due to their illiquidity and the complete lack of control or effective rights that a minority holder would then have. This was clearly not in the interest of shareholders, as the GDRs were trading at nearly $20. To put this into context, if shareholders tendered their Zagrebačka shares into the deal, they ran the risk that they would have 75 percent of their shares accepted and 25 percent of them returned. Consequently, the shareholders would receive $23.80 of consideration for 75 percent of their position and would be left with 25 percent in the illiquid and effectively disenfranchised stub at $15. The combined value of such a position would therefore be $21.60, not $23.80.

Prompted by concern over the inadequate offer (in terms of both price and percentage tendered for), we began to contact other shareholders and formed a "Committee of Independent Shareholders." Once formed, the committee controlled over 20 percent of Zagrebačka Banka and held more shares than Unicredito and Allianz combined. We articulated our belief, in a variety of public venues, that Unicredito should pay a higher price to acquire Zagrebačka, and that, most important, it should buy out 100 percent of the free float. In June of 2001, the committee put a substantial advertisement in the *Financial Times* and also in the Croatian-language business newspaper *Vecernji List*, announcing the committee's opposition to the deal. After consulting with local counsel, we also wrote and spoke to the Croatian SEC and the Croatian Central Bank because we believed that under Croatian law, Unicredito had an obligation to offer to buy 100 percent of the shares.

Gradually, our efforts began to pay off. Unicredito finally agreed to extend its offer to 100 percent of the Zagrebačka shares. This step in itself was a substantial improvement. In addition, through media pressure and continuous talks with the Zagrebačka management and Supervisory Board, we succeeded in convincing Unicredito to agree to allow Zagrebačka to pay a 2001 dividend. The bank declared a $0.70 dividend per GDR (a compromise, as we proposed a $1.30 dividend), which further enhanced the terms of the deal.

We were able to substantially improve the terms of the deal through the dividend payment and by extending the offer for 100 percent of the outstanding stock. These two changes increased the total consideration from the effective value of Unicredito's initial bid of $21.60 to $24.55, an improvement of 13.6 percent. Our investment in Zagrebačka, from the time of purchase in the first half of 2000 at an average price of $15.40, generated a 59 percent return in a period when emerging markets were down almost 10 percent and world markets were down 25 percent. This is a powerful example of the importance of not only active but also activist investing.

Of course, as I've discussed, active investing in frontier markets requires extensive brokerage and custodial relationships and takes a great deal of time and effort, which is why I believe the best approach is to hire a frontier markets' specialist. But for those who want to do it themselves, read on.

8

Do-It-Yourself Investing
in Frontier Markets

Investing in frontier markets is considerably more complicated than investing in mainstream emerging or developed markets, which is of course one reason why bargains in frontier markets abound—and why those who want to capture these bargains usually enlist a manager to help them do so. But if you're willing to do the work, you can gain exposure to frontier markets on your own in several ways. You can invest directly in frontier market companies whose shares trade in developed markets. You can invest directly in frontier market companies whose shares trade in their local equity markets, if your brokerage account can trade in these markets. Or you can invest indirectly in a frontier market through its currency or debt, or through commodities essential to that country's growth.

Frontier Companies Listed in Developed Markets

The easiest way to add direct frontier exposure to a portfolio is to invest in companies that operate in frontier markets but whose shares are either listed on a developed market exchange, or are locally listed but available via American depositary receipts (ADRs) or global depositary receipts (GDRs) that trade in a developed market. Not only does this afford the convenience of trading through your existing traditional brokerage account, but it also offers the advantage of trading in U.S. dollars or other developed-market currencies, eliminating the need (and the associated risk) of converting funds to frontier local currencies.

While this strategy certainly does not provide access to all frontier opportunities, it does capture a range of options. For instance, more than 200 companies, from over thirty countries, offer ADRs or GDRs. The largest of these, such as Colombia's Ecopetrol and Argentina's YPF, trade hundreds of thousands—or even millions—of ADRs per day. Most frontier ADRs and GDRs, however, are much smaller and less liquid than that. Table 8.1 lists, by sector, a sampling of other large frontier market ADRs/GDRs.[1] Each company has a greater than $500 million market capitalization, although its ADRs/GDRs may trade very thinly.

If you were to analyze a list of every available ADR/GDR, you would see that while banking is by far the most represented industry, an investor could construct a fairly well-diversified frontier portfolio from ADRs/GDRs alone. Notably underrepresented on this list are consumer products companies, which often trade only on local exchanges.

Table 8.1
Selected ADRs/GDRs of Frontier Market Companies with Market Caps >$500 Million

Sector	Country	Company	Market Cap (US$ billions)
Consumer Discretionary	Cambodia	Nagacorp (Hotels and Gaming)	1.3
	Greece	Jumbo (Specialty Retail)	1.2
Consumer Staples	Ukraine	MHP (Poultry)	0.8
Energy	Pakistan	Oil & Gas Development Co.	4.6
	Kazakhstan	KazMunaiGas Exploration Production	3.1
Financials	Qatar	Commercial Bank	4.1
	Nigeria	Guaranty Trust Bank	2.3
Health Care	Hungary	Richter Gedeon (Pharm.)	2.8
Industrials	Sri Lanka	John Keells (Conglomerate)	1.3
Information Technology	Argentina	Mercadolibre (Internet)	4.4
Materials	Colombia	Cementos Argos	3.9
	Peru	Minas Buenaventura (Metals & Mining)	1.4
Telecommunication Services	Argentina	Telecom Argentina	3.2
	Kazakhstan	KCell	0.7
Utilities	Romania	Electrica	1.0

A different but related opportunity lies with those companies that are headquartered in developed or mainstream emerging markets but derive their revenues almost solely from operations in frontier markets. These are not common, but they do exist—take UK-based oil companies such as Tullow Oil and SOCO International, which derive all of their revenues from Africa and Vietnam, respectively, or Swedish cellular phone company Millicom, which derives all of its revenues from frontier markets in Central and South America and Africa.

PriceSmart is another example of this type—and its 1997 IPO afforded U.S. investors an early opportunity to invest directly into a pure play on a world-class frontier market retailer.

Case Study: PriceSmart

PriceSmart, headquartered in San Diego, California, owns and operates thirty-eight wholesale clubs in twelve frontier markets in Central America, South America, and the Caribbean. PriceSmart's model, like other chains of its type, is to offer a limited number of products (usually in bulk), cut costs through operational efficiencies and low overhead (its stores are little more than well-lit warehouses), and pass on the savings to customers.

PriceSmart has its roots in the very origins of this warehouse, or wholesale, club model. Sol Price essentially created the warehouse retail concept when he founded FedMart in 1954. He and son Robert launched the eponymous Price Club chain of warehouse clubs in 1976, ultimately merging their company with Costco in 1993; the merger was rocky from the start, and Costco spun off Price Enterprises to Messrs. Price shortly thereafter. Sol and Robert opened their first PriceSmart club in Panama in 1996 and began expanding across Latin America and the Caribbean soon thereafter.

This connection to Sol Price was one of the first things that attracted me to PriceSmart. In the eyes of the industry, no one does the warehouse club better. James Sinegal, Costco's co-founder and longest serving CEO, started his career moving mattresses at Sol's FedMart for $1.25 an hour, and says that Sol had more influence on his career than anyone. Sam Walton, founder of Wal-Mart, said in his memoir *Made in America*, "I guess I've stolen—I actually prefer the word 'borrowed'—as many ideas from Sol Price as from any-body else in the business," including, he admits, the idea of Sam's Club. PriceSmart shares a business model with Costco and Sam's, though the average size of its stores is 50,000 to 90,000 square feet, smaller than its competitors, in order to better fit the needs of its smaller markets.

What also drew me to the company was the proven success of the warehouse club format in Latin America and the Caribbean. PriceSmart same-store sales have grown at almost 12 percent annu-ally for the last six years, well above the same-store sales growth of Latin American retailers overall. Total club members are increasing at a fast 11 percent per year, which shows that stores continue to attract interest.

I was further encouraged by PriceSmart's expansion potential. PriceSmart entered the Colombian market in 2011, and it plans to expand further there—a move that could double the company's foot-print, given that Colombia's GDP and population is larger than the combined GDP of the other eleven countries in which the company operates. The opportunity is likely larger even than this; I see no rea-son why PriceSmart would not eventually enter Chile and Peru. U.S.-based Costco, BJ's, and Sam's combined have more than 1,300 ware-house clubs, while PriceSmart has only thirty-six, and PriceSmart operates in an economy about half the size of the United States. The company has plenty of room for expansion.

While I found PriceSmart's fundamentals exceptional, the market did not agree. The stock traded at just seventeen times earnings in March 2011, which I estimated could grow at 25 percent per year well into the future. After completing due diligence, we began purchas-ing shares of PriceSmart in June 2011. The market finally discovered this opportunity and the stock rerated, trading as high as forty times earnings by the end of 2013, by which time we had exited most of our position. The stock corrected sharply in the second half of 2015, making it once again attractive on a valuation basis. I think revenues could grow at double digits for the next five years—and this may be conservative given growth in the last five years. PriceSmart's return on equity is high at almost 20 percent, and the company boasts a strong balance sheet and a net cash position, so it is well prepared to deliver strong growth.

Investing in Frontier-Listed Equities

Only a limited number of frontier opportunities are listed in developed countries; many of the most attractive frontier equities trade only in their home markets. It is beyond the scope of this book to delve into the legal and administrative minutiae of opening local brokerage accounts to trade frontier-listed shares, but suffice to say I have found that developing strong relationships with local brokers and custodians is very important in frontier markets. And many of the structures required for foreigners to access some of these markets, such as participatory notes ("p-notes" for short), are available only to large institutional investors or professional investment managers.

Assuming your brokerage account can trade them, one place to look for attractive opportunities in frontier markets is the locally listed shares of a multinational's frontier market subsidiaries. Often, you can look to how the parent's mainstream emerging market subsidiaries fared in the past to help assess its frontier subsidiaries' prospects. This was certainly the case with Unilever.

Case Study: Unilever, Then and Now

My view that emerging markets provide a roadmap for frontier market investors applies as much to the bottom-up as the top-down. The investments I find in frontier markets today share many similarities with those I made in emerging markets many years ago. The British/ Dutch global consumer products company Unilever, for instance, has subsidiaries that trade in several emerging and frontier markets. Analyzing the past performance of Unilever's subsidiaries in mainstream emerging markets can tell us a lot about how its frontier market subsidiaries may perform in the future.

One of Unilever's emerging market subsidiaries is Unilever Indonesia. At the end of 2002, five years after the Indonesian rupiah collapsed, the market valued Unilever Indonesia at $1.55 billion. In simplistic valuation terms, this market capitalization divided across 212 million Indonesians represented a value of $7.30 per capita for Unilever Indonesia—a very low price, at least relative to the developed world, for a leading producer of shampoos, body lotions, and laundry detergents.

This $7.30 valuation looked even cheaper when you consider the country's economic growth trajectory. From 2002 to 2012, Indonesia's nominal GDP grew by over 16 percent annually, and its per capita GDP grew over 14 percent annually, from $922 to nearly $3,600. As a country evolves from a rural, agrarian, subsistence economy into an urban, manufacturing-centric economy, its per capita income grows. Once you have an incremental dollar of disposable income in your pocket, you begin to move up the S-curve of discretionary consumption items.[2]

Over that period of 16 percent nominal GDP growth, Indonesia developed a consumer class, and the first place its disposable income went was to what we in the developed world consider basic necessities. If you eat it, drink it, wear it, bathe with it, brush your teeth with it, or wash your clothes in it—that's where the first discretionary dollars (or in this case rupiahs) go. Soap manufacturers' sales—and earnings—soar once people consume two bars of soap per year versus no bars of soap per year. Over the 2002 to 2012 period, Unilever Indonesia's earnings grew at over 17 percent per year—in line with nominal GDP growth—which over ten years led to a near quintupling of earnings.

At the end of 2015, Unilever Indonesia had a $20.5 billion market capitalization—thirteen times its market capitalization thirteen years previously—with no change in the number of shares outstanding. This is partly the function of a rerating of its P/E multiple from fourteen times earnings at year-end 2002 to forty-seven times earnings in 2015, but the bulk of the company's increased market value was driven by the growth of its earnings, which was fueled by the growth of disposable income of the Indonesian consumer. Today, Unilever Indonesia's value per capita is about $80, over ten times what it was in 2002.

With that in mind, consider an investment in Unilever Indonesia versus its parent over the last fifteen or so years. As figure 8.1 highlights, while an investor would have gained some exposure to the Indonesian growth story (or the broader emerging market growth story, for that matter) via an investment in Unilever the parent company, that investor would have benefited much more handsomely from

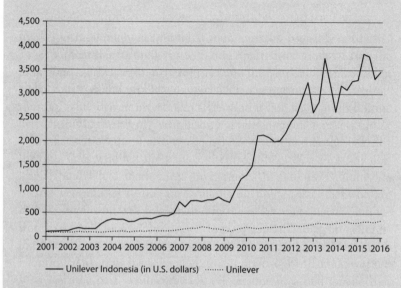

Figure 8.1
Performance of Unilever parent vs. Unilever Indonesia (indexed to 100).
Source: Bloomberg.

owning the local subsidiary over the long term. Including dividends, Unilever Indonesia rose over 3,300 percent, twelve times more than did its parent.

Today, I see a similar opportunity in another Unilever subsidiary, Unilever Nigeria. We can look to Unilever's experience in Indonesia to see why.

For starters, both countries have large populations—Indonesia now has over 250 million people and Nigeria over 170 million—which present significant opportunities for Unilever. At the start of 2016, Unilever Nigeria was valued at $821 million, or about $4.50 per capita, about where Unilever Indonesia was valued at the end of 2001 (figure 8.2). By this measure, the valuation of Unilever Nigeria relative to the size of its market lags Unilever Indonesia by about fourteen years.

On a macroeconomic basis, Nigeria's 2014 U.S. dollar GDP per capita was $3,300, about equal to Indonesia's. On a PPP-adjusted basis, Nigeria lags Indonesia by a decade (Figure 8.3). Unilever Nigeria is attractively valued on this top-down metric, based on the historical experience of Indonesia. This suggests an attractive long-term

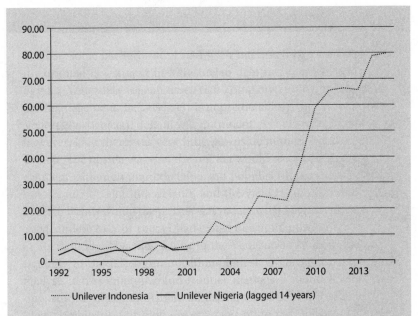

Figure 8.2
Market capitalization per capita, Unilever Indonesia vs. Unilever Nigeria (lagged fourteen years). *Source*: Bloomberg; UN Population Division.

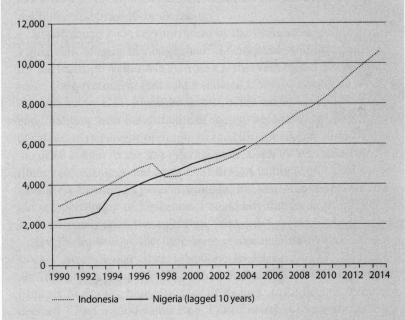

Figure 8.3
PPP-Adjusted GDP per capita comparison, Indonesia vs. Nigeria (lagged ten years). *Source*: IMF.

outlook for Unilever Nigeria's market capitalization if the country continues along its current growth trajectory.

From a microeconomic perspective, the parallels between Unilevers Indonesia and Nigeria are compelling: solid global corporate governance, world-class product development, and excellent marketing and distribution strategy, all provided by parent Unilever. Unilever has an extremely successful track record selling bars of soap in developed and emerging markets around the world for over 100 years; so, as with frontier subsidiaries of multinationals in general, my concern is less with the company and more with the state of the economy. Can Nigeria grow nominal GDP at 16 percent per year (in line with Indonesia), generating enough growth in consumer income to provide Unilever Nigeria the opportunity to sell 16 percent more product per year with 16 percent (or higher) earnings growth per year? If so, we could easily see each consumer in Nigeria valued not at $4.50 but at $60 or $70, as we saw in Indonesia. Unilever Nigeria could well be worth over $10 billion in ten years' time, quite an attractive return for its shareholders.

Of course, just because Nigeria today in many ways resembles Indonesia ten or fifteen years ago does not guarantee that Nigeria will grow at 16 percent—or even 12 percent or 8 percent—per year over the next decade. Every opportunity carries a different set of risks, and that is what frontier investment managers spend their days researching and analyzing. The thesis remains the same, however: Frontier market companies often follow the trajectory of similar companies in mainstream emerging markets, providing a roadmap for investors.

Multinationals with locally traded frontier subsidiaries are rather rare (Nestlé is another example), but many markets have local companies, traded on local exchanges, that are as strong as, if not stronger than, their multinational-subsidiary competitors. Their growth prospects are similar, and the local companies can sell at even more attractive valuations than the multinational subsidiaries—again, if your brokerage account can trade shares in these markets.

A Caveat on Pursuing Frontier Exposure
Through Multinationals

Many developed and mainstream emerging market multinationals such as Unilever are pursuing the allure of the frontier market customer. For a multinational to be an attractive investment proxy for frontier growth, however, it is crucial to consider just how much business the company conducts in frontier markets. Broadly speaking, the percentage of revenues from frontier market operations for most multinationals is at low levels— roughly 5 percent.[3]

This caveat highlights why it is often better to gain frontier exposure by investing in frontier-dedicated companies rather than emerging or developed market companies with some frontier operations. Shoprite, the South African–based retailer, illustrates this point. Shoprite posted stellar 28.1 percent sales growth in the second half of 2013 for its supermarkets in the fourteen other African countries in which it operates (all frontier markets), versus only 7.6 percent growth for its supermarkets in South Africa. Sales outside of South Africa, however, represented only 16 percent of total revenues; so while Shoprite's frontier markets business is growing quite rapidly, contributing nearly one-third of company-wide annual sales growth, this is not enough (yet) to carry the day. The stock still trades on the strength or weakness of its South African operations—a risk for those looking to this emerging market company for frontier market exposure.

Investing Directly in Frontier Markets Means
Buying—and Selling—in the Local Currency

When you buy a share of stock on a foreign stock exchange, you pay for that stock in local currency. In some cases, you can hedge this foreign currency exposure back to your home currency. But often no market exists on which to implement this hedge, in which case owning a foreign stock exposes you, from the day you buy until the day you sell, to up or down moves in the stock price as well as to fluctuations in the exchange rate between the local currency and your home currency.

You are also exposed, on the day you buy and the day you sell a locally listed stock, to the liquidity (or lack thereof) of the underlying foreign exchange market—it may be straightforward to buy Nigerian naira or Kenyan shillings with your dollars or euros, but what about selling them back? You never know if a frontier market country is going to impose currency restrictions. A country's central bank will from time to time be a source of liquidity for local brokers, but if it curtails its willingness to buy back its own currency because it does not want to give up its foreign currency reserves, then it becomes very difficult to convert out of that local currency. Argentina has a strict policy that investors are allowed to take out of the country only $5,000 per year, so if you buy local Argentine equities in size and ever want to sell them, you may not get your money back for a very long time.

Owning a frontier market stock directly thus can mean taking on currency risk as well. This currency risk, which I discuss further in chapter 12, becomes an additional consideration in your investment analysis. Fortunately, what makes a specific stock attractive oftentimes also makes its underlying currency attractive (i.e., undervalued), or at least not unattractive, although occasionally I will come across an appealing equity investment in a country whose macroeconomic and/or political fundamentals I find less so. This is analogous to traveling in a boat upriver— you may still reach your destination, but it takes a lot more time and effort. When you buy a stock in a local currency, you are betting on both the boat and the direction of the river. Companies operating in favorable macroeconomic currents face a much lower degree of difficulty reaching their destinations.

Investing Indirectly in Frontier Markets: Frontier Currencies

Occasionally, the best way to express a view on a country—positive or negative—is by buying or selling that country's currency. The foreign exchange (or currency) market is the most liquid asset class in the world—trading over $5.3 trillion daily.[4] While developed market currencies are the most widely traded, emerging market currencies are becoming a larger share of the global foreign exchange market. The Mexican peso rose to become the eighth-most-traded currency in 2013. The Chinese yuan (also known as the renminbi) notably jumped from the twenty-ninth-most-traded currency in 2004 to the ninth-most-traded in 2013.

Frontier currency markets are understandably much less liquid than mainstream emerging or developed currency markets. The most-traded currencies in 2013 in my frontier universe were the Hungarian forint, ranked twenty-fourth, and the Czech koruna, ranked twenty-sixth. But these currencies can still be much more liquid than their associated equity markets. The forint, for instance, trades about $9 billion per day, whereas the average daily volume of equities traded on the Budapest Stock Exchange is about $40 million. Other frontier currencies trade even less volume, or not at all; but views on a currency can also be expressed through a country's short-term treasury bills, whose interest rate spreads over U.S. Treasuries reflect the market's view on the country's currency prospects versus the U.S. dollar. Currencies and fixed income in frontier markets—as in emerging and developed markets—can be attractive ways to invest indirectly in these markets' growth, but only if they offer equity-like returns (more on this in chapter 9).

Capturing Frontier Growth Indirectly by Investing in Commodities

Another indirect way to capture the growth in frontier markets is to invest in the commodities required to fuel and sustain this growth.

Young, growing populations eat more food—demanding more wheat, corn, and rice, and the fertilizer to grow them. And as standards of living rise in frontier markets, diets become richer, and people eat more meat. Per capita meat consumption in China, for instance, more than doubled from 1989 to 2009. Larger livestock herds require more feedstuffs, particularly corn. One additional kilogram of beef requires feeding roughly seven additional kilograms of corn to the associated cow. China now feeds 70 percent of its corn crop to its livestock and only 5 percent to its people.

Young populations in growing markets also drive more cars, which require more steel, aluminum, and palladium to build; more oil to fuel; and more cement to build the roads and bridges on which to drive. Young people also marry (more weddings mean higher demand for gold for gifts and dowries) and start families (requiring more copper, cement, and lumber to build new houses).

What is the best way to invest in the growth in commodity demand in frontier markets? Investors can buy shares in developed or emerging market commodity producers, or even (in some cases) the shares of frontier market commodity producers and exporters—but investing in the underlying commodities themselves is oftentimes the best way to profit from the growth in these markets. In the past, we have held positions in precious metals, industrial metals, soft commodities, and energy-related commodities that we felt would benefit from frontier market demand growth. Owning a long position in a commodity can also hedge the risk of a steep price hike in that commodity for those frontier markets that must import that commodity in large quantities (see Inflation Risk in chapter 12).

Corporate Sustainability

Some final advice if you go it alone: as you analyze potential investment opportunities in frontier markets, it is important to look beyond the financials and current growth prospects of a company and try to determine whether the company's success is sustainable. As a long-term investor, I care about sustainability; ultimately, whether a company can maintain its success depends on its ability to continuously deal with environmental, social, and governance issues. Successful management of these factors allows a company to avoid potentially costly and/or disruptive events, which would also affect its financial health.

When assessing a company, I suggest you look carefully at each of the following ten sustainability factors:

1. The company's sustainability policy
2. The company's corporate governance policy
3. Independence of the company's board of directors and audit committee
4. Management/employee ownership of equity
5. Employee relations
6. The company's social responsibility policy including child labor, health, safety, and human rights
7. The company's environmental policy
8. Use and promotion of renewable energy
9. Contribution to local economic development and community involvement
10. The company's policy on diversity and gender equality

This list can be applied to all of your holdings globally, but it is especially helpful in frontier markets where differences are most stark. I encourage you to add a sustainability checklist to your analytical toolbox.

* * *

Whether you hire a manager or go it alone, investing in frontier markets can bring a wealth of benefits to a global portfolio. It also involves additional risks, the topic of chapters 11 and 12. But first: While the principal attraction of frontier markets is the opportunity to invest in growth equities at a good price, frontier markets offer a number of other ways to make money. These strategies—which few investors focus on—include special situations in distressed debt, which I discuss in the next chapter, and privatizations, which I discuss in chapter 10. A warning: Some of the examples in these next two chapters (particularly the case studies) are fairly complex in their financial discussion.

9

Special Situations in Distressed Debt

I have invested in debt for almost as long as I have invested in equities. But I never invest in debt just to earn the semiannual interest payments—to "clip the coupons"—unless, of course, the coupons are substantial. For bonds trading at face value (e.g., a $1,000 bond trading at $1,000, usually referred to as trading at par or at 100 cents on the dollar, "100" for short), these coupon payments represent my only source of return, since the most I will likely receive when I sell the bonds or when the bonds mature is their face value. And the low single-digit coupon rates of most bonds trading at par today are not a particularly attractive return, in my view, for the risk they entail.

Instead, I always look for debt investments with equity-like (i.e., double-digit) returns. Since few bonds offer double-digit coupons, equity-like returns are available (although not guaranteed) only from bonds selling at prices significantly below par. Bonds trading at par have yields equal to their coupon rates, so if I buy a bond with a 7 percent coupon at par, my current yield (the percentage return on my investment from the bond's interest payments) will be 7 percent. But bonds selling at prices below par offer yields higher than their coupon rates, so if I buy that same bond at 50, its 7 percent coupon now pays me a much more equity-like yield of 14 percent on my investment. And if I hold that bond to maturity and the issuer repays the bond's principal in full (100 cents on the dollar), my "yield to maturity" is amplified by this additional return on my initial investment. Even if I sell the bond before maturity, any price I get above my original cost of 50 increases my return (of course, any price below my cost reduces my return).

The catch is that a bond usually trades significantly below par only when its issuer is a company or country in financial trouble (real or perceived), which is why such bonds are referred to as "distressed." And the resolution of this trouble usually involves a bankruptcy or other restructuring—a so-called special situation.

My first job on Wall Street after business school was on the "high yield and special situations" desk of PaineWebber, a U.S. brokerage and asset management firm that has since been bought by UBS. "High yield" refers to bonds with high coupon rates, typically issued by companies with below-investment-grade credit ratings that must offer higher coupons to attract lenders. In the late 1980s, high-yield corporate bonds offered equity-like returns even when they traded at par, from just their coupon payments. The only bonds more attractive than high-yield bonds were distressed high-yield bonds, which traded at a deep discount to par. When I started Everest Capital in 1990, another class of distressed debt had just been born—publicly traded sovereign debt known as Brady bonds.

Case Study: Brady Bonds and the Tequila Crisis

In the 1960s and 1970s, governments funded themselves principally via commercial bank loans. Banks considered loans to governments "money-good," or certain to be repaid; former Citibank chair Walter Wriston even coined the famous phrase, "Countries don't go bust," (to which an IMF official portentously replied, "Yes, but their bankers do"). By the 1980s, though, many countries did default (including the People's Republic of the Congo, my first sovereign customer from my Swiss banking days), and a market for distressed sovereign debt developed. From the restructuring of some of this debt, Brady bonds were created.

Brady bonds were securities issued in exchange for defaulted sovereign commercial bank loans, named after former U.S. Treasury Secretary Nicholas Brady, who proposed the first outline for these debt-reduction plans in 1989. Such plans were implemented for Argentina, Brazil, Bulgaria, Costa Rica, the Dominican Republic, Ecuador, Mexico, Morocco, Nigeria, the Philippines, Poland, Uruguay, and Venezuela. After decades of ruinous economic policies involving protectionism, corruption, and wasteful spending, these countries were reforming—but they needed a lifeline in order to reduce their debt burdens and, ultimately, re-engage global capital markets to finance their future growth. Brady bonds were their lifeline.

The creation of the Brady bond market coincided with a general shift toward free markets worldwide. With the fall of Communism, the leaders of many countries realized that state planning was not a successful means of growing their economies and providing jobs for their citizens. The late 1980s and early 1990s saw a remarkable increase in free-market capitalism and open trading around the world, especially in Latin America. This move toward open markets and capitalism was spurred by the growth of Western-trained economists— outwardly focused professionals schooled at top U.S. and European universities—who joined government bureaucracies and ministries and staked their professional lives on growth and on integration with the world economy.

Many of the countries that defaulted had not only gone through this transformation to free market capitalism; of equal magnitude to the changes in their economies were their moves to democracy. Military dictatorships went from universal to rare. Even Mexico, long burdened with a corrupt and dominating controlling political party, in 1994 conjured the unprecedented spectacle of arresting former high-ranking party officials in a wide-ranging assassination probe.

The face value of all Brady bonds issued was approximately $150 billion (almost 90 percent denominated in U.S. dollars and the rest in G7 currencies). Most individual Brady bond issues were in the billions of dollars of face value—some over $10 billion. Their large size spurred one of the greatest attractions of Bradys: They were much more liquid than other corporate or sovereign distressed debt. Even on the most chaotic trading days, Brady bond bid/ask spreads of one point (versus one-quarter to one-half point in quieter times) were narrower than the bid/ask spreads on normal trading days for most U.S. corporate distressed debt.

Brady bonds incorporated a number of innovations, and creditors could choose from a menu of new securities in exchange for their past obligations. Bonds offered fixed coupons or coupons that floated at a spread (typically 0.875 percent) over LIBOR (the London Interbank Offered Rate, the interest rate that banks charge one another, which is widely used as a benchmark). Some bonds paid interest in cash, and others accrued but did not pay out interest for a certain period. Maturities varied, with some bonds repaying principal in one "bullet" payment at maturity while others paid off portions of principal over many years.

We monitored the Brady market for the first few years but thought the sovereign risks were fairly priced into the bonds (Venezuela is the only significant Brady position we held prior to 1995, in part because its bonds were already trading at yields to maturity approaching 30 percent). Then, in December 1994, Mexico—no longer able to maintain its fixed currency peg—devalued the peso. Investors immediately headed for the exits and sold whatever they could, launching the so-called Tequila Crisis. Mexico had made a classic financing mistake: funding current expenditures and long-term investment with short-term liabilities. Suddenly Mexico found itself with all of its short-term creditors demanding payment and no fresh funding in sight.

This was a classic liquidity crisis; worse, it produced the so-called Tequila Effect—the spread of panic caused by the Tequila Crisis to other countries. Thus by the first quarter of 1995, many Bradys traded not at yields of 10 to 12 percent as they did in 1993 and the beginning of 1994, but at incredibly distressed yields of 22 to 33 percent. These were levels demanded of only the junkiest of developed market corporate borrowers, and when bonds trade at these yields, the market is assuming an extremely high risk of near-term default. Eventually, these countries would either default on their debt or survive the turmoil—in which case the prevalent mood would swing from fear to greed as investors bid up bond prices chasing these high yields.

The Brady market now had my full attention. I was looking not to make macroeconomic wagers, though, but to take advantage of event-oriented opportunities that would produce very good returns if the countries avoided default and would break even if they did default. We ultimately put on a number of attractive Brady-bond capital structure arbitrage trades in early 1995. Many of these situations were analogous to opportunities in corporate distressed securities that proved very profitable for me in the past. In Venezuela, for instance, we constructed an options-based capital structure arbitrage using two bonds with similar prices and yields but with very different downsides in the case of default. We thus had default protection without sacrificing the upside of extremely depressed bond prices. In the interim, the position earned a low teens current yield.

We also found attractive outright long positions in collateralized Brady bonds, which had U.S. Treasury zero-coupon bonds (commonly called "zeros") deposited with the New York Federal Reserve Bank, whose maturities coincided with the Brady bonds' final (bullet) maturities. A holder of such a bond was therefore guaranteed to receive at least par for the bond at maturity if the issuing country were to default and pay no intervening coupons, and if there were no recovery for the defaulted portion. In effect, a collateralized Brady bond was a hybrid security with a stream of coupons bearing the credit risk of the underlying country and the principal bearing the credit risk of the U.S. Treasury.

As U.S. Treasury zeros were a large, liquid market, we could readily determine the value of the principal guarantee. In addition, collateralized bonds often had guaranteed interest payments for a specified period (usually twelve to eighteen months) deposited with the agent bank that facilitated the bond exchange, so the value of the interest guarantee was also easily determinable. This created the anomalous situation in early 1995 that some Brady bonds, after subtracting out the value of their collateral, were trading for 20 to 30 percent of face value—levels beneath where defaulted loans traded for most of the 1980s—and yet the bonds were not in default (table 9.1).

So, for example, an investor could buy a Venezuelan par bond at 43.63 and resell or "strip" the collateral of 22.44, thus buying the net sovereign risk at a little over 21 cents on the dollar. Even defaulted ex-Soviet bank debt (later assumed by Russia) and Algerian debt traded in the twenties, and debt issued by Ivory Coast, Nicaragua, Yugoslavia, and North Korea traded in the teens. All of these countries were in default on interest and principal (Algeria was in default on principal only).

Some argued that the sovereign risk created by stripping a collateralized Brady from its collateral was not exactly the same as a regular

Table 9.1
Representative Brady Bonds and Their Collateral Values, First Quarter 1995

Security	Market Price	U.S. Treasury Zero Coupon	Interest Guarantee	Total Collateral	Net Sovereign Risk
	A	B	C	D = B + C	E = A – D
Argentina Par	40.50	12.90	5.00	17.90	22.60
Brazil Par	36.25	12.10	0.00	12.10	24.15
Bulgaria Disc	41.75	11.90	6.90	18.80	22.95
Mexican Par	47.00	15.25	8.76	24.01	22.99
Venezuela Par	43.63	14.94	7.50	22.44	21.19

noncollateralized claim, because the stripped Brady lacked the principal at maturity (the principal being the collateral in the form of a U.S. Treasury zero). While this argument was technically correct, in practice, because of the very long maturities of those Brady bonds (twenty-five to thirty years), the net present value of the claim on principal was very small—discounted at a rate of 23 percent, $1,000 due in 25 years is worth only $5.65 today, or about half of 1 percent of face value. The value of that last cash flow was therefore minute.

Opportunities like these, in both long positions and arbitrages in Brady bonds, were some of the most profitable of my career, in part because the conventional wisdom in the immediate aftermath of the Tequila Crisis—that the bulk of Brady bonds were on the brink of imminent default—was wrong. But what amazed me is not so much how wrong the conventional wisdom was, but how fast it changed. By the end of 1995, our Venezuelan par Brady bonds had moved from 43 to 57½, for a total return (including a 6.75 percent coupon) of close to 50 percent. By September 1996, the Wall Street Journal was exhorting its readers to "Hold on to your Brady bonds—they could soon become prized collectors' items," describing how Mexico, Argentina, Brazil, and the Philippines were retiring Brady debt through refinancings and buybacks.[1] Many of these refinancings were similar to the arbitrages we put in place, with countries going long (buying back) their higher-yielding bonds and shorting (issuing additional) more expensive, lower-yielding bonds. By the end of 1996 yields on Brady bonds had declined dramatically; I found them fully valued, and we exited our remaining positions in early 1997.

Case Study: The Debt of the Former Yugoslavia, or How to Make Money from CNN

Conventional wisdom also played a major role in another profitable distressed sovereign debt opportunity. In the former Yugoslav Republics, an area I know well, the images of a war-torn Bosnia obscured excellent credit fundamentals that became obvious with the war's end.

As I mentioned in the introduction, I grew up mostly in Switzerland, but as a kid and a teenager in the 1960s and 1970s I spent my summers with my grandparents in Yugoslavia. In the West, the perception was that things in Yugoslavia weren't so bad—but I knew firsthand how difficult life was there. For instance, Yugoslavia's Communist economic system had supposedly been reformed, and the workers owned their businesses. But everyone on the ground knew this was a joke; the high-ranking members of the Communist Party who were managing those companies clearly had very important perks. I could see this every summer in Kraljevica, the small seaside village on the Adriatic near the island of Krk where my grandparents lived. I would watch party members arrive in their big corporate cars and spend their holidays in vacation homes provided by their worker-owned companies. But ironically, by the 1990s, this perception had reversed: The reality on the ground in most of the former Yugoslavia was better than the perception of it in the West. And this misperception ultimately created an investment opportunity.

Yugoslavia comprised various regions, called republics, and in the 1990s the country started to break up as each of the republics declared independence. Each republic became a country by the end of the decade, but not without conflict and bloodshed. Slovenia was the first to declare its independence, in 1990, and the dissolving Yugoslavia was soon engaged in a nearly decade-long series of civil wars (later called the Yugoslav Wars) beginning with the Ten-Day War in Slovenia in 1991. The wars became a fixture on Western media, with a particular focus on one republic: Bosnia.

Televisions showed a constant flow of images of the Bosnian War from 1992 to 1995, and the world's perception was that the civil war there had spread to all of the former Yugoslav republics. Investors tuning into CNN saw daily updates under the banner BALKAN TRAGEDY, and believed that all of the former Yugoslavia was a war-torn wasteland.

The reality, however, was that the other former republics—the newly independent countries of Slovenia, Croatia, Serbia, and Montenegro (formed in 1992) and Macedonia—had experienced little or no destruction, and even Bosnia had just a few hot spots that were shown over and over again. Although my grandparents had passed away by this time, my remaining family and friends in the country confirmed that what I was seeing on TV was not what they were experiencing in their neighborhoods and cities. What's more, Bosnia represented less than 10 percent of the GDP of the former Yugoslavia. Politically Bosnia was a basket case, but economically it was insignificant.

The investment opportunity created by this misperception was in the collective debt of the former Yugoslav republics. This debt was an ideal candidate for my style of investing: It was a misunderstood situation with low downside risk. Ultimately, it was a very lucrative investment and one that paid off much more quickly than I had anticipated.

The debt was issued under the New Financing Agreement (NFA) signed in 1988 by the six Yugoslav republics—Slovenia, Croatia, Serbia, Montenegro, Macedonia, and Bosnia—to refinance loans previously made to those republics and to the National Bank of Yugoslavia (the country's central bank). The original principal was $7.5 billion, but this shrank to $4.2 billion between 1988 and 1990 through buybacks and debt-to-equity swaps. Despite the dissolution of Yugoslavia, the republics of Slovenia, Croatia, Serbia, and Montenegro continued servicing their portions of the NFA debt. But in 1992, the United Nations Security Council imposed harsh sanctions—financial and otherwise—on the newly created country of Serbia and Montenegro (the "new" Yugoslavia), and these sanctions forced Serbia and Montenegro to stop servicing its portion of the debt. Croatia stopped servicing its debt shortly thereafter. The NFA debt was then in default, awaiting a restructuring.

I started studying the NFA debt in the spring of 1995. What immediately piqued my interest was that the liability of the NFA obligors was joint and several, meaning that each republic was liable as principal debtor for *all* NFA obligations. This obliged every republic to negotiate with the NFA's creditors to escape liability for the entire debt. Various methods helped establish what the "fair share" of the debt for each republic would be. The IMF had proposed allocations for each republic, which I used as a starting point in my own analysis. However, because

I knew the richer northern republics of Slovenia and Croatia were anxious to finalize their shares of the NFA debt in order to normalize their financial standing and tap international markets again, I believed that they would take larger shares than the IMF proposed (15.8 percent and 27.8 percent, respectively) and modified my calculations accordingly. (Indeed, in September 1995 Slovenia agreed with NFA creditors to assume 18 percent of the debt.) I also assumed allocations to Serbia and Montenegro slightly higher than the IMF's, and correspondingly reduced my estimated allocations to Bosnia and Macedonia.

In addition to the claim of 100 cents per dollar of principal outstanding, creditors were also owed approximately 18 cents of unpaid interest. This past due interest (PDI), which was to be apportioned among the republics, would continue to accumulate until the debt was restructured. I expected the restructuring of the NFA debt to take place by year-end 1996, by which time the past due interest would have grown to twenty-five. In my analysis, I divided this twenty-five cents among the five republics using the same percentages as my estimated principal allocations. I then set out to put a value on the restructured debt.

Just as one would value a holding company in a corporate restructuring by summing the value of its subsidiaries, in this case I tallied the value of the pieces of debt to be allocated across the various republics to come to my estimate of the true value of the aggregate NFA debt. This sum-of-the-parts analysis bolstered my thesis that "Yugoslavia Inc." was trading at a steep discount to the value of its parts.

Slovenia. Of all the former Yugoslav republics, Slovenia was in the best shape, with its export-oriented economy in excellent condition. Its share of the NFA debt (approximately $750 million) was very small compared to its foreign exchange reserves of over $2.5 billion. On all economic indicators, it was an economic powerhouse, comparable or superior to the Czech Republic, the central European country with the best credit. And Slovenia was untouched by the war. I therefore assumed Slovenia's debt would trade at a spread of 200 basis points (2 percent) over LIBOR, making its share of the principal plus past due interest worth ninety-five cents on the dollar. Slovenia's portion of each dollar of total outstanding NFA debt was worth over twenty-one cents by itself, or half the cost of my investment, and since Slovenia on a standalone basis would be such a high-quality, low-risk credit, I was confident we would likely recoup this portion of our investment quickly.

Croatia. This is where I believed the greatest misperception existed. Because part of eastern Croatia had been the scene of fighting, the market unduly discounted Croatia's credit. In reality, with the war over, I believed Croatia's tourism-derived hard currency earnings would quickly increase from $750 million in 1994 to their pre-1990 level of over $4 billion per year. Croatia's foreign currency reserves of over $2 billion were higher than the $1.3 billion of NFA debt it would likely assume. Its total debt level of about 25 percent of GDP was comparable to Poland's, which carried an investment-grade credit rating (BBB). I assumed Croatia's debt would trade at seventy-five or a spread of 5 percent over LIBOR, but believed it could do much better over time.

Serbia and Montenegro. The UN's economic sanctions had a negative impact on Serbia's economy. Strong agriculture and hydroelectricity sectors helped it survive, however, and created the foundation for a slow recovery. Contrary to common belief, Serbia did not suffer much war-related destruction at this time (it would suffer much more a few years later). If my estimate of Serbia's principal allocation proved accurate, Serbia's postrestructuring debt-to-GDP ratio would be better than neighboring Bulgaria's, whose debt traded at forty-seven and at a yield of 19 percent. I used a very conservative price of thirty for Serbia's debt, assuming the possibility of a partial write-off for some of the debt.

Macedonia. Macedonia was a similar case to Serbia, although I thought the low absolute amount of debt (Macedonia's estimated 6.2 percent share of the NFA was about $200 million) would allow for debt reductions through debt-for-equity swaps. For example, Macedonia's government tobacco company was worth probably as much as its entire debt outstanding. A foreign strategic buyer could wipe out all of Macedonia's NFA debt allocation if the government privatized the tobacco company. I placed a value of thirty-five cents on the dollar on Macedonia's debt.

Bosnia. Bosnia suffered the bulk of the war's destruction—but I thought this would also ensure Bosnia would receive massive aid from the United States and the European Union. Many Muslim countries had already pledged important reconstruction aid as well. I thought Bosnia might extinguish its debt at low prices with a buyback law, similar to what Nicaragua—another war torn country—did with its debt. So I assumed a price of ten for Bosnia's debt, the price at which Nicaragua completed its buyback.

Table 9.2 summarizes all of my valuations and gives my total value for the NFA debt post restructuring.

Using my pricing assumptions I came to two conclusions. First, our NFA position had little downside because the debt attributable to Slovenia and Croatia, the two most easily analyzed and most predictable pieces, were together worth over forty-eight—more than the price for all the NFA debt. So even if the values of the three remaining republics' debt went to zero—a highly unlikely scenario—we would not lose money. And we were likely to receive those two pieces quickly, as both Slovenia and Croatia were anxious to separate themselves from their joint and several obligations. Second, even with my conservative assumptions, the upside on the NFA was substantial: At my estimate of sixty-six we could make a return of over 60 percent. Recalling my experience with corporate

Table 9.2
Yugoslav New Financing Agreement Sum-of-the-Parts

Republic	My Estimated Allocation of Principal	Estimated Principal + PDI Obligation (par = 100)	My Assumed Price After Restructuring (cents on the dollar)	Value Post-Restructuring	
	A	B = A × 125	C	D = B × C	
Slovenia	18%	22.5	95	21.4	more than cost
Croatia	29%	36.3	75	27.2	of entire NFA
Serbia/ Montenegro	38%	47.5	30	14.2	
Macedonia	5%	6.2	35	2.2	
Bosnia	10%	12.5	10	1.3	
Total NFA	100%	125.0		66.3	

reorganizations, I saw this as akin to the stock of a holding company trading at a 35 percent discount to its intrinsic value because one subsidiary, contributing less than 10 percent to its parent's value, was having serious problems.

In the fall of 1995, near the end of the war in Bosnia, we initiated positions in the former Yugoslav debt at prices in the low thirties. At that time, very few other investors were buying the debt. Other investment managers did not want to touch it. Brokers would not even bother trying to pitch it. Bloomberg quoted the head emerging markets debt trader for a major London bank saying about the debt, "People have not done their homework. Suggest this [investing in Yugoslav debt] to management in New York and their first knee-jerk reaction is, 'Forget it.'" It is just this kind of situation, where reality is so different from popular perception, that I believe offers excellent risk-adjusted return potential in frontier markets.

Once Slovenia announced its restructuring agreement in September 1995, the NFA debt rose to thirty-five to thirty-seven. After rallying as high as fifty at year-end 1995, the debt traded down to forty-three in early 1996; Serbia had filed a lawsuit in London demanding an injunction to stop the debt restructuring without a simultaneous negotiation of the division of the former Yugoslavia's assets. My sense, however, was that this was a minor blip that would not disrupt my return scenario. In conducting our analysis, we retained New York and London counsel with experience in prior sovereign debt restructurings and international law. Our attorneys concurred that Serbia had very little chance of slowing the restructuring.

Confident that the restructuring could continue, I saw an opportunity to add to our position in the immediate aftermath of the lawsuit and the ensuing sell-off caused by misinformed and pessimistic press reports. In March, we purchased more NFA debt at 43 cents on the dollar, versus my estimate of its true value of 66, for a claim of principal and past due interest that had now grown to 120. Serbia's injunction demand was denied, and the restructuring continued through the second quarter of 1996, with Croatia reaching an agreement to assume 29.5 percent of the NFA—a slightly greater share than I forecast.

Despite the very wide gap between perception and reality, the market changed its view very quickly once it recognized this discrepancy. Slovenia received an excellent "A" investment-grade rating by Standard

& Poor's in May 1996, confirming my forecast, and the Slovenian bonds traded up to ninety-eight, where we sold them. Croatian debt traded on a when-issued basis above ninety, much better than I had anticipated. The aggregate NFA traded at the equivalent of seventy-five (including the value of the Slovenian distribution), 13 percent above my target of sixty-six, and up 74 percent in three months and 100 percent since the previous fall. Soon brokerage firms were producing research reports once again extolling the virtues of Slovenia and Croatia, and investors felt safe buying these now-popular credits at their now-low yields. We were happy to sell our bonds to these investors once the inefficiency in the market disappeared. It was time to move on.

Obviously, my knowledge of the region helped me in this investment, and this illustrates why it is so important for frontier market investors to spend time in these regions and with the locals. Time on the ground allows you to weigh what the media and the consensus are saying about a situation versus the reality.

Corporate Bonds

Relatively few in number for now, frontier market corporate bonds offer a unique opportunity for investors willing to do the bottom-up credit analysis. Frontier corporate bond issuers are often underresearched by traditional fixed-income investors, and so their credit risk may be mispriced as investors handicap them with their country's sovereign credit rating ceiling. And if their country is in financial turmoil, as was Argentina in 2002, corporate bonds may be selling at distressed prices even when the issuer is in good fiscal shape.

I went to Argentina for the first time in 1983. I was visiting some cousins of my father who fled there after the Communists took over Yugoslavia in 1946. Refugees from across Europe came to Argentina after World War II because it was a very prosperous country. It had been spared the damages of the war and was at the time one of the richest countries in the world—the third-richest per capita in some rankings. My relatives had gone there thinking that they would stay a couple of years, and yet here they were twenty-five years later. Argentina had slowly decayed under Perón, but even in the 1980s it was still looking pretty good in my eyes.

Since then Argentina has further deteriorated, a clear example of how bad politics and bad governance can turn a rich country into a basket case. However, we found opportunities over time in Argentina because it still possesses very strong underlying agricultural riches and the human capital of a well-educated population.

Crises often lead to opportunities, so after Argentina's bank runs and debt defaults in late 2001 culminated in the 2002 depegging and devaluation of the peso, we looked for opportunities in Argentine stocks—and found better opportunities in distressed corporate bonds. As I mentioned at the beginning of this chapter, distressed bonds can offer equity-like returns—and corporate distressed bonds can sometimes be more attractive than stocks. Indeed, in 2002, some Argentine stocks seemed richly valued.

The panic created by this financial crisis afforded very good opportunities to buy bonds well below their intrinsic value given the issuers' strong asset values and business franchises. In one such case, Perez Companc, we were able to buy a company's bonds at distressed levels and short its common stock, which was still overvalued, as a hedge.

Case Study: Perez Companc Distressed Corporate Debt

In 2002, Perez Companc was the second-largest integrated oil and gas company in Argentina, with operations throughout Latin America. Its domestic portfolio of assets weighted heavily toward energy production, transmission, and distribution. The Perez Companc family started the business in 1946 as a transportation company, which grew into an industrial conglomerate and later transitioned into an energy conglomerate with proven reserves of over one billion equivalent barrels of oil.

Perez Companc was attractive for several reasons. First, the core business earned U.S. dollars when it sold energy commodities into the international markets, but it paid its bills in Argentine pesos, which had depreciated over 60 percent since the beginning of 2002. Second, the company had assets outside the country. Not only did the company hold almost $500 million in cash outside of Argentina, it also had oil and gas assets located throughout the rest of Latin America that I estimated to be worth almost $1 billion. Third, by buying the distressed bonds, we were buying the company at astoundingly cheap valuations through the debt. Finally, the bond indentures fell under New York law and New York jurisdiction, which made me very comfortable that our rights as a creditor would be upheld in a U.S. court of law.

In May 2002, we purchased the Perez Companc Floating Rate Notes of November 2002 at a price of sixty-two. With approximately $2.2 billion of debt outstanding, the market value of the debt was $1.36 billion ($2.2 billion × 0.62). Subtracting $500 million of cash, the enterprise value of Perez Companc through the debt was only $860 million (i.e., by buying the bonds at sixty-two cents on the dollar, we were paying $860 million to own the assets of the company). In 2001, the business generated $700 million of EBITDA, and I conservatively estimated that the company would generate $500 million of EBITDA in 2002. In effect, we were buying the business through the bonds at 1.7 times EBITDA, while other international oil and gas equities were trading at 5 times to as high as 12 times EBITDA. At the same time, Perez Companc's common stock was trading at $6.50 per share for a market capitalization of $1.4 billion. The equity market was valuing the business at 6.2 times EBITDA while the debt market was valuing the business at 1.7 times EBITDA—a huge discrepancy (table 9.3).

After extensive modeling of various scenarios, we shorted thirty cents worth of common stock for every dollar invested in the bonds,

Table 9.3
Perez Companc Capital Structure Arbitrage

(US$ in millions)			
Senior Debt			
Face Value	$2,200		
Price as % of Face Value	62		
Market Value	$1,364		
Face Value of Debt	$2,200	Market Value of Debt	$1,364
Market Value of Equity	1,400		
Cash	−500	Cash	−500
Enterprise Value of Equity	$3,100	Enterprise Value of Debt	$864
2002E EBITDA	$500	2002E EBITDA	$500
EV/EBITDA Through the Equity	6.2×	EV/EBITDA Through the Debt	1.7×

as a hedge to the long bond position. I concluded that, given the value of the underlying assets, the downside on the bonds was forty-five, and if the bonds were to trade at these levels, the common stock would be worth zero.

Although the company had short-term debt of over $1 billion, most of the debt was trade related and held by large multinational banks. As I had seen in other situations in emerging markets, the banks were willing to roll their loans if the business was sound but management just needed more time to pay down debt. Furthermore, most of the banks had relationships with Perez Companc that dated back many years. With a clear understanding of the indenture and sound legal advice, I believed that our bonds would be repaid. Additionally, all of Perez Companc's debt (including the bank debt) was senior unsecured, so the company could offer security to the existing holders in order to get them to roll into a new note.

My analysis of the business was validated in mid-July 2002 when Brazilian oil giant Petrobras bid approximately $8 per share for the Perez Companc family stake, representing 59 percent of the economic ownership and 81 percent of the voting control in Perez Companc. Petrobras was offering to pay approximately 6.8 times EBITDA, and during a conference call it explained that the Perez acquisition was extremely attractive on a valuation basis compared to many other potential investments it had analyzed. Although the common shares of Perez Companc traded up on the announcement, the shares fell back to pre-announcement levels when investors realized that Petrobras had no intention of buying out the minority shareholders, but would buy only the family shares.

In late September 2002, we sold the bonds at ninety-eight and covered the stock at an average of $4.65 per share, producing a total return of approximately 68 percent and making a profit on both sides of this capital structure arbitrage.

* * *

In the Perez Companc trade, we benefited from the large discrepancy in the way debt and equity markets were looking at the same situation. With Brady bonds and the debt of the former Yugoslav Republics, we profited when reality proved much better than either conventional wisdom or media-driven investor perception. Opportunities like these to earn equity-like returns in distressed-debt special situations add another arrow to my investment quiver, but they rarely occur anymore in developed or even mainstream emerging markets. They are much more likely to be found in frontier markets, which are less researched and less understood. And in those countries without investable equity markets, or whose equities are too illiquid to trade in sufficient size, distressed debt opportunities provide an attractive alternative investment option.

10

Privatizations

In 1982, in a country behaving like a typical emerging market, investors were spooked by a government that was expropriating privately owned businesses by fiat. The newly elected president had just nationalized some of the largest private businesses including steel, defense, industrial, and consumer electronics companies, as well as thirty-nine banks. He installed government bureaucrats into top corporate management posts and began looting the banks to fund his pet projects.[1] In short, he acted like any good president of a banana republic. He actually nationalized his country's banks several months ahead of another emerging market; President Lopez Portillo nationalized Mexico's banks in September 1982, after studying this country's bank takeover.[2]

So what was this exciting, dangerous country? France, led by Socialist president François Mitterrand.

By 1986, France's new conservative government under Prime Minister Jacques Chirac began installing more market-friendly managements in the nationalized companies and then reprivatizing them. All the noise and smoke of the previous four years scared away skittish investors, but those intrepid enough to navigate the minefields were rewarded with a near tripling of the French market during that dicey period. More important for France's economy, French companies were once again in private hands.

Privatizations transfer ownership of a business or other state-owned asset from the government to the private sector. They include public offerings of state-owned companies as well as private sales to third parties; as an investor, I am most interested in the former. Privatizations take place in developed as well as developing countries, and they can be very large; in fact, eleven of the world's twenty largest initial public offerings through 2015 were privatizations of state-owned enterprises (twelve if you include the U.S. government's 2010 IPO of General Motors). These companies—six developed market telephone and electric utilities, four Chinese banks, and a Russian oil company—were listed either on their country's already well-established equity exchanges or in London, Hong Kong, or New York.

Privatizations in developing markets can present very attractive investment opportunities, especially in those markets overlooked by, or unappealing to, other investors. But it is in frontier markets, where shares of newly privatized companies often debut on young and poorly followed public equity markets, that many of the most undervalued, and therefore most attractive, privatizations can be found. I have invested (mostly profitably) in many such opportunities, in which governments utilized a host of mechanisms including auctions, vouchers, and privatization funds to promote their nascent public equity markets and encourage outside investment in their formerly state-owned enterprises. As the following cases show, privatizations—especially in frontier markets—can offer outstanding bargains to those willing to do the additional work.

Case Study: Egyptian Privatizations, 1996 and 2004

On two separate occasions over the past two decades, Egypt's privatization programs provided attractive investment opportunities. The current political situation in Egypt may provide additional such opportunities in the future.

I first traveled to Egypt in 1988 and—as anyone who has been to Cairo can attest—you can feel the bustle of its population as soon as you step out of the airport. Traveling to the countryside, you can also sense the potential for growth, and when we have invested in Egypt, we focused on those industries that I felt would benefit from this growth. Of course, the upheavals of the past few years have hampered

Egypt's economy, but the country still has significant potential if it gets its house in order.

It was 1996 before I finally invested in Egypt. For decades prior, Egypt had followed a socialist economic policy with the predictable results of low growth, misallocation of resources, low foreign direct investment, and a moribund—and at times, shuttered—stock market. Valuations in 1996 were very low, with the Egyptian market trading on an average P/E multiple of eight times earnings with juicy 9 percent dividend yields. Egypt was a classic value play; yet even with value plays, I like to identify a catalyst that might bring out the value.

In this case, the catalyst was the government's decision to privatize a number of state-owned companies in order to raise revenues and jumpstart economic growth. These were not small privatizations. In June 1996, the government auctioned a 5 percent stake in Amreyah Cement (22 percent was already in public hands, and the government was seeking a strategic buyer for an additional 40 percent stake) at a price of forty-six Egyptian pounds (EGP), representing a P/E multiple of 6.5 and a dividend yield of over 11 percent. We participated aggressively in this auction and were one of the few foreign buyers directly allocated shares.

Along with the very attractive price, after years of underinvestment and slow growth in the previously statist economy, cement demand was rising rapidly as economic growth accelerated. Furthermore, Amreyah had sold out its production well in advance; the industry was an oligopoly, and the government was granting lucrative tax incentives to boost production. Hence, we were buying a growth stock selling at a deep-value multiple with a strategic buyer on the horizon likely to pay a significantly higher price and bring a more aggressive management style.

Another partially privatized company with great promise was North Cairo Mills, one of the largest flour companies in Egypt. Facing a rapidly growing population, the government decided to liberalize the flour market, removing price controls to encourage growth. We approached the Egyptian government in late July 1996 and purchased a block of stock of North Cairo Mills at eighty-seven EGP per share (at about six times earnings and a dividend yield of over 12 percent)—lower than what we would likely have paid on the open market. The government benefited too, by monetizing an additional portion of its stake in the company without paying brokerage fees or causing any market impact.

During this period, several Egyptian companies issued Global Depositary Receipts (GDRs)—certificates for shares of their stock held in foreign banks and traded in London—to increase liquidity and attract more foreign investors. General investor enthusiasm for Egypt gained momentum and amplified the inefficiencies in the Egyptian market; new buyers were blindly snapping up Egyptian shares in the open market, giving us the opportunity to reduce certain positions at very advantageous prices in order to fund purchases of cheaper stocks in the continuing privatizations of government stakes.

After selling our last Egyptian holdings in 1997, we monitored but did not actively reinvest in Egypt for many years. I was dissuaded by Egypt's ensuing lackluster economic growth, its currency depreciation, and its stalled reform agenda. President Hosni Mubarak attempted to address structural reforms under the premiership of Dr. Atef Ebeid in 1999, but this reform effort did not take, and the country's economic troubles worsened. A slowing global economic environment affected tourism revenues, weak commodity prices resulted in unfavorable terms of trade, and a series of devaluations from 2000 to 2003 weakened the currency by nearly 50 percent and pressured fiscal accounts.

In late 2003, however, Mubarak began to readdress the structural reform agenda, appointing a new board to the Central Bank of Egypt and introducing policies to further liberalize trade. He also appointed market-friendly, pro-reform prime minister Dr. Ahmed Nazif in July 2004. (The youngest prime minister in the Republic of Egypt's history, Nazif served as prime minister until January 2011 when he was sacked by Mubarak during the Egyptian Revolution; Mubarak himself was sacked two weeks later.) As the prior government's Minister of Communications and Information Technology, Nazif had successfully accelerated the liberalization of the telecom sector. Nazif's appointment convinced me that this effort to spur sustained economic growth was serious.

In contrast to 1999's stalled reforms, Nazif's efforts benefited from strong economic tailwinds, namely a strong current account surplus fueled by high oil prices (Egypt was a net exporter of oil) and a significant improvement in tourism revenues (tourism, which accounted for nearly 7.5 percent of Egypt's GDP, rose over 50 percent in the year ending June 2004).

Given all this, and encouraged by the government's privatization efforts, we initiated positions in several already-listed Egyptian equities during the second quarter of 2004. These companies provided strong earnings growth, high dividend yields, compelling valuations, and potential M&A opportunities. The companies we invested in included the following:

Mobinil. a cellular phone service provider. Operating in a duopoly with approximately 50 percent market share, the company was poised for a potential acceleration of growth given an underpenetrated market (10 percent) that largely reflected several years of lackluster economic expansion, and no new competition on the horizon. I expected the company to continue to offer a relatively high dividend yield of 7–8 percent over the next two years and post 15 percent earnings growth in both 2005 and 2006. When we initiated the position, Mobinil traded at a 2005 estimated P/E multiple of eleven times and an EV/EBITDA multiple of 4.6 times, relatively attractive valuations versus emerging market peers.

Orascom Telecom. which experienced strong cellular subscriber growth through its ownership of 31 percent of Mobinil as well as various other successful, high-growth operations in Algeria, Pakistan, and Iraq. As the most liquid stock in the Egyptian market, I believed it would be among the first to attract investor attention, and it would also provide a natural hedge against negative surprises on the reform front due to its fast-growing and profitable cellular operations elsewhere in the region. We bought the stock when shares were trading at a compelling 5.3 times 2005 estimated P/E and 4.2 times EV/EBITDA with approximately 20 percent earnings growth in both 2005 and 2006. The stock was attractively valued when compared to both local and other emerging market telcos.

Orascom Construction Industries ("OCI"). which capitalized on the significant changes occurring in the region from both higher oil prices and the war on terrorism. OCI was the largest construction company in Egypt with operations throughout the region, including an aggressive expansion into the oil-rich Gulf States as well as Libya, Algeria, Afghanistan, and Iraq. In addition to its successful construction business, the company also owned profitable cement operations in Egypt and Algeria, which together accounted for nearly 35 percent of consolidated revenue and over 40 percent of EBITDA. We invested in OCI when the stock was trading at an estimated 2005 P/E of 7.3 times and an EV/EBITDA of 6.3 times with nearly 30 percent EPS growth expected for 2005 and 2006.

During the third quarter of 2004, the government announced several important measures, including tariff reform and a new bill that would reduce corporate and individual tax rates as well as loopholes and tax evasion. The government also announced its intention to accelerate the privatization of state-owned companies in order to streamline government finances and cover any shortfall in revenues from its fiscal reforms. As the market took notice of the accelerating momentum of the new government's reform agenda, our Egyptian holdings rose quickly, more than doubling in the following year.

By 2006, Egypt's privatization push began to run out of steam, and was officially suspended in 2010 after selling only seven companies in the previous four years.[3] Negative public sentiment is currently stalling any renewal of privatizations in the near term, but the government understands the need for outside investment to spur growth, so I will continue to monitor this market.

* * *

Privatizing state-owned companies in frontier and emerging countries benefits both the companies involved and the nascent (or, in the case of Egypt, mothballed) markets in which they trade, fostering the growth of equity markets and the participation of local investors.[4] However, although privatized companies outperform their state-owned peers, those companies that are still run by their preprivatization managements perform worse than those with new managements brought in from outside.[5] My team's on-the-ground research certainly supported these findings.

In 1994, for instance, one of my partners traveled to Russia on a research trip. He visited a large company outside St. Petersburg that formerly built parts for intercontinental ballistic missiles. That day, no one was building anything. St. Petersburg had great universities and a great many very smart people, so the workers at this company were brighter than the average Russian. The managers were sitting around a conference room table, trying to figure out how to "privatize" their company (essentially steal it from the state) as they had seen other managements do at some oil and other state-owned companies. But this company did not produce oil; it produced missile parts—old, useless technology. So he asked the managers, "What else can you make?"

"We are going to show you," they said, "what we think we can do with our technology and resources." And they brought out and proudly unveiled a prototype of their proposed product: a microwave oven. This was 1994, but their microwave looked like the kind you could buy in the West in the early 1980s—it weighed forty pounds, it was clunky, and it had zero design elements. My partner wished them good luck. I do not know if they are still in business, but I doubt it.

* * *

Countries in transition—as Egypt was in the 1990s and 2000s—are great places to look for privatization opportunities. This is especially true for countries transitioning from centrally planned to market-based economies.

The fall of Communism in the 1990s kicked off a flurry of activity by Soviet-era centrally planned economies—including the Czech Republic, Estonia, Romania, Poland, Slovakia, and of course Russia—transitioning to market-based economies. These countries adopted varying approaches to opening their markets, and much of this activity was fraught with corruption, cronyism, and lack of transparency. Many state-owned assets (or the proceeds from their sale) ended up in the hands of a small number of the politically connected, rather than distributed more broadly throughout the population. Russia, for example, adopted the coupon methodology and distributed physical paper vouchers to its citizens. These vouchers represented ownership of a company, like physical stock certificates. As very few of these people understood the concept of private ownership of companies, their vouchers were ultimately scooped up by a small group of oligarchs, who went around physically collecting the vouchers and paying very low dollar prices for them in a period of hyperinflation when the U.S. dollar was considered more attractive than the ruble.

Like Russia, Poland was a frontier market in the early 1990s, attempting to transform from a state-run to a market economy. Part of Poland's metamorphosis included the direct or indirect privatization of over 7,000 state-owned companies. Because its citizens had so little savings with which to purchase shares in newly listed companies, Poland—like Russia and several other former Communist countries—distributed vouchers to its citizens tradable for shares in many of these companies. A group of poorly understood funds created by the Polish government to corral and manage a sprawling subset of these privatized companies turned into an interesting investment opportunity.

Case Study: Polish Privatization Funds

In 1995, Poland conducted a creative experiment in the wholesale privatization of 512 small- and mid-sized government-owned companies through an innovative mass privatization program designed to spread ownership of these state-owned companies across its citizenry. The companies were put under the control of fifteen closed-end-type funds called Narodowy Fundusz Inwestycyjny (National Investment Funds, or NIFs). All adult Polish citizens received certificates that gave them equal shares in the ownership of these NIFs.

The NIF program was also designed to provide corporate governance over the managements of the hundreds of underlying operating companies newly freed from state control. Because these companies would no longer have the government watching their every move, the NIF structure was meant to provide better oversight than would a new shareholder base of nearly 25 million unsophisticated investors.

The companies, mostly industrial, were allocated across the NIFs on a random basis, so that no one NIF was concentrated in any particular sector. (This was done for fairness, but it would not make the NIFs any easier to manage.) The government then chose the managers for these NIFs, tasking them with restructuring and improving the companies allocated to their respective funds. In February 1997, the privatization certificates and the NIFs began trading in the Polish stock market (the certificates automatically converted into shares of the fifteen NIFs at the end of 1998).

This privatization program was intriguing but complex. Each NIF controlled an approximately 33 percent stake in 35 of the 512 companies in the program and an approximately 2 percent stake in each of the other 477 companies. The complexity of this structure prompted few institutional investors or brokers to research the program in depth. But my team and I did—and concluded there was significant value in it. These companies had combined sales of more than $2 billion, but by the end of 1998, the combined market value of all of the NIFs had fallen to under $500 million.

Two of the NIFs that most interested me were the Zachodni and Foksal funds. I believed that the assets in the funds were good and that the companies they owned were essentially solid. After detailed analysis, we invested in these and several other selected NIFs and offered advice as a shareholder. As time went by, though, I recognized that while the NIF managers did a fine job of monitoring the companies they owned, they were paying too little attention to shareholder value (despite our recommendations). The managers would often invest fund assets in the underlying companies without first performing simple return-on-capital calculations. I believed that given their low valuations, the NIFs should use their excess cash to buy back shares. In particular, Zachodni held substantial cash, and the best use of that cash would be a stock buyback.

I realized that we would have to become more proactive to protect and enhance our NIF investments, and, after a few trips to Poland, I decided to build a business to try to better manage the NIF program. We created a venture, Everest Capital Polska, and set out to establish an office in Warsaw. As you can imagine, this gave me great insight into staffing a frontier markets office.

I was quite impressed by the high quality of the local professionals my team and I interviewed. Some of the young people had gone to the West, to the United Kingdom in particular, for schooling, studying free market accounting, economics, and business principles, and had come back to Poland to take advantage of the vacuum in managerial expertise from the Communist days. Poland now had young people in their twenties and thirties that had finished their studies—not of the Communist system but the capitalist system—and could compete very much on par with young professionals in the West. This incredibly fast transfer of skills, this leapfrogging of technological and managerial expertise, only adds to frontier markets' appeal. And now, with readily accessible Internet-based distance-learning services, frontier workers have at their fingertips knowledge and best practices from around the world.

Today we are seeing another phenomenon in frontier markets: People who went to work abroad are now returning to their home countries because the opportunities have dried up in the West. Expatriate workers in London are going back home to Kenya or Bangladesh. Workers from Latin America who came to the United States are going back to their home countries. Interestingly, 2013 was the first year that immigration from Mexico to the United States was flat—as many people are now going back to Mexico as people coming from Mexico. Mexico is not a frontier market, of course, but it is a good example of how talent is leaving the United States and western Europe and returning home: a reverse brain drain.

But back to Poland. With our office established and filled with young local professionals, the shareholders of the Zachodni and Foskal NIFs overwhelmingly elected Everest Capital Polska to replace their existing managers. We then substantially lowered the management fees paid by both funds and were in a position to institute stock buybacks subject to government approval. The announcement of our program of lowering fees and advocating stock buybacks induced other NIF managers to take similar steps, which in turn benefited some of the other NIFs in which we invested. Substantial value existed in these NIFs, which I estimated still traded at 40 percent to 50 percent discounts to their intrinsic value, offering 60 percent to 100 percent upside potential over the next several years. Taking over management of the NIFs, a level of shareholder activism new in eastern Europe, was the catalyst needed to unlock the value embedded in them.

* * *

Poland is now home to one of the most established and liquid stock markets of the former Eastern Bloc countries. Along with privatizing its state-owned businesses, Poland developed a successful pension fund program, and its pension funds—much more so than foreign investors—are the dominant drivers of its stock market today. Like Chile in the 1980s, Poland was able to grow its market because of this initial participation by the pension funds.

Romania also began its privatization process in the 1990s, but it took longer than Poland to shake off its Communist roots and transfer state-owned assets into the hands of its citizens. Romania's economy was very government-centric under Nicolae Ceausescu, who was much more of an autocrat than were any of the Polish Communist authorities. Ceausescu ran Romania in a very centralized, Soviet style, and so the country was in a much worse position economically when it came out of the Ceausescu regime in 1989. By the mid 2000s, though, Romania was well into its transition to a market-based economy, and one privatization program launched during this time proved particularly profitable.

Case Study: Romanian Privatization Fund Fondul Proprietatea

As part of the mass privatization program it started in the early 1990s, the Romanian government established five Social Investment Funds (SIFs), privatization funds stocked with nationalized assets, and then, as Poland did with the NIFs, distributed shares to the public. The government also established a unique investment fund, Fondul Proprietatea, in 2005, to pay the restitution claims of private individuals—including everyone from the former king, to formerly affluent Romanians, to the general Romanian public—for property and assets expropriated by the Communist regime since 1948.

The government, which retained a stake in Fondul Proprietatea initially, marketed the fund's stock to Romanian firms and encouraged the developing pension fund industry to take a stake as well. Over time, the government gave up its ownership, leaving Fondul Proprietatea shares in the hands of the Romanian public, Romanian institutions, the original restitution holders, and some foreign investors.

The SIFs and Fondul Proprietatea were run by local politicians and local portfolio managers, which engendered little confidence in shareholders and led to wide discounts to net asset value for their share prices. Following the 2008 global financial crisis, many of these funds traded at very significant discounts to NAV—in Fondul Proprietatea's case, a discount of 65 to 70 percent. So as part of its attempt to bolster a recovery in its capital markets and economy, the Romanian government decided to try something different with Fondul Proprietatea: outsource its management to a Western asset management company.

It chose Templeton, a large global investment manager, for what was to be the biggest mandate ever awarded by a sovereign wealth fund to a single manager in one go; at $4.3 billion, it was a big deal.

Templeton took over the management of Fondul Proprietatea, establishing a big local Romanian office and building a very large franchise. The discount to NAV in Fondul Proprietatea's share price has brought pressure on Templeton, however, because Templeton can be voted out as manager. Templeton has therefore been cutting costs in Fondul Proprietatea's operating companies and in the fund company itself.

Romania has fuel and food self-sufficiency, unusual for a frontier market. Its assets include Iron Gates, one of Europe's largest hydroelectric plants, which spans the Danube River between Romania and Serbia. Romania has 22 million people and 22 gigawatts of installed electricity generation capacity. That compares favorably with mainstream emerging market countries such as Poland, with 34 gigawatts of generation capacity for 39 million people; Turkey, with 57 gigawatts of generation capacity for 81 million people; or Mexico, which has 62 gigawatts of generation capacity for 120 million people. It also compares very favorably with countries like Egypt, which has only 27 gigawatts of generation capacity for 87 million people. With a gigawatt of generation capacity per million people, Romania is in an enviable position—and many of these generating assets, including Iron Gates, are held by Fondul Proprietatea. Based on its attractive assets and discount to NAV, we began purchasing shares of Fondul Proprietatea in 2011.

Taking It to the Street

As I mentioned in chapter 7, investing in frontier markets oftentimes requires an activist approach in order to maximize shareholder value. This may mean pressuring management to act in the best interests of shareholders, or taking more drastic steps like opening a local office and taking over management yourself. It may also mean agitating for the brokerage community to act in the best interests of its clients.

For several reasons we acquired shares of Fondul Proprietatea indirectly through a total return swap—a contractual agreement where a broker owns the underlying security and pays (or charges) the buyer the gain (or loss) on that security, plus any dividends received, in exchange for interest payments to the broker to finance the cost of the underlying security. Fondul Proprietatea management occasionally needs to take a shareholder vote on some common corporate activity such as distribution of dividends or proceeds from capital transactions. In order for certain votes to be valid, a quorum of at least 50 percent of the shares must participate. Recall that Romania originally distributed Fondul Proprietatea shares to locals as restitution for assets seized by the government, so many of the current holders of Fondul Proprietatea's shares are individuals who are not very market savvy or even market aware. On a previous attempt to distribute cash proceeds in November 2013, the company was unable to convene a quorum of the widely dispersed shares to vote on this piece of business, mustering less than the required 50 percent of the shares outstanding.

One bloc of market-savvy shareholders that did not participate in this vote were all the non-Romanians who, like us, owned shares through swap transactions and who therefore could not vote their shares directly. Only the brokerage firms holding the actual shares could vote, which, for reasons I find unacceptable—amounting to "We don't want to potentially hurt our other customers' feelings"—they never, ever did. We held a share swap with a large New York–based bank and, joined by another swap client, we pressured the bank to vote our shares, arguing that these votes were for common but essential business decisions that Fondul Proprietatea needed to make (plus, we wanted our cash payout). The bank ultimately relented, agreeing that not voting the shares would have a "material adverse effect" on its clients. The next vote, in February 2014, included the 2.4 percent of shares held by the bank, bringing the total to 52.0 percent of the outstanding shares, enough for a quorum; those present overwhelmingly approved the cash distribution.

Shareholder vote hurdles notwithstanding, Fondul Proprietatea shares have performed well. With pressure from international investors, a desire to increase the IPO process, and the threat of the manager being kicked out, the discount of Fondul Proprietatea's share price to NAV narrowed from 60 percent at the end of 2011 to under 33 percent by June 2015. The NAV rose 40 percent during that time as well, resulting in a more than doubling of Fondul Proprietatea's stock price. Fondul Proprietatea continues to repurchase and cancel shares in an effort to narrow the discount to NAV, and in April 2015 its GDRs began trading in London, which should further increase investor demand.

In Poland, we saw that as a country makes its final transition into a democratic capitalist society, these investment funds ultimately go away; they are broken up into their constituent parts or bought by bigger entities. Many shareholders would like to see the constituent parts of Fondul Proprietatea distributed to them as a stock dividend, as they would rather not pay Templeton's management fee—but Templeton is going to try to maintain Fondul Proprietatea as an operating fund for as long as it can earn its fee.[6] Nevertheless, just as in Poland, none of Romania's privatization funds—the SIFs or Fondul Proprietatea—likely will exist in the next five to ten years.

* * *

I look forward to finding additional investment opportunities as many of today's frontier markets launch or expand their privatization programs. The Vietnamese government, for example, plans to privatize several hundred state-owned enterprises in the coming years, although its pace has been lackluster to date. Pakistan launched a privatization program in 1991, which by 2006 had stalled; however, the June 2014 sale of the government's remaining 20 percent stake in United Bank Limited—Pakistan's first privatization transaction in eight years—looks to be the start of a renewed privatization push (I discuss Pakistan further in chapter 12). And Kenya set up a Privatization Commission in 2008 to renew efforts begun in 1992 to privatize over 200 "parastatals" (a term used across Africa for state-owned companies). These and other programs aim to invigorate their countries' economies and equity markets; investors can profit by helping them do so.

III

Risks and Opportunities
in Frontier Markets

11

Political Risks in Frontier Markets

North and South Korea—created in 1945 when the United States and the Soviet Union arbitrarily split the Korean Peninsula along the 38th Parallel following Japan's surrender—began their separate lives alike in many ways: same culture and language, roughly similar size, and, with the South's economy and population both about twice the size of the North's, a nearly identical GDP per capita.[1] South Korea was predominantly agricultural, while most of the natural resources, hydroelectric power, and manufacturing were in the North. Yet today, South Korea's GDP per capita is nearly twenty times that of North Korea.[2] The principal cause for this vast discrepancy is politics.

When I look at an investment opportunity, I analyze its risks across three categories: political, macroeconomic, and microeconomic. This risk assessment framework is especially important in frontier markets, where governments and economies are often at very early stages of development or at important inflection points. Once I identify the risks of a potential investment, I have to decide what to do about them; some risks I try to avoid, some I try to mitigate, and some I embrace. In this chapter, I focus on the political risks of investing in frontier markets, including the risk of corruption. The next chapter discusses frontiers' macroeconomic and microeconomic risks.

Political Risk

Political risk in an investing context is the uncertainty of return on capital (or even return *of* capital) due to government actions, which include everything from elections—every election with more than one candidate poses some political risk—to governments able but unwilling to repay debts, to expropriation of privately held assets, to war. The common conception is that political risk occurs in nondemocratic, less developed countries, where the rule of law often bends to political will. Chrysler's secured bondholders, however—publicly denounced as "profiteers" by President Obama in April 2009 and in the end repaid just twenty-nine cents on the dollar for their first-priority claims—learned that political risk is increasing in the developed world even as it is decreasing in the developing world. The Swiss National Bank painfully reminded me of that same lesson in 2015. Although the political environment in frontier markets is generally improving, crises do still erupt.

Political risk sometimes devolves into nothing more than headline risk (discussed in the next chapter), such as in 2014 with Turkish President Erdoğan's saber rattling—his attempt to ban Twitter or his calling Israel more barbaric than Hitler. This shook the markets but had little long-term effect on valuations. Other times, government policies—or reactions to those policies—can destroy value, as was the case in the Arab Spring uprising in Egypt in January 2011; one study showed that during the Arab Spring, one of the best indicators of subsequent stock market performance was the number of participants at sit-in demonstrations.[3] Such events can affect not only the targeted country's markets but neighboring markets as well, by association (although the impact of the Arab Spring on the Gulf Cooperation Council [GCC] markets was essentially headline risk).

I learned firsthand the extent to which political risk can destroy value during the 1998 Russian debt crisis; indeed, Everest Capital's losses in the third quarter of 1998 from its Russian investments stand as the worst in dollar terms in the firm's history. Russia in 1998 resembled a company whose management is found to have committed fraud. Russia then was like Enron in 2001 when everything—its stock, bonds, receivables, and even its pensions—collapsed.

Case Study: Russian Debt Crisis of 1998

Until as recently as 1997, Russia was a frontier market.[4] Its journey to emerging market status began when the Soviet Union officially dissolved in December 1991, at which point Russia assumed the USSR's seat on the UN Security Council—as well as the USSR's debt. Russia's ensuing transition from a centrally planned to a market-based economy started with a crushing bout of hyperinflation in 1992, launched by the elimination of price controls and exacerbated by a contracting economy, an out-of-control money supply, and a plunging ruble. Only after the October 1994 ouster of Viktor Gerashchenko, named a year earlier as "the worst central-bank governor of any major country in history" by then–Harvard economist Jeffrey Sachs, was Russia able to implement reforms to lower inflation and stabilize its currency.

As I discussed in chapter 9, I am always searching for investment opportunities with equity-like returns, even in debt markets, and I have at times held significant investments in distressed emerging market debt. In 1994, Russia had few tradable equities but plenty of sovereign debt; in fact, I had very successfully invested in Russian debt and Russian Treasury Bills (GKOs) from 1994 through 1996 (as well as in other eastern European debt such as the debt of the former Yugoslavia, also discussed in chapter 9). But because of low yields and an unattractive risk/reward profile, I sold most of our debt positions and had very little exposure to emerging market debt in general, and Russian debt in particular, by the second half of 1997 and into the first half of 1998.

By this time, Russia had brought inflation down to single digits and stabilized the ruble, but its economic policies still had many shortcomings, and its reforms had stalled. By June 1998, President Boris Yeltsin had replaced his prime minister and cabinet and, with the new prime minister Sergey Kiriyenko, appointed respected reformers like Anatoly Chubais and Boris Fyodorov to overhaul government finances and increase Russia's anemic tax collection. This was the most reform-minded and nonpolitical government that Russia had ever had. The yields on Russian dollar and ruble debt had nonetheless increased substantially from the beginning of the year, as the market believed that Russia needed international assistance to maintain stability until the positive results of reforms and higher tax collections kicked in.

On July 16 the IMF announced a $22 billion plan to stabilize Russia, saying that it fully supported the fiscal measures of the government and the continuation of the stability of the ruble as the anchor of monetary policy. The IMF plan was larger than the $10–15 billion that most analysts were expecting. Given the size of the plan, the implicit commitment of support by the G-7 nations, and—most importantly—the commitment of the Russian government to reforms and tax collections, I believed that Russian debt constituted an excellent investment, similar to Mexican government debt in 1995 after Mexico received its support package. I increased our Russian debt exposure substantially following the IMF announcement.

Investments are rarely riskless. In almost every case (except U.S. Treasury bills for a dollar-based investor), no matter how good an investment may seem, it can lose money. For each investment, therefore, I weigh the potential loss and the probability of losing if I am wrong versus the potential gain and the probability of gaining if I am right. This expected value of an investment is what I try to maximize across multiple scenarios.

I knew that there was a probability of loss in buying Russian debt even after the IMF awarded its package, but I believed that it was moderate (about a one in three chance, as I describe further below). And the fact that a loss did occur does not mean that my probability assessment was necessarily wrong, just as a house fire does not mean that the home insurer made a bad probability assessment. Many talented investors and other financial institutions made the same judgment about the probability of a ruble devaluation, and I think my sense of the probability was about right.

Where I was certainly wrong was on the magnitude of the decline in Russian debt prices. For example, after the announcement of the IMF package the long-dated dollar bonds known as Principal bonds traded at forty-eight (cents on the dollar) or a yield of 15.5 percent. These bonds had traded at seventy-five at their peak in 1997, and I believed that they would trade at sixty to sixty-five once stability had returned to Russia. With an annual coupon of 5.8 percent (and a current yield of 12 percent) these bonds could provide a total return of 36 percent over a six-month period. On the downside, even if Russia devalued, I believed that the bonds would trade no lower than forty-two, with a yield similar to the yields of other countries, such as Indonesia, that had devalued and were in a position similar to Russia's. Furthermore, before the Russian elections in 1996—a time when a return of the Communists seemed a real risk—the former Soviet debt (Vneshekonombank), which Russia assumed and was at that time in default, traded at thirty to thirty-five. So even if the ruble devalued and Russia was perceived as poorly as Indonesia, I felt the downside on the bonds was in the low forties (a 10 to 15 percent loss). Even in the very unlikely case of a default, which I estimated at a less than 5 percent probability, I saw thirty to thirty-five as an absolute downside (a 30 to 35 percent loss). The blend of those outcomes and probabilities, listed in table 11.1, gave the bonds an expected simple return of over 19 percent and an annualized return of over 39 percent.

I was wrong. Russia devalued and had not yet even defaulted on these bonds, yet they traded down to ten—an 80 percent loss. I did not contemplate the sequence of events in August: After the July IMF package, the Russian government made a few tactical mistakes that shook the market's confidence, such as reopening the GKO (Russian T-Bill) auctions, which they said they would not do just days earlier. At the same time, oil prices sank to new lows, adding further doubt

Table 11.1
Expected Return on Russian Dollar Debt

Scenario	Probability	Price	Coupon*	Absolute Gain (Loss)**	Expected Gain (Loss)
	A	B	C	D = B + C – 48	E = A × D
Stability	65%	62.5	2.9	17.40	11.31
Devaluation	30%	42	2.9	(3.10)	(0.93)
Default	5%	30	0	(18.00)	(0.90)
Expected Value of Gain					9.48
Expected Percentage Return (Expected Gain/Price=9.48/48)					19.75%
Expected Percentage Return—Annualized					39.50%

*Over six months (5.8 percent annual).
**From the mid-July, post-IMF announcement price of forty-eight.

about the success of the Russian plan. Russian bond and stock prices were declining, and Russian banks had to sell Russian government debt and bonds to meet margin calls on their leveraged positions, accelerating the bonds' decline.

Russia still had options. On August 13 and 14 one of my partners met with Central Bank and Ministry of Finance officials in Moscow to discuss constructive proposals, such as a new voluntary exchange offer for short-term ruble debt into dual-currency bonds that would alleviate the short-term cash crunch. They also discussed implementing a currency board.[5] Yet the following week, Russia announced a nonsensical plan comprising an uncontrolled devaluation, a unilateral restructuring (really a default) on its ruble debt, and a ninety-day moratorium on its foreign debt. At the same time, Yeltsin fired the reformist government and replaced Kiriyenko with Viktor Chernomyrdin, the former prime minister who had failed at reforms in the past.

The power change in Russia was most likely provoked by Russian banks that could not meet their payments on bank loans and margin debt owed to Western institutions. A number of Russian banks were controlled by a small group of business tycoons, the so-called oligarchs, who gained control of many oil and industrial companies in privatizations during Chernomyrdin's previous term as prime minister. The same group of oligarchs was targeted by the Kiriyenko government to start paying taxes that they obviously were not keen to pay. Furthermore, by mid-August some of the oligarchs' banks were on the brink of defaulting on their foreign-currency loans because of continuing margin calls. Facing the threat of having to pay taxes and the risk of their banks defaulting, the oligarchs essentially staged an unprecedented change of government—a de facto coup.

With a moratorium on foreign debt and a friendly prime minister, the oligarchs hoped for a government bailout; but the sloppy devaluation and default created a panic in the market. The loss of confidence in Russia was total; Russians were desperately trying to exchange their rubles for dollars while the political opposition tried to block Mr. Chernomyrdin's appointment. It was chaos.

I believe the Russian collapse was a seminal event for world markets, not because of the direct impact of Russia's imploding economy on the world (which was small), but because of the global credit contraction it sparked. Yields of other developing countries' debt rose dramatically, and the spread on the JP Morgan Emerging Market Bond Index widened from 4.5 percent over U.S. Treasuries in May 1998 to 14.5 percent by October. Bonds of emerging market countries traded at yields of close to 20 percent in dollars, up from 10 percent only months before. Such extremely high dollar yields forced local currency yields higher in Latin America and eastern Europe, worsening interest burdens and slowing growth.

The rise in emerging market yields also triggered a collapse in emerging market equities, raising the cost of equity financing for corporations and making new investments less likely or more costly in those countries, which could potentially delay privatizations. The spreading collapse in commodity prices affected not only many emerging markets but also Canada and Australia, whose currencies dropped to record lows, reducing global growth.

In my reflections on the events of 1998 for Steven Drobny's 2006 book, *Inside the House of Money*, in which I am profiled, I noted that Russia's simultaneous devaluation and default made no economic sense. It was unprecedented for a country to devalue and default at the same time, and it created a real panic. Russia got lucky when oil prices skyrocketed over 150 percent in 1999. If that had not happened, Russia would still be suffering from its actions of the summer of 1998. I have yet to hear a convincing rationale for why Russia did what it did, but Yeltsin was not the sharpest economic mind that has ruled a large country.[6]

Russia should have done in 1998 what many Asian countries did in 1997, which was to devalue but not default. Instead, the example of the unilateral Russian default and devaluation may have prompted other countries to abandon the model of free markets and globalization. In September 1998, Malaysia made its currency nonconvertible, removing itself from the world's foreign-exchange market and trapping foreign investors in Malaysian stocks. The Hong Kong authorities, through massive equity purchases, basically nationalized 10 percent of their stock market in order to protect their currency.

These profound changes to the investment landscape prompted me to sharply modify my investment stance. At the time, I was not forecasting a financial Armageddon, but I nonetheless reduced our exposure and moved more than 40 percent of our portfolios into cash to capitalize on new opportunities created by the myriad market dislocations. I wrote in our third quarter 1998 investor letter that I believed the market turmoil might last for a few more months, probably until early 1999, but that this turmoil—as with other past dislocations such as the junk bond market crash in 1990–1991 and the Mexican devaluation in 1994–1995—would produce unprecedented opportunities for my bottom-up, value-driven investment style. And it did; 1999 produced the best returns in the twenty-year history of our emerging markets fund.

In that same letter, I also reminded my investors that they weren't the only ones who felt the pain of my investment decisions; my colleagues and I had made large investments in our funds alongside them, even adding to our investments on July 1, just weeks before Russia's implosion. We fully shared in the losses that quarter, and we were extremely focused on preserving our capital and again generating the returns to which our investors—and we—were accustomed. I continued to apply the same investment philosophy that had worked so well in the past, while applying the lessons I learned during that quarter—most importantly, because political risk can cripple a country's entire capital structure, I learned to look at a frontier country, in aggregate, like a single company, and to limit exposure accordingly.

* * *

Soon after the Russian crisis, elections in Venezuela were set to disrupt the political status quo in that country, but on-the-ground political due diligence ultimately protected our portfolios from losses. The lesson I learned from this adventure: Follow the walk, not the talk.

Case Study: My Midnight Meeting with Hugo Chávez

I had the chance to meet with Venezuelan President Hugo Chávez in Caracas in early 1999, shortly after he took office and four years after I first invested there. Prior to Chávez's election, I thought that Venezuela's political risk was overpriced (i.e., prices were discounted too heavily for the actual political risk); this regime change necessitated a fresh assessment.

First, some background. I had been interested in Venezuela since my original investment in Venezuelan debt in 1994, when my analogy for Venezuela was an asset-rich company run by an unpredictable management. Because of this unpredictability, the market treated Venezuelan debt as if default was imminent. As I describe in chapter 9, however, I felt there was very little downside to these bonds even in a default. The upside was that the market would recognize that the government, although unpredictable and populist on the surface, would not see any benefit in a default, and the yield required to hold Venezuelan bonds would drop. This was in fact what happened starting in 1995, and by May of 1997, I had exited our bond positions.

By then I had become active in the Venezuelan stock market, particularly in the telecommunications industry. Through comparative analysis across emerging and frontier markets, I found several great opportunities in Latin American telecom stocks. Many exhibited the ideal combination of high growth rates of 20 percent or greater per year (phone companies in emerging economies can be fast-growing businesses because of pent-up demand for service) and low valuations based on P/E multiples, enterprise value-to-EBITDA (EV/EBITDA) multiples, and price-to-book ratios.

In particular, I was very intrigued by the Venezuelan government's 1996 public offering of a large share of Compañía Anónima Nacional de Telefonos de Venezuela (CANTV), the Venezuelan phone company. The government had sold a stake in CANTV in 1991 to a consortium led by GTE (then the largest independent U.S. phone company, merging with Bell Atlantic in 2000 to become Verizon), for $33 per share, a 43 percent premium to the November 1996 public offering price of $23. At the $23 offering price, CANTV was valued at 7.6 times 1997 earnings and at an EV/EBITDA multiple of 3.4 times for a business growing 20 percent annually. Because of investors' unduly gloomy perception of Venezuela, I could buy this great growth story at an extremely attractive valuation—so I did.

Several brokers at the time were recommending Asian telecom stocks—in particular Thai Telephone & Telecom (TT&T), a major Thai phone company whose stock had dropped over 70 percent from its May 1995 high. Because of its huge price decline, brokers deemed TT&T a good value. Now, I often search for bargains among securities or markets that have had steep declines, but my analysis showed that even at its lower price, TT&T traded at a P/E ratio of thirty-three times and on an EV/EBITDA multiple of fourteen times. Having dropped sharply, this Thai telecom stock was still valued at a more than 300 percent premium to the Venezuelan phone company's stock. I saw no good reason for this very large discrepancy in valuations, and, in the end, the market agreed. From November 1996 to June 1997, TT&T dropped another 65 percent while CANTV rose 80 percent. The brokerage community's consensus on TT&T was wrong; valuations still mattered.

Despite its higher share price, CANTV was still inexpensive in 1997, and Venezuela's macroeconomic prospects were improving. Venezuela was the largest oil exporter to the United States but had not fully exploited its oil and gas potential because it did not allow foreign oil companies to operate in the country. The government eventually decided to sell oil concessions, realizing that it could improve its production efficiency and receive immediate dollar proceeds. In June 1997, the government oil company auctioned twenty oil fields for over $2 billion, instantly increasing the country's foreign reserves by 15 percent. The government anticipated an additional $6 billion in foreign direct investments on the fields over the ensuing five years, which would create a powerful multiplier effect. This initial sale was to be followed by auctions of other oil and mineral rights, driving additional foreign direct investment (FDI). FDI inflows soared in 1997, but oil auctions were suspended after Chávez's election in 1998 until 2010, and FDI inflows plummeted (figure 11.1).

Containing inflation had been a high priority for the government, and the result was a strong currency. While common wisdom says that a strong currency can make a country uncompetitive, this was not the case for Venezuela, where the large majority of exports were dollar-denominated natural resources like oil, coal, and aluminum. A strong currency made imports more affordable, increasing middle-class consumption and encouraging greater social stability. Within this macroeconomic context, CANTV and our other Venezuelan stocks still appeared to be excellent investments.

Contagion from the Russian crisis in the summer of 1998 spread quickly across Latin American equities, and CANTV was not immune. Its stock price dropped by over 75 percent from its peak in

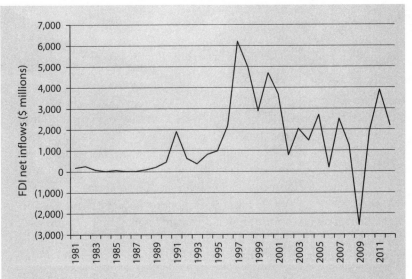

Figure 11.1
Venezuelan FDI net inflows. *Source*: World Bank.

1997 to its trough in August 1998, even though its revenue and free cash flow actually increased in 1998. Venezuelan bond prices also dropped sharply. Despite these price declines—in fact, partly because of them—I was still excited about our Venezuelan equity positions, and in November we began repurchasing Venezuelan debt.

As part of our ongoing political due diligence on the country, one of my partners had met with Hugo Chávez in the fall of 1998, when Chávez was a presidential candidate. My partner was impressed with what he heard in that meeting, especially since Chávez's pro-invest-ment attitude was so different from the consensus view of Venezuela in New York at the time.

Chávez won the presidential election in early December 1998 and took office in February 1999. We then requested another meeting with him, which was to be held in early April 1999 at Venezuela's stunning, hundred-year-old Palacio de Miraflores. My partner and I arrived at the presidential palace wearing Chavista lapel pins, which we had bought from a Caracas taxi driver. Chávez was originally scheduled to meet with us for lunch, but the meeting was delayed by, among other things, a three-hour televised speech that he decided to give, extem-poraneously, that afternoon. We were invited to Chávez's television studio, conveniently located in the presidential palace, to watch the broadcast. My Spanish is fluent, and I thought it was quite an impressive speech and a very professionally run operation.

We finally sat down with Chávez at midnight that night in a spacious Spanish-style room filled with portraits of Simón Bolívar. Chávez even referred to himself as the new Bolívar during our two-hour meeting, which we conducted entirely in Spanish. Chávez was quite charming, and he said everything that a foreign investor would hope to hear: Venezuela would continue to honor free markets; he would solicit foreign investment in Venezuela's equity and fixed income markets, as well as foreign direct investment in the country's oil and gas industry; and, most importantly, he would honor Venezuela's debt. Even though the talk in New York was that Chávez was against foreign investors and that Venezuela would likely default on its debt, on the strength of this meeting we decided to hold onto our Venezuelan bonds. And indeed, during Chávez's first three months in office, the bonds rallied over 25 percent.

Alas, Chávez's true stripes eventually emerged; the pro-investment posture he took during our April meeting was just for show. The first sign of this insincerity came at a follow-up meeting in Caracas when my partner met with some other officials in Chávez's administration. This meeting was conducted in English, and as we pried deeper into the administration's planned programs, Chávez's finance minister José Alejandro Rojas turned to one of his colleagues and asked—in so many words, and in Spanish—"Why do we have to meet with these idiots?" I suppose it did not occur to him that we spoke anything but English, even though our original meetings with Chávez took place in Spanish.

Not long after these meetings with Chávez and his ministers, Chávez began doing exactly the opposite of what he said he would do. Knowing that actions speak louder than words, we quickly sold our Venezuelan holdings and avoided sharp losses as Chávez's populist actions rattled Venezuela's equity and bond markets.

We eventually repurchased CANTV stock in 2001, by which time valuations had dropped to an extraordinarily cheap 1.5 times EV/EBITDA. I was not the only one to notice how cheap CANTV was trading—it was subject to a hostile takeover bid from AES

Corporation in the fall of 2001, and CANTV's board proposed an ill-conceived share buyback and special dividend to combat the takeover attempt. In an open letter to the board of directors of CANTV, we strongly rejected CANTV's proposal because it involved a complicated trust structure that would benefit majority shareholders (e.g., Verizon) at the expense of minority shareholders (e.g., us). Our letter proposed "two simple and fair options for the board to pursue in maximizing all shareholders' value: I) institute a special dividend followed by an increased regular dividend; or II) sell 100 percent of the company to the highest bidder."

Chávez ultimately renationalized CANTV in 2007, as well as dozens of other companies soon thereafter, including much of the oil, steel, cement, agriculture, and finance industries—spending the country's reserves to buy companies, then wasting the country's natural resources through mismanagement. If only Chávez had behaved as Lula did in Brazil, privatizing rather than nationalizing industries and allowing private companies to explore resources, Venezuela's current hyperinflation might now be closer to Brazil's 10 percent inflation rate.

Early in his presidency, Chávez's approval ratings reached as high as 80 percent. By early 2002, however, his ratings had dropped to below 30 percent, and Chávez was even briefly removed from office in a military coup following protests outside the presidential palace by over a million Venezuelans. (His political career began with his own failed coup attempt in 1992.) Wildly popular after his death in 2013, Chávez's approval ratings hovered near just 52 percent during his last five years in office.

* * *

In-person meetings with presidential candidates and officeholders in frontier and emerging markets—in their native language, if possible—are a great primary source for top-down country analysis. These politicians may not walk their talk, but at least you know firsthand what they said.

One of my partners met with three of the candidates in the 2011 Peruvian presidential election, including the eventual winner Ollanta Humala. During the first half of a one-hour meeting, Humala sounded very moderate. During the second half, however, he shifted to the left, pounding the table and shouting, "Peru's mineral wealth belongs to the people!" The leftist nationalist Humala we saw during his 2006 presidential campaign (and his failed coup attempt in 2000 against then-president Alberto Fujimori) ran the second half of the meeting. Which Humala would show up to run the country? Would he go the route of Chávez or Lula? We did not know, so we took a wait-and-see approach. Fortunately, the Humala of the first half of the meeting reported for duty, and his moderate governing has substantially decreased Peru's political risk and improved its investment attractiveness.

Political risk tends to increase around elections, although it is best to monitor it continuously. Sometimes markets misprice political risk, which can influence an investment decision. We saw overpriced political risk in Pakistan prior to its 2013 elections and in Russia in 2014. Political risk was certainly underpriced in Zimbabwe in 2003. It may fluctuate between over- and underpriced in Rwanda at least until the 2017 presidential election, depending on whether President Kagame attempts to stay in power and whether the markets believe that would be good for the country. Political instability can also lead to other risks such as higher inflation (one mani- festation of lower economic stability), particularly in developing countries.[7]

A potential political risk that investors will need to monitor in both developed and developing markets is income inequality and its potential to foment political unrest. One way to do so is by looking at a country's Gini index. A country with perfectly evenly distributed income would have a Gini index of 0, and a country where all of the wealth is held by one person would have a Gini index of 100. According to the CIA's "World Factbook," Sweden has the world's lowest Gini index (i.e., the most equal income dis- tribution) at 23.0. Most Scandinavian and European countries' Gini indices are below 35.0.[8] The world's highest Gini indices belong to Lesotho (63.2) and its all-encompassing neighbor South Africa (63.1) where, despite the South African government's post-apartheid attempts to reduce poverty and inequality, thousands of "service delivery" protests by the poor and unem- ployed rock the country every year. Interestingly, all of the Arab Spring countries have Gini indices below that of the United States (45.0), birth- place of the "Occupy" movement (Egypt's Gini index is 30.8).

Corruption Risk and Investor Protection

Government corruption, and its impact on companies, is another source of political risk when investing beyond the United States and western Europe.

The World Bank defines corruption as the abuse of public office for private gain, which can include bribery, theft of state assets, and nepotism. Corruption undermines macroeconomic stability, stifles foreign direct investment, and increases the cost of doing business; it also hurts the environment and (disproportionately) the poor.[9] While such political corruption is not unheard of in developed markets, it clearly exists in emerging markets, including some of the largest ones such as China, India, and Russia. But for investors who have decided to invest in emerging markets, corruption in frontier markets is surprisingly not much different from corruption in the largest mainstream emerging markets.

To many, frontier markets are the Wild West of the investment world. But in reality, today's frontier markets (not just investable frontier markets) are likely no more corrupt on average than the largest emerging markets— the BRICs—according to Transparency International's Corruption Perceptions Index, which rates how corrupt a country's public sector is thought to be on a scale from 0 (highly corrupt) to 100 (very clean). The highest-scoring countries in 2015 were Denmark (91) and Finland (90). The United States scored a 76. Two-thirds of the 168 countries rated scored below 50. The BRICs averaged 35.5, lower than the frontier markets' average score of 35.6. Both the BRICs and frontier markets have improved their average scores over the past ten years (figure 11.2).

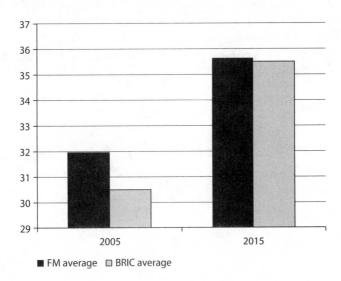

■ FM average □ BRIC average

Figure 11.2
Corruption Perceptions Index. *Source*: Transparency International; Authors.

Just as there is corruption risk in the public sector, there is the risk in the private sector that the government will not uphold the rights of minority shareholders. As I mention in chapter 2, the IFC's Doing Business Project publishes an annual Strength of Investor Protection Index, which rates 189 countries from 0 (low) to 210 (high) on their business regulation environments. While the average investor protection rating for all frontier markets is 4.8, the average rating for the thirty-eight frontier markets that have adopted the OECD's Principles for Corporate Governance (5.6) nearly matches the average rating of the BRICs (5.8).

Corruption and investor protection issues are risks that are prevalent in, but not unique to, frontier markets. These risks should pose no greater a deterrent to investing in a diversified portfolio of frontier markets than to investing in the BRICs.

* * *

Because politics play such a pivotal role in the formation and continued health of frontier economies and markets, political risk in frontier markets often trumps—and certainly influences—other investment risks. As we saw in Russia and Venezuela, governments can destroy or expropriate value by fiat. The best way to address political risk is to conduct thorough country due diligence, meet with the people in government who pull the strings, and then decide if this is a country you want to invest in. But because political risk involves uncertainty, you also may want to mitigate its effects by diversifying it across a number of countries. As we will see in the next chapter, however, some investment risks in frontier markets transcend borders.

12

Other Risks in Frontier Markets

Certainly, bad politics can trump good economics, especially in younger economies or economies in transition. In addition to political risk, frontier investing gives rise to two additional types of risk: macroeconomic (inflation risk, currency risk, and systemic risks spilling over from events in developed markets) and microeconomic (market liquidity risk and custody and settlement risk). Frontier markets also entail one real but typically overpriced type of investment risk—headline risk—that can obscure attractive investment opportunities.

Inflation Risk

Historically, rising inflation has benefited frontier equity markets as a group. An extensive study of returns across asset classes from 1948 through 2009 found that in periods of rising inflation frontier equities were the best-performing asset class; further, the swing in returns between periods of rising inflation and periods of falling inflation was greater for frontier equities than for any other asset class except (just barely) commodities.[1] Even though inflation in frontier markets has recently been more moderate (as discussed in chapter 3), higher growth can lead to higher inflation, and so it is important to carefully analyze and monitor inflation on a country-by-country basis. Doing so can help not only to identify risks but also uncover areas of opportunity.

Inflation comes in two forms: expected and unexpected. Expected inflation does not pose additional risks because, well, it is expected. Unexpected inflation, often caused by rising commodity prices, does pose risks to frontier investors. Commodity inflation can benefit commodity exporters, which include many frontier markets, but it poses risks to countries that are net commodity importers. The risks are most dramatic in countries that import versus export oil or food. Thus, inflation risk in frontier markets is essentially oil and food price risk.

Investors can benefit from changing oil prices in several ways. I may want to take positions, for instance, that would benefit from a rise in oil prices. There are two different kinds of long oil positions: those that benefit when oil prices rise on strong demand, and those that benefit when oil prices rise on weak supply. If oil is up on demand from growing economies, this is good for everyone. If oil is up because of supply disruptions, say because of a crisis in the Middle East, this is good for Nigeria and Kazakhstan, because they benefit from higher oil prices.

Or, if I owned oil-sensitive stocks, I may want to hedge against a decline in oil prices through a combination of downside protection on oil or short positions on some of the big oil majors that are correlated with the price of oil. This approach requires careful attention to monitor and reassess the best hedge for one's long oil-related exposure. Investors can short oil in other, less direct ways—for instance, while oil stocks suffer from lower oil prices, airlines on the contrary benefit from declining fuel prices, which feed through very quickly to their stock prices. So owning oil producers and airlines can create a natural hedge to changes in oil prices. (These positions benefit not just from dropping oil prices; with the enormous pent-up demand for air travel, airlines will continue to be beneficiaries of strong frontier market growth.)

Inflation (or deflation) generated by moves in the price of oil is important if it spans a long period. If oil goes up or down and then stabilizes, the inflationary impact is temporary and tends to be digested by the markets much better than prolonged upward or downward trends.

Food inflation risk can be mitigated by hedging food prices either directly, through futures contracts on rice or wheat, or indirectly, by shorting stocks of food companies (such as Kellogg's and Hershey's) whose profits fall as the costs of their raw ingredients rise. But the biggest food inflation risk in frontier markets is that it becomes political risk. As I mentioned in chapter 3, food expenditures as a percentage of total consumer spending are much higher in frontier markets, especially in the poorest countries— where dependence on imported food means that a sharp enough rise in food prices can destabilize society. Recall that the doubling of wheat prices from June 2010 to January 2011 helped trigger the Arab Spring.

One inflation risk I hope always to avoid is hyperinflation, loosely defined as double-digit monthly price increases (Zimbabwe's hyperinflation peaked in November 2008 at an estimated 79 billion percent per month[2]) and caused mainly by governments with poor restraint printing too much money. Hyperinflation is rare, but even excessively high inflation should sound warning bells. The official inflation rate in Venezuela skyrocketed to over 60 percent annually in 2014 from the high teens in late 2012, exacerbated by collapsing oil prices and destructive currency controls. The Venezuelan government has since stopped publishing inflation data, but the IMF estimates inflation in Venezuela could reach 720 percent in 2016. As an investor, I want to be out well before inflation threatens to become hyperinflation.

Growing economies generate moderate inflation, which adds no meaningful additional investment risk. Price shocks in imported commodities, or the threat of hyperinflation in poorly managed economies, pose the greatest risks.

Frontier Currency Risk

Currency risk is the risk that investments held in foreign currencies will lose money due to fluctuating exchange rates. As with most frontier market risks, currency risk can be avoided, mitigated, or embraced.

At the security level, you can avoid frontier market currency risk altogether by investing only in your home currency. This is easier to do in frontier debt markets, where most bonds are denominated in hard currencies (mainly the U.S. dollar, the euro, and the yen). Most frontier market direct equity investments can be made only in their local currency. To find a frontier market hard currency equity you would need to find a company with an ADR or GDR or that operates in a frontier market but trades on a developed market's stock exchange. PriceSmart (see chapter 8) is one such company, operating exclusively across twelve frontier markets but traded in the United States. A company like PriceSmart still exposes you to operating currency risk from those countries with floating currencies in which the company does business; however, when you sell your shares, you will receive dollars. You can also avoid currency risk by investing in companies in a country that has pegged its currency to the U.S. dollar, such as Qatar, Saudi Arabia, and the United Arab Emirates. Your risk in this case is that the currency peg may be broken.

Emerging markets in the 1990s opted for pegged exchange rates, which they were forced to break due to the buildup of dollar debt. Today most mainstream emerging markets have floating currencies, which provide them a much more stable macroeconomic environment. The bulk of frontier markets, however, still peg their currencies. Investors are thus surprised to hear that frontier markets often entail less currency risk than emerging markets. This is because most such pegs have been very safe (such as in Saudi Arabia, Qatar, and the United Arab Emirates); these are strong countries with very solid current account surpluses, mainly because oil had been very resilient at over $100 per barrel. And while oil remained so stable, the currencies of many frontier markets had very little dollar fluctuation. As oil dropped below $50 per barrel in 2015, however, these currencies, long a source of stability for frontier investors, have come under increased pressure.

Sometimes investors can mitigate currency risk by hedging their currency exposure back to their reference currency through vehicles such as currency forward contracts, currency options, and so forth. Shares on the Nigerian Stock Exchange, for example, are denominated in Nigerian naira, but investors can hedge their naira exposure back to the U.S. dollar or euro. So if you purchase a Nigerian stock and hedge your naira exposure when the U.S. dollar is worth 160 naira—as it was from 2011 to 2014 until running up to 200 naira in 2015—you can be sure that at whatever price you sell the stock in naira, those naira will still be worth 160 per dollar. (Technically, you will not get the exact same exchange rate because you will have to pay the differential in interest rates between the naira and the U.S. dollar; this will be the cost of your hedge.) Or you can embrace the currency risk, owning stocks or bonds in a local currency and receiving the benefit (or detriment) of an appreciated (or depreciated) currency at the time of sale.

One currency risk that is actually a political risk is so-called transfer risk—the risk that once you sell a security, you may be unable to convert your sale proceeds from the local currency into your home currency or transfer your cash balances out of the country. This is an example of how different risks can be interrelated; an analysis of currency risk must take into account the political landscape, and because this particular risk also affects the companies you own if they cannot convert and repatriate their profits, currency risk becomes a necessary part of your microeconomic analysis as well.

Systemic Risk from Events in Developed Markets

Although frontier markets do offer significant diversification, they are still subject—like all markets—to increased correlation during a global crisis. Global economic and financial integration provides growth and development opportunities for frontier markets, but this integration can also mean the economic problems of one country or region become a problem for others. Even though frontier markets historically have had a lower correlation to developed markets than have emerging markets, figure 12.1 shows that correlations increased sharply during the 2008 financial crisis when markets around the world fell precipitously, and again in late 2011 to early 2012.

From the start of 2008 until the trough in early March 2009, developed markets fell by 51 percent as measured by the MSCI World Index; emerging

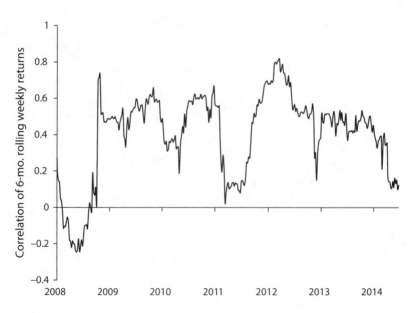

Figure 12.1
Market correlations increase during times of stress. MSCI FM Index vs. MSCI World Index. *Source*: Bloomberg.

markets fell by 58 percent; and frontier markets dropped by 65 percent (figure 12.2). Frontier returns decoupled from the rest of the world during the global recovery, though, so that while emerging markets rebounded to their year-end 2007 levels by late 2010 and developed markets recovered by early 2013, frontier markets were still 28 percent below their year-end 2007 levels through the second half of 2015. Note that at the start of 2016, while frontier and emerging markets had yet to recover from the dip in global markets following their August 2014 peak, developed markets were still above their pre-crisis levels.

Systemic risk is tough to avoid. Frontier markets are not immune to the impact of major events in the rest of the world, and as frontier markets become more globally integrated this risk may increase.

Market Liquidity Risk

Purchasing an attractive investment is only half the job—and not the most important half. A successful investment is a round trip.

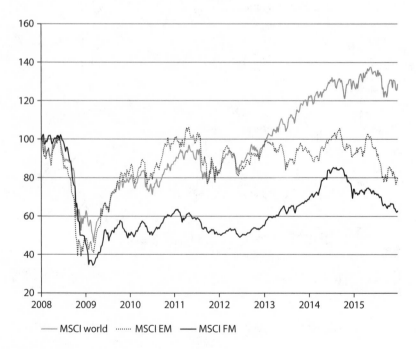

Figure 12.2
World, EM and FM performance (including dividends), 2008–2015.
Source: Bloomberg; Authors.

Over the years, I have had dozens of world leaders, academics, CEOs, and investment professionals speak at my investment conferences to educate my clients and stimulate thought and conversation on a wide range of investing topics. One of the most popular speakers, Ed Viesturs, has no particular expertise in investing, but is a master in managing risk.

Ed Viesturs is America's leading mountain climber. For Ed, risk management is a matter of life and death, where a lost mitten or a torn tent at altitude can render you incapable of returning to base camp. Ed has successfully summited Mount Everest seven times, but this is not his greatest mountaineering achievement. Fourteen mountains in the world rise over 8,000 meters (just over 26,000 feet), and Ed has successfully climbed all of them. In fact, Ed is the first American to climb all of these mountains without supplemental oxygen.

As impressive as these accomplishments are, what really struck me and my audience was the number of times that Ed has halted a climb before reaching his destination—sometimes a stone's throw from the summit. When climbing a mountain, the important question for Ed is not "How am I going to get to the top?" but "How am I going to get back down alive?"

"Getting to the top is optional," he told us. "Getting down is mandatory."

For frontier market investors, an illiquid market may force you to pay more than you would like for a stock, or may even keep you from buying that stock altogether. But worse, when it comes time to sell, an illiquid market may force you to settle for a much lower price than you would like, especially when trying to sell a sizeable holding. Worse still, it may prevent you from selling altogether, as investors saw in the Egyptian uprising in early 2011 when the Egyptian stock market shut down for eight weeks, or in the summer of 2015 when the Greek stock market closed for five weeks because of fears of Greece's exit from the eurozone.

One characteristic of frontier markets is in most cases their lower levels of liquidity. By definition, most frontier markets are smaller and often much less liquid than mainstream emerging markets or developed markets, with the exception of markets deemed frontier for other reasons (such as restrictions on foreign investment, as with Saudi Arabia). The only way to avoid liquidity risk is to avoid illiquid markets. But since illiquidity is by definition common in frontier markets, market liquidity risk in frontier investing should be embraced. After all, the patient investor usually is highly compensated for taking this risk. The impacts of market liquidity risk can be mitigated by diversifying across companies and countries.

As frontier market volumes—and thus liquidity—increase over time, market liquidity risk will decline. Frontier markets are only just beginning to attract what I believe will be significant institutional financial flows, as investors rebalance their asset allocations to include frontier markets. The same phenomenon occurred in today's mainstream emerging markets such as Brazil and India, which had low liquidity just fifteen to twenty years ago.

It is very important to match the liquidity of an investment vehicle with the liquidity of its underlying investments. A fund that offers daily or weekly liquidity can be very seductive for an investor, but if the fund invests in illiquid stocks that could take weeks or months to liquidate, this may create a dangerous situation if redemption requests start pouring in. In that case, the fund may enter a vicious circle of forced selling of more—and more illiquid—holdings at distressed prices.

Custody and Settlement Risk

Custody and settlement risk encompasses an assortment of uncertainties investors face when attempting to buy, hold, and sell securities in frontier markets. Custody risk is the risk of loss if the custodian holding your investments files for bankruptcy, goes out of business, or otherwise loses or absconds with your assets. Settlement risk (which bookends custody risk) is the risk that the securities you paid cash for are not delivered, or that you are not paid the cash for securities you delivered. (Settlement risk in frontier markets is a close cousin of transfer risk, mentioned above.)

Each country has its own rules and laws, so the degree of custody and settlement risk varies widely by market, as does the degree of adherence to a regulatory framework or even enforceability of the rule of law. In some markets, you may have to sue a custodian in its local jurisdiction in a court system that favors locals over foreigners or that runs on bribery. Each country has its own bankruptcy code, so if a custodian goes bankrupt, it is questionable whether you will get your securities back. It may be that a country commingles assets in a bankruptcy, or—worst case—the assets just disappear. Some countries label securities holdings so that the securities are held in your name at the custodian and recorded as such at the exchange. In some markets, foreigners cannot hold shares at all but must invest through derivatives such as swaps, adding another layer of risk: the swap counterparty.

Settlement risks outside of custodian bankruptcy arise from antiquated processes and technology (increasingly rare), human error or malfeasance, or disruptions on the local exchange due to downed networks, power outages, political actions, natural disasters, and so forth.

Custody and settlement risk events are unpredictable but sporadic. The best defense against these risk events is due diligence and vigilant monitoring, especially in person. In one such meeting we had in Kigali, the employees of a Kenyan custodial bank expanding into Rwanda were extremely professional and went above and beyond to address our due diligence queries. Their team leader, who had just personally shepherded a batch of dividend checks through Rwanda's central bank, delayed her annual vacation to meet with us. All else being equal, this kind of service wins my business.

Of enormous benefit, too, was that my multinational team could speak twenty-two languages, which allowed us to interact directly with custodian, exchange, and government employees in most of the markets we followed. My team's fluency in Bulgarian, Croatian, Macedonian, Serbian, Arabic, Urdu, French, Portuguese, and Swahili, for example, was particularly advantageous in eastern European, Middle Eastern, and African frontier markets where we have invested, even in those markets that regularly conduct business in English. Having native speakers who know the vernacular can go a long way toward cutting through bureaucratic red tape to get to the root of an issue (or, in Swahili, "Wacha mchezo, tuongee vizuri").[3]

Headline Risk

Headline risk is clearly a risk of a different sort from the others I discuss above. It comes in two forms: the risk that a high-profile news story (such as the BP oil spill) will affect a company's—or an entire country's—stock market performance (and possibly its intrinsic value); and the less quantifiable reputational risk to investors once it is discovered that they are invested in the country or company in the headlines.

One high-profile media event with little economic impact that should not affect markets, but does, is soccer's World Cup. A study by Goldman Sachs found that since 1974 the winning team's home equity market outperforms global markets by an average of 3.5 percent in the month following the victory, only to underperform by an average of 4 percent in the year after the event. Conversely, runners-up (i.e., losers of the final match) underperform for a few months after the match but make up those losses by the one-year anniversary of the loss.[4]

On the other hand, headline events that investors assume will have a powerful impact on equity markets may have little lasting effect on the actual markets. Take, for example, the tragic garment factory collapse in Savar, Bangladesh, on April 24, 2013, a ghastly example of the consequences of greed and criminal disregard for human safety that dominated the media that spring. Rana Plaza was a four-story retail and banking building atop which its owners illegally built four additional stories to house several garment factories. The day before the collapse, inspectors discovered cracks in the walls, and the retail stores and bank offices evacuated their employees. The garment factories' owners, however, told their workers that the building was safe, and that they would dock a month's pay from anyone who did not report to work the next day. The owners now face murder charges. Had these factories been owned by publicly traded companies, their shareholders rightfully would have been wiped out.

The Dhaka Stock Exchange Index, however, includes less than 5 percent garment- or textile-related stocks by market capitalization. It rose 18 percent in the two months following the factory collapse and over 33 percent in the year after the disaster. By the way, the doomsayer media's predictions that the rest of Bangladesh's garment industry could not recover from the negative publicity proved overdone, as garment exports increased 16 percent from April 2013 to March 2014.[5] With all this media attention, one would have thought that every garment factory in Bangladesh was a disaster waiting to happen; but many factories, including the factory I toured—pictured in chapter 4—are state of the art and provide safe jobs to Bangladeshi workers. The more pertinent headline risk from the Rana Plaza tragedy is that which engulfed twenty-nine developed-market apparel retailers including Walmart, Benetton, and Carrefour when word spread that they had sourced merchandise from the illegal factories.

Investors face headline risk of a similar sort: making headlines themselves for the investments they hold. An organization called the Asset Owners Disclosure Project now tracks and publicizes the investments in high-carbon assets of over 1,000 pension funds and over 270 university endowments to empower pensioners, students, and alumni to agitate for change. Some universities are now outsourcing their endowment management, in part to avoid the headaches of headline risk from their investments.[6] One large brokerage firm even advocated a "replication strategy" to avoid the headline risk of investing with managers who themselves make headlines for being invested in controversial assets.[7]

This may sound like an ethical matter, but headline risk and ethics are in fact two separate issues. If an investor or an investment committee decides to avoid certain industries (say, gambling or tobacco) because of the nature of the products they sell, this is a decision based on the ethics of the investor. But if an investor decides to avoid certain companies for fear of being discovered to own these companies, that is a business decision based, not on ethics, but on fear of headline risk. Many investment committees, for instance, are debating whether to divest fossil fuel–related companies. They may believe these companies are harming the environment, or they may sell these holdings simply to avoid the headline risk of owning them. (In either case, if committee members are then filmed driving to work in full-size SUVs, they may face additional headline risk.)

As investors, we need to remember that media outlets are paid to sensationalize the news, increasing the probability and severity of headline risk. The headlines need not even be true. The death of King Abdullah bin Abdulaziz of Saudi Arabia made the headlines regularly; the Saudi market dropped 3 percent in November 2012 on news of the king's death, only to rebound when he appeared on Saudi state television three days later greeting members of the royal family. Subsequent reports of his demise elicited more limited market reactions, although the market fell over 6 percent on the day he was admitted to the hospital in December 2014. Following his death three weeks later, the Saudi market actually traded up 0.7 percent for the day and nearly 10 percent over the next month.

Looking beyond the headlines can be profitable, as with the debt of the former Yugoslavia (discussed in chapter 9). Likewise, the media constantly bombarded us with images of 9/11 and the war in Afghanistan yet ignored the economic stimulus from the inflow of aid and commerce to neighboring Pakistan in the months and years that followed.

Case Study: Investing in Pakistan After 9/11 and Now

The attacks on New York's World Trade Center on September 11, 2001, reminded the world that the blurring distinctions between developed and emerging markets are not only economic; terrorist attacks are no longer remote events in faraway lands. Of course, we had seen terrorist activity in other developed markets such as in the United Kingdom, but nothing on the scale of 9/11. After the initial shock, it became clear that the U.S. government planned to take whatever actions were necessary to find the attackers and bring them to justice. This ultimately led to the war in Afghanistan—and America's nearest and newest ally in this war was Pakistan.

The United States' staunch commitment to bring the perpetrators of the attacks to justice reassured investors, and U.S. stocks quickly recovered their losses following 9/11. I believed the U.S. government's actions would also change the dynamics of Pakistan's external debt and would ultimately have a positive impact on Pakistan's currency and equity markets, so in late 2001 we revisited the investment case for Pakistan.

For many years prior to 2001, I had followed the Pakistani stock market, and I always thought it represented an intriguing opportunity. Many of Pakistan's large-cap stocks traded at extremely cheap valuations, and their lofty dividend payouts were unparalleled in any other market. But I was always deterred by Pakistan's macroeconomic environment and the political and currency risks of investing there. The Pakistani rupee (PKR) became a floating currency in 1982, and for every year since it had depreciated against the U.S. dollar—sometimes by more than 17 percent—handicapping any return on investment for dollar-based investors.

In the third quarter of 2001, Pakistan owed the equivalent of 60 percent of its GDP in external debt, and, more worryingly, the high servicing costs on this debt represented 30 percent of its exports. Saddled with current account deficits since 1957 and a projected budget deficit of more than 5 percent of GDP, there was widespread skepticism from the international markets that Pakistan would be able to honor its foreign obligations in a timely manner. A unilateral default seemed almost inevitable. However, the United States' post-9/11 collaboration with the Musharraf government to fight terrorism provided an environment conducive for Pakistan to request the rescheduling of its debt. In December 2001, the Paris Club—an informal forum of nineteen of the world's largest creditor nations that meets regularly (in Paris, hence the name) to renegotiate the debt of troubled debtor countries— agreed to a generous $12 billion restructuring of Pakistan's multilateral debt (one-third of its total foreign debt) to ensure that the country maintained political stability during the conflict in Afghanistan.

In addition, the IMF started a new three-year program that provided Pakistan with additional funding. These initiatives were beyond even the most optimistic scenario I had scripted for the country.

I realized that there was potential for a virtuous financial circle. A little known fact about Pakistan is that, like many other developing nations, foreign remittances from Pakistanis living abroad are an important component of current account inflows. While the rupee was depreciating against the dollar, Pakistani expatriates reduced their remittances to levels sufficient only to assure the subsistence of the families left behind. Once the foreign debt situation improved and a substantial amount of additional aid was received or promised, the rupee started to appreciate, reversing its twenty-year trend. Foreign remittances quickly picked up in volume as offshore dollars flowed in to take advantage of the stronger currency. Overseas Pakistanis were sending home more of the earnings and savings they had accumulated abroad. Remittances to the country more than doubled, from $1.5 billion in 2001 to $3.5 billion in 2002.

This favorable climate substantially alleviated the pressure from high interest rates and inflation. Short-term rates fell from 11 percent in early 2002 to less than 3 percent in the first quarter of 2003. At the same time, the credit spreads on Pakistan government bonds denominated in U.S. dollars tightened to less than 7 percent over U.S. Treasuries, and local bank deposit rates collapsed under the flow of new liquidity coming into the local market. In September 2002, the foreign currency reserves of Pakistan's central bank reached an all-time high of $9.5 billion.

In this environment of falling rates and a strengthening currency, but without a large local market accessible to foreigners for purchasing bonds with long maturities, the Pakistani stock market was the most attractive asset class for foreign and local investors.

Two stocks in particular attracted my attention: Pakistan Telecom and Hub Power. Pakistan Telecom was the fixed-line telephone operator in Pakistan as well as the leading cellular phone company. Mainly because of the very low teledensity of the country and the success of its cellular business, the company was growing earnings at a healthy 10 percent per year. Despite its robust potential, though, the stock was trading at depressed ratios of 5 times P/E and 2.5 times EV/EBITDA. Even more attractive to me, the dividend yield was close to 15 percent.

Since the Pakistani government controlled Pakistan Telecom and the dividend payments represented over 5 percent of the government's revenues, I believed that the payout ratio—the portion of earnings earmarked for dividends—was safe. To find a company with these kinds of numbers is unheard of in a developed market. I've never seen a stock like that in the United States or in Europe in my thirty-year career—but that's the type of opportunity you can find in frontier markets; you're buying growth at an extremely reasonable price. With only a few people analyzing a situation, you can have pricing anomalies like this. We initiated a position in Pakistan Telecom in late 2001 at a price of PKR14.25 per share.

Early in 2002, we invested in Hub Power at PKR20.4 per share. Hub Power is Pakistan's second-largest independent power producer, operating power stations in the eastern part of Pakistan and selling its electricity to the government. Like Pakistan Telecom, Hub Power traded at a cheap valuation of less than five times P/E and four times EV/EBITDA, with a dividend yield approaching 25 percent. Even in a business that is not fast growing, if you earn a dividend yield of 25 percent, you are going to recoup your whole investment in four years. Again, that's unheard of in developed markets. Although the business was not a fast grower, the company's off-take agreement with the government and some commitments of a guaranteed yield to shareholders at the time of its IPO made Hub Power a unique, high-yielding investment.

With the macro environment in Pakistan improving, the outlook for these two companies strengthened dramatically as well. By year-end 2002, Pakistan Telecom shares had reached PKR26.00 and Hub Power closed at PKR40.10. For the full year 2002, the Karachi market returned 112 percent in local currency and 118 percent in U.S. dollars. We began selling the Hub Power position in early 2003 and the Pakistan Telecom shares in early 2005.

The market continued to rally, gaining another 420 percent in dollars from 2003 through March 2008. But it was hit especially hard during the 2008 financial crisis; from its peak on April 4, 2008, to its trough on January 26, 2009, the Karachi Stock Exchange KSE 100 Index lost 75 percent of its value in dollars—back to levels not seen since 2003. Business fundamentals were still sound across many industries, and I found several attractive equity investments among the ruins.

Several years into the recovery, though, investors still avoided the market in droves. One reason was that the Pakistani central bank had run a very tight monetary policy in 2011, when Pakistan faced the twin inflationary perils of high oil prices and high food costs. Tight monetary policy and high interest rates encouraged savings into the fixed-income market, so domestic savers, a key part of any frontier economy, had very little money in the stock market. Earning an 18 percent interest rate (in effect, their risk-free rate) makes asset allocation simple, because nothing could beat that risk-free rate. With fixed-income yields at 18 percent, earnings yields (i.e., the inverse of the price-earnings ratio) on Pakistani stocks rose to 25 percent.

Price-earnings ratios of four times earnings were once again prevalent in Pakistan at the end of 2011, and dividend yields were often in excess of 10 percent. Bargains abounded: Pakistan Telecom, which peaked at PKR90 per share in March 2005, reached a low of PKR10 in December 2011; we began repurchasing shares in late 2011 and early 2012. As debt yields fell below 15 percent, earnings yields also fell, and the implied price-earnings ratio moved to six times earnings. This expanding market multiple translated to a 50 percent return, before factoring in any growth—and in 2012, Pakistan was beginning to enjoy decent GDP growth from the recovery following the 2008 crisis.

Many foreign investors still refused to look at Pakistan due to geopolitical risk, even though the implied earnings yield would decline in sync with the fall in the cost of debt, improving the price-earnings ratio of the market. Too bad for them; fast-forward twenty-four months to the end of 2013, and the Pakistani stock market was up over 160 percent, partly due to the price-earnings rerating as the cost of equity and debt fell. In 2014, twelve-month fixed-income yields had fallen to 9.5 percent, and dividend yields had compressed (although they were still attractive in the context of the global search for yield). This finally caught the attention of foreign investors—several years late. Of the $125 million per day of turnover in the Pakistani stock market today, about $25 million is from foreigners. This is dramatically different from the end of 2011, when foreign investment was nearly non-existent.

Pakistan remains beset with poor macroeconomics. It is a constant recipient of IMF packages. It has a very significant budget deficit, as it has one of the lowest tax revenue-to-GDP ratios in the world (of countries with a recorded tax intake), at about 9 percent. This reflects a traditional society rarely willing to enter into compacts that require it to pay taxes, and it has left the government dependent on external financing. At the same time, the high price of oil led to a very significant current account deficit for Pakistan (as well as other parts of the subcontinent including India), although lower oil prices since late 2014 should ease this deficit. The current account deficit finances oil, but also fertilizer—vital to Pakistan, where agriculture remains a very significant part of GDP.

Against this poor macroeconomic situation, Pakistan has had some very significant political changes recently, with the first peaceful transition of civilian power since independence in 1947 without the interference of the army. This move toward democracy in a population of 180 million people makes Pakistan one of the final frontiers of global investing. A key thesis for investing in a frontier market is that growth in disposable income increases discretionary consumption beyond the necessities, and with a GDP per capita of about $1,300 in U.S. dollars ($4,800 PPP-adjusted) in 2014, Pakistan is at a very interesting point on its disposable income curve.

The Karachi Stock Exchange's All Share Index returned 250 percent from 2012 to 2014 (212 percent in U.S. dollars) despite the country's difficult geopolitical and macroeconomic situation, which means that political risk need not always stand in the way of outstanding returns.

Beyond Headline Risk: Adventure on the High Seas

Lesson learned: Sometimes frontier markets investment research involves more adventure than originally planned.

In January 2006, I traveled to Nigeria to conduct due diligence on a prospective oil exploration investment's operations in the Gulf of Guinea off the coast of West Africa. I have invested in Nigeria since 1996—first in debt and later in equities. Nigeria is a large country, the most populous in Africa and the seventh-most-populous in the world. With a population of over 170 million, it has more people than France, the United Kingdom, and Canada combined. Nigeria's economy ranks about twentieth in the

world, as large as Sweden, Poland, or Argentina. Nigeria is a large oil producer—2.5 million barrels per day.

As my research team and I did hundreds of times each year, on this trip
I conducted on-the-ground due diligence—and in this case on-the-water
as well, with a visit to an offshore oil rig. From the city of Port Harcourt
on the Niger Delta, we took a helicopter to the Bulford Dolphin, a semi-
submersible offshore drilling rig owned by the Norwegian oil rig company
Dolphin Drilling and leased to the oil exploration company I was analyzing
(figures 12.3 and 12.4).

This oil rig made news in June 2006, five months after my due diligence trip, when it was attacked by pirates who kidnapped eight personnel (six Americans, one Canadian, and one Brit). Fortunately, all of the

Figure 12.3
View from a helicopter descending for a landing on the Bulford Dolphin rig in the
Gulf of Guinea. *Source*: Author.

Figure 12.4
On the Bulford Dolphin rig (before the pirate attack). *Source*: Author.

captives were released two days later, unharmed. The Bulford Dolphin, it seems, was star-crossed. On May 13, 2010, the $235 million rig—bought by an Indian company and renamed the *Aban Pearl*, then leased to Venezuela's state-owned oil company to drill in that country's offshore natural gas fields—sank off the coast of northeastern Venezuela in over 500 feet of water. All ninety-five of its crew were rescued unharmed, but the incident dealt a blow to President Hugo Chávez's plans to harvest offshore gas reserves.

* * *

Frontier investing is not without risk—but it is also not without opportunity. The next chapter explores some of the long-term investment opportunities, or megatrends, that I see now and ahead from frontier markets' continued growth and integration into the global economy.

13

Megatrends in Frontier Markets

Throughout my career, when I have found an attractive investment opportunity in a particular company or country, I have looked to see if the thesis of that investment might also apply across other companies or regions, thus creating an investable theme. Such themes typically occur across several markets at one time, or in predictable patterns based on what other markets went through during similar phases of development. Because some markets are ahead of others in their stages of economic growth, these themes may present new opportunities in one market as they come to fruition in another. We have seen similar "movies" before; the actors and locations might change, but the story is almost the same and will end in a similar fashion.

This chapter explores some of the long-term, top-down investment themes—or megatrends—I see in frontier markets today:

- The rise of the frontier markets consumer, and other demographic-related investment themes, including consumer staples, leisure travel, retail and luxury goods, residential real estate, and health care;
- Banking and financial services penetration; and
- Commodity producers on the verge of capacity booms.

Each of these megatrends should provide interesting potential investments in frontier markets for many years to come.

Rise of the Frontier Markets Consumer, and Other Demographic-Related Investment Themes

As I have discussed throughout the book, what makes frontier markets so attractive from an investment perspective is their fast growth, usually coupled with young and growing populations. This leads to rapidly expanding middle classes that will begin to demand more of the consumer staples that most of the developed and emerging world take for granted. In middle-income frontier markets (i.e., those whose populations are solidly middle class), consumption demand growth will migrate to more discretionary items such as travel and leisure, retail, and—for the wealthiest markets plus a few others I discuss below—luxury goods. I also see increased demand for residential real estate and health care in countries across income levels, although the most attractive investment opportunities in these areas will likely come from the wealthier markets.

Consumer Staples

I see tremendous growth potential in fast-growing consumer goods markets, in Africa in particular. Africa's middle class now comprises over 350 million people—larger than the entire population of the United States.[1] Their consumption of consumer goods is very low by global standards, and as disposable incomes rise, I expect consumption levels to increase. Multinationals such as Nestlé, Unilever (discussed in chapter 8), and Procter & Gamble, as well as many local brands, will cater to the African consumer's burgeoning demand for grocery, household, and personal care products and her expected move to premium product lines. Many of these companies can grow earnings at 20 percent annually for the next five to ten years.

Also on the rise in Sub-Saharan Africa is beer consumption (I discuss Rwanda's Heineken subsidiary Bralirwa in chapter 6)—although when one accounts for the size of each market's Muslim (nondrinking) population, the male/female split (men drink more beer than women), and the percentage of the population below eighteen years of age, food and nonalcoholic beverage companies may have a wider demographic appeal.

Travel and Leisure

Just as we saw in mainstream emerging markets, when discretionary incomes in frontier markets reach a certain level, the demand for travel and leisure-related products and services (airlines, hotels, gaming, etc.) should accelerate. The same macroeconomic forces that in the past decade proved profitable for emerging Asian airlines—significant demand growth with limited supply—will do the same for Central American and Middle Eastern airlines.

Particularly promising are countries with an established tourist market. In Saudi Arabia, for instance, one of the big revenue generators is religious tourism. The country is home to the holy cities of Mecca and Medina, two regular pilgrimage destinations. The Hajj—the pilgrimage to Mecca required of every Muslim who can afford it—occurs during one specific week each year, and the Umrah is a pilgrimage that Muslims can make at any time throughout the year. Saudi Arabia has about three million visitors just for the Hajj and about 10 million religious visitors altogether each year, renting hotels and spending money.

It is difficult to invest in the religious tourism theme in Saudi Arabia. There are a few stocks (such as construction companies) that as of this writing only Saudi and Gulf Cooperation Council (GCC) nationals and large foreign institutions can purchase, but smaller outsiders should be able to buy soon. In the meantime, we can invest in this theme indirectly. For example, one company we have invested in has exposure to the hospitality and landlord business in Mecca as well as the ticketing, lodging, and logistics for a popular Saudi scholarship program (education is a theme in emerging markets that may subsequently play out in frontier markets).

Retail and Luxury Goods

Farther up the income curve, consumers' appetites for retail brands grow, and frontier markets consumers are the retail and luxury goods consumers of tomorrow. Although GDP per capita levels in most frontier markets lag behind those of emerging and developed countries, strong economic growth, highly attractive demographics, and greater urbanization rates should drive the growth of the aspiring middle-class frontier markets consumer.

The GCC countries, for instance, have the demographics and economic growth to support a sustained rise in consumer spending, especially on fashion retail. The Dubai Mall is the world's largest shopping mall and combines retail and leisure travel into one destination. It attracts over 90 million visitors a year, four times more than Disney World's Magic Kingdom, making Dubai Mall the most-visited tourist attraction in the world after Istanbul's Grand Bazaar (91 million annual visitors). Growth in the GCC also benefits publicly traded fast-food restaurant chains.

Frontier markets already are growing in importance for the luxury goods industry. These include the wealthier countries—the Middle East is now the tenth-largest luxury goods market globally, ahead of Russia, according to Bain & Company—but also countries whose income levels are still low but whose upper middle classes are expected to expand with their growing economies. Over the last several years, Louis Vuitton and other luxury brands have opened stores in Ulaanbaatar, the capital of Mongolia. As I mentioned in chapter 3 and discuss again below, Mongolia's mineral wealth is expected to drive one of the world's fastest economic expansions in the coming years. And Nigeria was the fastest-growing market for champagne from 2006 to 2011, posting a compounded annual growth rate of 22 percent, according to Euromonitor International. Nigeria is now among the top twenty champagne markets in the world.

Residential Real Estate

When a city becomes a regional economic hub, its economic growth surges. Hong Kong and Singapore are two examples of cities that became hubs in their regions, and economic hubs such as the United Arab Emirates (UAE) have the potential to repeat these successes. Other frontier market hubs include Tbilisi, Kigali, Nairobi, and Panama. Investments in residential real estate in these hubs should do well as their economies grow.

As with most frontier investments, you can find great bargains in the real estate sector. Several attractive property development companies in the UAE saw their stocks drop over 80 percent from their 2008 peaks, and yet their profitability has reached all-time highs. In 2015 they still traded on average over 65 percent below their peaks (figure 13.1). Dubai in particular is becoming a central hub for the Middle East / North African (MENA) region, and real estate developers could benefit as global companies begin opening offices there to service their fledgling Iranian operations.

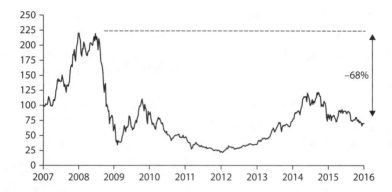

Figure 13.1
UAE real estate developers' performance, 2007–2015 (indexed to 100).
Source: Bloomberg; Authors.

Even after a strong run-up in 2013 and early 2014, Dubai real estate prices are still cheap compared to cities like London, New York, Hong Kong, or Singapore. Prime real estate in Dubai sold for under $700 per square foot in 2015 compared to $2,700 in New York and $4,400 in London.[2]

In the coming years, the UAE will spend enormous amounts on real estate development and other infrastructure build-out, particularly in Dubai for World Expo 2020 and Qatar for the 2022 World Cup and proposed pipeline projects. Construction companies in the UAE as well as property developers and theme park owners could see their businesses, and stock prices, do well.

Saudi Arabia has a significant housing shortage by emerging or developed market standards, given its large and growing population, its density, and its land mass. The Saudi government estimates the country has a shortage of one million residential units, and it is working to bridge that gap. One way to invest in this Saudi residential real estate build-out is through cement companies. Other ways include through publicly traded companies that own land or listed construction companies involved in civil engineering, water and waste management, and infrastructure construction.

Iraq experienced a massive shortage of residential units following the war, estimated at 2.5 million units according to the Ministry of Construction. It plans to spend $1 billion on housing between 2014 and 2017, and it is in talks with a couple of large regional real estate developers to manage these residential building projects.

Egypt also has a housing shortage. The Egyptian government announced a massive $40 billion project to build one million residential units in Cairo (although these plans will likely be curtailed sharply), which should benefit cement companies. Egypt also has several listed companies involved mainly in residential real estate development.

The top three rules of real estate are: location, location, location. As locals and expatriates migrate to frontier market economic hubs, they all need places to live. And this can mean great places to invest.

Health Care

As incomes rise, people spend more on health care services, including hospitals, pharmaceuticals, and health insurance (see figure 13.2).

The GCC countries in particular have historically underspent on health care but present attractive investment opportunities in health care in the coming years. The Saudis are poised to spend large sums on education and health care because the country has a young population—and one with some health challenges. For example, Saudi Arabia has one of the

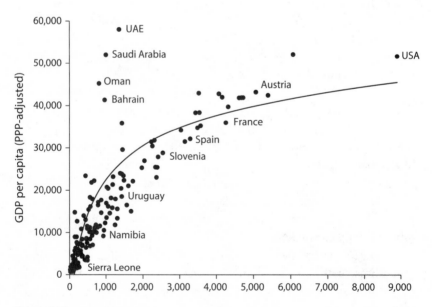

Figure 13.2
Health care spending and GDP per capita. *Source*: WHO; World Bank.

highest rates of obesity and diabetes in the world, almost on par with the United States. This is a structural health care issue that the country needs to address, especially since diabetes is showing up not just in older people, but younger people, which affects the efficiency of the workforce.

Despite the importance of health care for the Saudis, they are suffering a shortage of services. They have 2.2 hospital beds per thousand people, which the government wants to raise to the emerging markets' average of 3 to 3.2 beds per thousand people. Four Saudi health care companies trade publicly (mainly hospitals and inpatient/outpatient services), as well as a few listed medical care insurance companies and branded generic pharmaceutical companies (which have the sole license to distribute specific medications).

Like Saudi Arabia, the UAE also has a shortage of hospital beds per capita. Abu Dhabi now mandates that all people be covered by health insurance, which is adding to health care demand. A couple of foreign-listed companies operate in the UAE with hospitals offering inpatient and outpatient services. Qatar also has a listed company with direct exposure to health care through hospitals.

Lower-income frontier markets also present interesting opportunities in the health care space. The pharmaceutical industry in Bangladesh is a $1.5+ billion per year industry growing at over 20 percent annually, and this is on pharmaceutical spending of less than $10 per person per year. As Bangladeshis' incomes rise, their purchasing power goes up, and their spending on pharmaceuticals goes up. Bangladesh is party to the World Trade Organization's TRIPS Agreement (Trade-Related aspects of Intellectual Property rights), which affords Bangladesh exemption from intellectual copyright protection on pharmaceuticals. What this means is that Bangladesh, as a least developed country, is exempt until 2033 from having to honor other countries' patent protections. So if Pfizer spends billions of dollars to develop a drug, Bangladeshi pharmaceutical companies can actually reverse engineer—which is a polite way of saying copy—that product in Bangladesh as long as they sell it in the Bangladeshi market only. That advantage gives them the ability to meet 97 percent of the domestic demand for pharmaceutical products in Bangladesh.

Once you can afford enough food for your family and a roof over your head, your next purchase as a frontier market consumer is health care, which is why I view health care as an attractive long-term frontier investment theme.

Banking and Financial Services Penetration

Frontier market banks are often attractive from a top-down and a bottom-up perspective. Frontier economies enjoy low banking penetration rates, and banks can do particularly well as these economies grow. And many of these banks boast strong franchises and cheap valuations relative to their developed and emerging market peers.

Banks are also one way to profit from promising frontier markets with otherwise illiquid or inaccessible equities. "The banking sector tends to disproportionately benefit from the reform momentum," former Georgian prime minister Lado Gurgenidze told my investors at a recent investor conference, "and tends to exhibit growth rates far, far above the nominal GDP growth rates for many years in a row once such a cycle begins." And, Gurgenidze says, because large international banks actually tend to fare poorly in these frontier markets, the best investment opportunities lie in investing in attractive local banks.

Gurgenidze should know: He is also the former chairman of the Bank of Georgia and the Bank of Kigali in Rwanda, and the current chairman of Liberty Bank in Georgia. Georgia and Rwanda share several traits that bode well for their banking sectors, including very strong political will to reform, small but fast-growing GDPs, and low banking-assets-to-GDP and credit-to-GDP ratios. "When you reform and when you govern responsibly," according to Gurgenidze, "you tend to enjoy these growth rates—7 to 7.5 percent for the last few years in Rwanda—come what may."

Georgia and Rwanda ranked first and second, respectively, as the top reformers in making their regulatory environments more favorable to business, as measured by the World Bank's latest Five Year Measure of Cumulative Change in Doing Business indicators between 2006 and 2011. "Investing in the banking sector of such frontier markets is a leveraged play on their growth and development," noted Gurgenidze. "Economic liberalization tends to trigger a long cycle of banking sector growth at rates exceeding that of the nominal GDP."

Gurgenidze also pointed out that (from a bottom-up perspective) once a bank's market share reaches 30 percent, "you pretty much have an indestructible franchise. You have to try very, very hard to damage your franchise at that point." Gurgenidze is very familiar with the examples that back this up. "Bank of Kigali has crossed that [30 percent] threshold," he told us. "Bank of Georgia has stayed at 34 percent for the last four years, and come hell or high water, there's no dislodging that bank from its position."

Banks play a vital role as countries progress from agrarian, subsistence economies into urbanized, industrial economies with growing disposable incomes. Empirical studies show that as a country begins to lower inflation through structural and supply-side reforms, its long bond yield (a measure of the cost of risk of an economy) falls in line. And as interest rates fall, the middle class can start engaging in long-term financial planning.

When real interest rates drop below 10 percent, which might mean nominal rates of between 15 and 20 percent (Indonesia is a good example of this), populations begin to trust in their own currency, and capital flight decreases. Capital stays in an economy and leads to the creation of credit. And credit is what drives an economy—not indebtedness at the levels that the developed markets or some emerging markets find themselves, but credit starting from a low single-digit percentage of GDP and generated through urbanization and household formation.

Penetration is a key factor in the frontier market banking sector. If you are a subsistence farmer, you do not need a bank account. When you get your first salaried job, however, you then begin to engage with the financial sector of the economy. As the economy grows, this banking penetration picks up dramatically. Rwanda's banking penetration, as measured by total loans to GDP, is a low 15 percent—one reason why I liked Bank of Kigali.[3] Elsewhere in Africa, Ghana, Nigeria, and Kenya also stand out as some of the lowest-ranked countries on both total-assets-to-GDP and total-loans-to-GDP. Interestingly, Mexico, Indonesia, Colombia, and Peru (two mainstream emerging markets and two smaller emerging markets that I classify as frontier) are also among the lowest-penetrated countries in terms of loans-to-GDP.

A key measure when looking for banking opportunities in frontier markets is the value of an individual to a country's banking sector (figure 13.3). Unsurprisingly, frontier markets today mimic their predecessor emerging markets. In the mid-1980s, the value of each member of Turkey's population to its banking sector was about $20; in 2014 that number reached over $1,000. As individuals begin to use credit cards and take out loans for household products—televisions, refrigerators, bicycles, mopeds—and ultimately auto loans and home mortgages, they become worth much more in net present value to the banking sector. This banking penetration is paralleled in the corporate world with corporate loans for the creation of small and medium enterprises (SMEs) and in the public sector with long-term infrastructure spending.

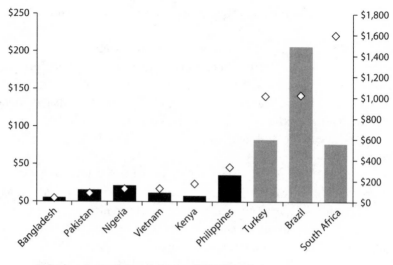

Figure 13.3
Market capitalization of banks per capita of select markets, 2014. *Source*: IMF; Bloomberg.

In most frontier markets, the banking sector's ability to grow profits rises dramatically as the sector develops, raising the sector's market value. So as a country makes the transition from a semiskilled agrarian labor force to an industrialized, disposable-income consumer base, I would monitor the growth of its credit to GDP as well as its loan growth, and track the ability of the banking sector to monetize this growth through its profitability. Looking at market capitalization to GDP of the banking sector as well as profitability as a percentage of GDP through the credit cycle can also help gauge future loan growth.

But there can be too much of a good thing. Loan growth can accelerate to unsustainable levels when an economy hits the sweet spot of middle-class growth (generally considered about $4,000 per capita). We saw, for example, overexpanded credit growth in Bangladesh in 2010, when credit to GDP expanded too drastically—the banking sector extended too many loans. The result was a cycle of nonperforming loans. We saw this in Vietnam as well, where bank credit to the private sector experienced one of the fastest expansions any economy has ever undergone, from 33 percent of GDP in 2000 to 115 percent of GDP in 2010. This resulted in a substantial banking sector bust and a collapse of bank assets, predominantly fueled by the property bubbles of 2008. Dubai is another classic example of a banking sector where loan growth and total credit to GDP got out of control. What we want to see, instead, is a slow rise in credit to GDP, as with India from 1990 to 2005 and China from 2002 to 2010. China has now undergone very substantial credit creation, the result of many years of orderly credit expansion as it brought people into the banking sector.

Another important part of the frontier markets' banking sector is its adoption of technology. In Nigeria, for example, the banking sector is a massive user of diesel fuel, because every bank needs generators in the basement to keep its computers running in the event of brownouts caused by the unreliability of Nigeria's power grid. As the power grid improves, and with reliable twenty-four-hour electricity, Nigeria's ability to deliver a more profitable banking sector will improve dramatically as well.

In frontier markets, necessity is oftentimes the mother of invention—as we've seen in Kenya. Let's say you wanted to send 100 Kenyan shillings from Nairobi to someone in Mombasa. Traditionally, the only way to transfer the money was to entrust your shillings to a bus conductor who would invariably take a healthy 30 to 40 percent commission. Of your hundred shillings, you hoped that maybe 60 or 70 shillings would reach your intended recipient at the other end. Then in 2007 Vodafone, through its Kenyan mobile subsidiary Safaricom, developed M-Pesa, a mobile wallet ("pesa" is the Swahili word for money) that allows users to transfer money through a text message. M-Pesa has 85,000 agent outlets across the country who facilitate the mobile wallets, and users now can transfer any amount from ten shillings (about ten U.S. cents) to $70 with a text message, which is certainly preferable to a bus conductor. And business customers can now use M-Pesa to transfer up to $500,000 per transaction. Mobile payments are actually more widespread in Kenya than in most of the Western world, which has not been forced by necessity to adopt such innovative technology.

Imagine the incremental return on equity for a banking sector that does not have to build out a brick-and-mortar footprint of one branch per 10,000 people. Safaricom has over 14 million active M-Pesa users who together transfer over $1 billion per month. M-Pesa's revenues accounted for 20 percent of Safaricom's total revenues in 2015 and are growing at over 25 percent per year. Safaricom stock has soared from under three shillings at the beginning of 2012 to sixteen shillings at the start of 2016.

The banking/financial services megatrend is attractive on many counts: Frontier markets are underbanked; demand for banking services will grow as economies expand; this growth is currently available at very cheap valuations; and technology will continue to bring down costs and bolster profits.

Commodity Producers on the Verge of Capacity Booms

Many frontier markets are on the verge of booms in the production and export of recently discovered natural resources. While extraction technologies such as hydraulic fracturing ("fracking") have allowed mature resource markets such as the United States (and likely China in the future) to retrieve previously uncommercial resources, more advanced and cheaper exploration technologies have also led to discoveries of new energy reserves and mineral and ore deposits around the world, mostly in frontier markets (see figure 13.4).

At present, a handful of publicly traded commodity producers have operations centered wholly or overwhelmingly in frontier markets. Many are local frontier companies raising capital or partnering with multinationals to invest in production facilities and distribution infrastructure. This increased production and exportation will lead to a surge in GDP for many commodity-rich countries, which will in turn create investment opportunities in those markets beyond the commodity producers.

A caveat on this megatrend: Commodity prices are volatile and move up and down in cycles, sometimes very abruptly. Oil rose from $10 per barrel in 1998 to $140 per barrel by the summer of 2008—and then dropped

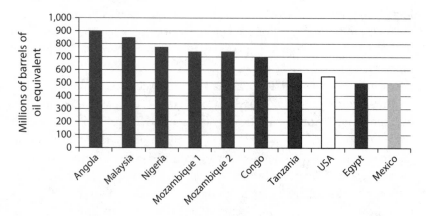

Figure 13.4

Ten largest hydrocarbon discoveries, 2013. *Source*: Forbes; Tudor Pickering Holt.

75 percent to under $40 by the end of the year. It then rebounded back to over $100 per barrel in 2011, and after the world acclimated to several years at this price, the 50+ percent drop back to near $40 per barrel by year-end 2015 was sharp—but not unprecedented. And because almost all of the world's megadiscoveries of hydrocarbon and mineral reserves are in frontier markets, where their lower-cost structures make drilling and mining these discoveries profitable even at lower price levels, these will be the most attractive marginal projects to develop once prices stabilize. Any rebound in prices from recent lows will make developing these reserves even more attractive.

Onshore Oil: Nigeria

Investing in indigenous onshore oil companies in Nigeria could be one of the most attractive opportunities over the next commodity cycle. Nigeria is the largest and one of the oldest producers of oil on the African continent, but focus is shifting from Nigeria's international producers to the locals, and this shift will be beneficial to the local economy. Back in the 1940s and 1950s, international oil companies discovered oil in Nigeria and then essentially wrote their own petroleum laws stating that they could keep their acreage nearly forever without having to spend money. In any other country, oil companies have to fulfill certain requirements in order to maintain their leases, which are usually for three to five years; they can renew the leases, but they have to keep spending or relinquish some acreage. In Nigeria, international oil companies have been just sitting on blocks of land above perfectly good oil, but because they have only a certain amount of capital—and Nigeria is not always the best place for them to invest it—this oil has been neglected.

The majority of Nigeria's budget comes from oil, and the country has now realized the urgency of reforming the law and reinvigorating investment in the sector. The Petroleum Industry Bill (PIB), in the works since 2008, will force oil companies to divest any blocks they are not using when it becomes law. So oil companies have begun selling some of these neglected assets to raise cash and to establish a track record of valuation metrics. That way, if they are forced to sell under the new law, they can point to these previous transactions to benchmark the value of their assets. Companies like Shell, Chevron, and Eni have been the most active sellers of these blocks, and local indigenous companies have been the favored bidders.

Local buyers are also attracted to these assets because they receive favorable tax treatment. If Exxon is producing oil, the tax rate (after cost recovery) is a steep 85 percent or so. For fields that are older or considered marginal, the tax rate drops to 55 percent. But if you are a local indigenous company, you can apply for "pioneer tax status," which offers five years of no taxes followed by accelerated cost recovery. This is the most attractive tax treatment of all. Nigeria has over 100 industries that offer pioneer tax status, so it is not unique to oil, but it is very attractive to an oil company. Nigeria has awarded pioneer tax status to fifteen local private and public oil companies (including publicly traded oil company SEPLAT, discussed below).

Oil reserves that have already been drilled and discovered—some of which may even have produced oil before being shut down or neglected—are being valued by the market at under $5 per barrel. Even after extraction and transport, this oil will be profitable if and when oil rises above $50 per barrel. This is a huge opportunity for locals willing to take the risk and able to line up the cash. A number of private companies active in this sector could mean more IPOs on the horizon and thus more opportunities for foreign investors to participate.

For publicly traded oil companies, consolidation in Africa's oil sector has begun. In June 2014, a company controlled by Qatar's royal family acquired Heritage Oil for $1.5 billion, paying more than $5 per barrel for Nigerian oil reserves that Heritage had purchased from Shell, Total, and Eni for under $2 per barrel less than two years earlier. This followed Glencore's April 2014 acquisition of Caracal Energy, a London-listed oil company with assets in Chad, at a nearly 60 percent premium.

The risks in Nigeria's oil sector (in addition to falling oil prices) include theft and terrorism. Nigeria is still victim to militant attacks against its oil assets, although not as many as in the past. Most are carried out by MEND (the Movement for the Emancipation of the Niger Delta) militants. These were the guys with assault rifles in rubber dinghies hijacking offshore oil rigs (see chapter 12). While the militants seek to disrupt oil operations by attacking offshore oil platforms and onshore pipelines and production facilities, the biggest ongoing issue for oil producers in Nigeria is "bunkering," where thieves tap into the pipelines to siphon and steal oil to sell on the black market. Producers have ways to mitigate bunkering, however. SEPLAT, a Nigerian oil and gas development company listed in Nigeria and London, lost nearly a third of the oil it produced to bunkering when it first acquired its oil leases—the company was still paying to produce this oil but was not getting any revenue for it. SEPLAT brought these bunkering losses down to 9 percent by increasing patrols but also by investing in hospitals and free clinics in the community. Improving relations with the locals is well worth it; such initiatives are cheap for a company that makes millions of dollars an hour but mean so much to the people they serve.

Nigeria is also one of the world's largest producers of natural gas (a by-product of its oil production) but has little infrastructure or pipelines to deliver it, so it flares (burns off) almost half of all the natural gas it produces. Under its Gas Master Plan, Nigeria is building a series of natural gas-fired power plants that will use this otherwise wasted gas to produce much-needed electricity rather than just CO_2 emissions. Nigeria privatized fifteen state-owned electricity generation and transmission companies in late 2013, and plans to privatize the new gas-fired plants as well. Other than SEPLAT, however, which expects to more than quadruple its 2013 natural gas production to over 500 million cubic feet per day by 2017, foreign investors have few ways—for now—to profit from the improved utilization of Nigeria's gas resources.

Onshore Oil: Kenya

Oil companies have recently made significant discoveries onshore in Kenya—essentially an entirely new hydrocarbon province. And because oil exploration and production are much cheaper onshore than offshore, breakeven for development of these projects occurs at much lower oil prices. Previously, no oil had been found in Kenya at all (wells were drilled and abandoned in the 1970s and 1980s). In 2012, however, oil was discovered in Kenya for the first time—upwards of a billion barrels of proven oil, which alone is enough to warrant its own pipeline. Kenya is planning the pipeline now, to run from Lake Turkana in northern Kenya (absolutely gorgeous but in the middle of nowhere) to the northern port city of Lamu.

This pipeline will also finally provide access to the several billion barrels of oil discovered in Uganda in 2010. Because Uganda is inland, its oil has been stranded, but a pipeline from Kenya could bring that oil to market. And a pipeline project in Kenya and Sub-Saharan Africa would likely qualify for assistance from the African Development Bank, the World Bank, and the IMF through low interest loans, or the International Finance Corporation might take an equity stake and fund it that way.

Unlike in Nigeria, so few locally listed companies are involved in East Africa's oil exploration and extraction that we must look for less direct ways to invest in this theme. One way is through cement companies. If you are building roads and drill pads in the middle of nowhere, you need a lot of cement—very high-margin cement. The cement sector is also a play on GDP growth more generally, as economic growth fuels further cement demand. And as incomes rise, consumers will buy more things—dairy products, beer, and so on. Kenya has one of the most liquid equity markets in Sub-Saharan Africa, with a host of publicly traded consumer products companies as well as banks.

Offshore Natural Gas: Mozambique

Two of the world's largest hydrocarbon discoveries in the past decade have been discoveries of natural gas off the coast of Mozambique—up to 70 trillion cubic feet of recoverable reserves—bringing Mozambique's total gas reserves to over 100 trillion cubic feet. Even with no additional discoveries, Mozambique may rise from an energy importer only a decade ago to a major global liquid natural gas (LNG) exporter a decade from now.

LNG projects are already bringing enormous foreign direct investment (FDI) inflows to Mozambique, especially given the energy-hungry markets of India, Japan, China, and the ASEAN countries just across the Indian Ocean. Indian state-run companies Bharat Petroleum, Oil India, and ONGC have purchased sizeable stakes in Mozambique's offshore gas fields. The Thai state-owned petroleum company PTT bought a company that owned part of the discoveries in Mozambique, so Thailand is also lining up to secure supply. These state-owned oil companies buy a stake in the underlying assets, which gives them a percentage of the discovered reserves and future production. In exchange, they help fund the construction of LNG facilities.

A typical LNG facility requires capital expenditures of $3–5 billion. Given the volumes of natural gas discovered and its voracious neighbors, Mozambique will build several LNG facilities, and the capex from these projects alone will likely double Mozambique's $16 billion GDP. This impact on GDP is similar to the impact on Mongolia's economy from the development of the Oyu Tolgoi copper mine in the Gobi Desert (see discussion later in this chapter).

Mozambique also has vast deposits of high-quality metallurgical coal (i.e., coal used to make steel rather than used as fuel), which were minimally mined by small international or local companies until global mining giants Rio Tinto and Vale invested in them in 2011. (As it so happened, Rio wrote off most of its investment in 2013, and sold the assets to a group of Indian state-owned mining companies in 2014.) Despite coal prices at less than half their 2011 peak, Mozambican coal production is expected to increase tenfold over 2010 levels once planned railway and port improvements are completed.[4]

Mozambique has had its problems in the past. From its independence from Portugal in 1975 to its first democratic elections in 1994, the country was riven by civil war. But the country has now transformed and is very stable, and companies are happy to invest there: Eni, the Italian oil company, has invested there, as has Anadarko, the U.S. oil company that made the initial gas discovery. Vale is there too. The list goes on. These publicly traded companies are emboldened by the host of countries (including India, Thailand, Italy, Korea, and Japan) whose state-owned national oil companies invest there as well. They recognize that Mozambique plans to finance its future with the money from these state-owned investors, and that this will ensure the government's careful attention to the success of its LNG business.

As of this writing, only four small companies trade on Mozambique's stock exchange, but the country has publicly traded sovereign debt, and it will be issuing more. Mozambique's current account deficit, at 40 percent of GDP, is the largest in the world. This deficit is currently funded by FDI, which should continue. If you want to invest in Mozambique's future growth, buying the debt could be one way to do it. Mozambique issued its first Eurobond in 2013, which as of early 2016 traded at a nearly 14 percent yield to maturity, and as GDP begins to reflect natural gas sales, this and any new debt should do quite well. The Mozambican metical, the local currency, might also appreciate, as may local property values.

Neighboring southern Tanzania also has natural gas discoveries, not as big as Mozambique's, but still big enough and profitable enough to warrant LNG production if oil returns to $70 per barrel.[5] Farther north, exploration wells are being drilled offshore of northern Tanzania and Kenya, targeting additional hydrocarbon prospects along East Africa's coast.

Metals and Minerals

Mongolia's booming economy is an example of the effects of commodity development and capital expenditure. The Oyu Tolgoi copper mine has completed construction and is ramping up production (see chapter 3). The roughly $10 billion capital expenditure on this mine equaled about two times Mongolia's GDP at the time of construction, and for something as routine as the first monthly payday, the mine operator had to go through the central bank to issue more currency because it had such a large payroll to meet.

Right now, Oyu Tolgoi is one of the five largest copper mines globally; when it reaches full capacity, it will be one of the top three—impressive for a country with such a small population and GDP. The tax revenues from the mine are massive, and the government still owns a third of the equity of the mine itself. The success of this mine is also attracting more money and exploration to Mongolia. Once Rio Tinto achieved first-mover status, other smaller companies began coming to Mongolia to test the waters.

There is an energy boom in Colombia, and as in Kenya, cement is one way to invest in it, in part because the Colombian government is reinvesting oil revenues and tax receipts into infrastructure projects. Colombia's efforts to expand its oil and gas production have been very successful, doubling output from 500,000 barrels per day a decade ago to a million barrels per day today, although slumping prices have discouraged exploration recently. (Colombia is not without its share of militant attacks. FARC and ELN guerillas launch over a hundred attacks on pipelines there every year, although both groups are in peace talks with the Colombian government as of this writing.)

Local cement providers will benefit on two fronts from this infrastructure investment. One of the biggest issues facing Colombia is logistics. The country is very hilly, and mountain ranges divide the three main cities of Bogotá, Medellin, and Cali, making intracountry transport very expensive. It can cost less to transport bulk cargo 15,000 kilometers from Asia to the port of Buenaventura on Colombia's Pacific coast than to deliver that cargo the remaining 500 kilometers from the port to Bogotá. Colombia is using its energy revenues to blast tunnels through mountains, build bridges over rivers, and upgrade or build afresh a proper highway network. Not only will local companies supply much of the cement for the tunnels, bridges, and roadways, but they will reduce their own transportation costs because their cement trucks will be able to drive a straighter path on better roads. And for a commodity that sells for around $100 a ton, a pretty low value given its weight, this cost reduction could lead to a substantial uplift in margins.

* * *

Several of these themes may very well play out concurrently in a given frontier market, as consumption themes correlate strongly where young demographics are involved. Growing populations need housing, groceries, clothing, and cars, for instance, which will filter into the banking system through mortgages and personal loans.

Once I identify attractive long-term investment themes like these from a top-down perspective, the next step is to use bottom-up fundamental analysis, including on-the-ground research, to identify specific opportunities within these themes that can take advantage of discrepancies between perception by the outside world and the reality on the ground.

14

Frontiers of Frontier Markets Investing

The world is a big place, and much of it is frontier markets. These markets are home to the fastest-growing economies and the young, expanding populations that will foster this growth for many years to come. These are the markets where truly global investors should want to invest.

One obvious barrier to investing in an otherwise attractive country is the lack of a public equity market that is open to outside investors. While most of the world's 195 countries have stock exchanges open to their citizenry, not all are open to foreign investors (some also have debt markets but no equity markets, or are home to companies listed on another country's exchange). But that leaves dozens of potential future investable frontier markets, several of which I discuss below.

* * *

Public investing in new markets is generally slow to evolve, usually starting with sovereign debt followed by publicly traded stocks. The growing investor interest in frontier markets, and the ability of new exchanges to deploy best-in-class market technology, will speed the progression of noninvestable countries into the global investable universe.

Table 14.1
Noninvestable Country Watch List

Algeria*	Armenia*	Bhutan*
Chad	Cuba	DR Congo
Eritrea	Guinea	Guyana*
Iran*	Kyrgyzstan*	Lesotho
Libya*	Malawi*	Myanmar*
Niger	North Korea	Paraguay*
Saudi Arabia**	Suriname	Syria*
Tajikistan	Uzbekistan*	Yemen

* Market open to locals only.
** Market open to locals and large foreign institutions.

I keep a watch list of countries that do not yet have investable (for me) equity markets, shown in table 14.1 above. In some countries, such as Chad and Myanmar, I have invested in companies whose stocks trade on another country's exchange. A number of these countries may have begun trading by the time you read this.

Even in the last five years, this list has changed significantly. Rwanda came off the list when its first publicly available stock (Bralirwa, the brewery and beverage manufacturer majority owned by Heineken that I discussed in chapter 6) began trading on the newly established Rwanda Stock Exchange in 2011. Rwanda's exchange currently lists six other stocks. Laos opened its stock exchange in late 2010 and lists four companies: a bank, a power producer, an oil company, and a small conference and entertainment company. In early 2012, Cambodia opened its stock exchange with its first listing, the Phnom Penh Water Supply Authority; its second listing, a garment manufacturer, began trading in June 2014. And Sierra Leone's stock exchange began trading in 2009 with one stock, a state-owned bank, which remains its sole listing. An inauspicious start for some of these markets, but I expect additional companies to list shares as more foreign investors arrive.

And more changes are coming. Saudi Arabia opened its stock market to large qualified investors outside of the Gulf Cooperation Council (GCC) in June 2015 (GCC citizens can invest in Saudi stocks since 2007, and certain foreign investors—including us—could invest indirectly through swaps as of 2008). With a market capitalization of nearly $600 billion, the Saudi market was the second-largest still closed to foreigners; the largest is China's Shanghai Stock Exchange. It is larger than the markets in Russia and Mexico, and nearly as big as Singapore.

The biggest market remaining on my watch list is Iran. At almost $100 billion, Iran's stock market is twice the size of Greece's and catching up with Austria. More on Iran below.

Bhutan, closed to tourists until 1974 and still closed to foreign investors, is an extraordinary country—one of the most beautiful places on earth, and still pristine. Bhutan strictly regulates movement within the country, banning independent travel and allowing only "high value, low impact tourism" through approved Bhutan travel operators. When I visited the capital of Thimphu in 2007, I couldn't resist visiting the stock exchange to check things out. The exchange was a bit sleepy, as you can see from the picture I took of it (figure 14.1). Bhutan has operated its stock exchange since 1993, and it looked as if it hadn't had a technology upgrade since opening day. The exchange currently trades twenty-one stocks available only to local investors, but eventually it will open up to foreigners. I hope that this happens soon, as this could be an interesting country in which to invest.

Are There Places Beyond the Frontier of Frontier Markets Investing?

Many investors are barred from investing in certain markets by their government (the U.S. government prohibits investing in Cuba or Iran, for example) or their investment committee (recall the anti-Apartheid divestments of South African holdings by university endowments and others in

ROYAL SECURITIES EXCHANGE OF BHUTAN LTD DATE: 12 MAR-2007				
STOCK PRICE				
COMPANY	ISSUE	PRICE BUY PRICE	SELL PRICE	LAST SALE PRICE
BBCL	100			100
BBPL	100			100
BCCL	1000			6001
BOL	100	140		100
BFAL	100			510
BNB	100			1650
BPCL	1000			100
BTCL	100	580		170
DPCL	100			120
DPOP	100	400		100
DSCL	100			3272
DSML	100			429
EBCC	100	150		100
PCAL	100			700
RICB	100	400		350
STCB	100	200		900

Figure 14.1
Bhutan stock exchange, March 12, 2007. *Source*: Author.

the 1980s). But take George Bush's 2002 "Axis of Evil" (Iran, Iraq, and North Korea) or Condoleezza Rice's 2005 "Outposts of Tyranny" (Belarus, Burma, Cuba, Iran, North Korea, and Zimbabwe). In less than a decade, we have witnessed one member drop out of the Axis of Evil (Iraq) to become an attractive, if illiquid, market; Zimbabwe has overcome its era of hyperinflation and reopened its stock exchange; and Burma (now Myanmar) is undertaking a reform agenda that is opening its markets to foreign investors (see below). Investment barriers erected by government or committee decree can also be the quickest to come down—literally at the stroke of a pen.

One could imagine that, if and when Cuba and the United States negotiate an end to the U.S. embargo, and were Cuba to espouse capitalism and allow foreign ownership of local companies, Cuba could be a very attractive market (at the right price, of course). I visited Havana in November 2015 to meet with academics and Finance Ministry and Exterior Relations Ministry officials. The city combines 1970s-era block architecture with an amazing downtown called Old Havana. Many of the buildings were in a state of advanced disrepair, and the whole city could use a coat of fresh paint. While the streets displayed some beautiful American cars from the 1950s, most of the vehicles I saw were inexpensive Soviet brands (Lada, Moskvich) and Asian imports.

Soviet-era automobiles notwithstanding, Cuba is not poor. By World Bank estimates, Cuba has a U.S. dollar GDP per capita of $7,000, and its $20,000 PPP-adjusted per capita GDP sits between Turkey's ($19,000) and Chile's ($22,000). It is a mostly urban, almost entirely literate, healthy population. It will have to hurry, though—the median age in Cuba is forty, and with a fertility rate as low as Japan's it is not getting any younger. The officials I met are aware of the country's issues, and the government has begun to address them—it has, for instance, created a special economic zone near Havana on the port of Mariel—but I think establishing manufacturing will be a challenge due to the small size of Cuba's domestic market.

Tourism, however, is another story. Cuba hosts three million tourists a year now and is planning for five million a year by 2020. I think these numbers are low. The old town is a gem. If you know Cartagena (Colombia), this is Cartagena on five times the scale. Many streets made me feel I was in Italy rather than the Caribbean. Nowhere else like old Havana exists in the Caribbean, and as relations with the United States normalize, I see tremendous opportunity for tourism growth.

Iran already has several thriving stock markets, the largest being the Tehran Stock Exchange. Iran has a large (77 million), young (median age of twenty-eight), and educated population, and sits atop the world's second-largest natural gas reserves and nearly 10 percent of the world's oil.[1] If Iran abides by its agreement with the P5+1 (the five permanent members of the UN Security Council—the United States, China, Russia, France, and the UK—plus Germany) on its nuclear program, restrictions on investing could be lifted on an economy the size of Australia.

Much closer on the investable horizon is Myanmar, an example of the speed at which government reforms can lead a country into the global marketplace.

The Return of Burma/Myanmar to the World Stage

Burma (now Myanmar) was for centuries a major player in the Southeast Asian region and an important trade route between China and India. The country was a British colony from the late 1800s until gaining its independence in 1948. By 1962, however, the first of two military juntas took over the country and established a socialist state. During its British occupation, Burma was one of the richest countries in Southeast Asia; by 1985, when I first traveled there, it was one of the poorest. Not only did Burma look very much like a frontier territory—it was as if I was visiting another world.

At that time, Burma had an authoritarian regime in place that exercised very tight control. Visitors first had to enter the country in order to get a visa to travel within it. This visa was good for a maximum of seven days, and so when I arrived I had the choice of waiting for a flight to tour the country (such flights were often canceled), or negotiating with a pickup truck driver to take me to various destinations. I chose the latter, and with a couple of fellow backpackers, I rented a truck and driver and we went on to see Burma.

We traveled tens of hours in the back of this truck (figure 14.2). We first visited Rangoon, the capital city at the time (Rangoon is now called Yangon; the capital was moved in 2006 from Rangoon to the then largely unbuilt city of Naypyidaw). We then drove into Burma's interior, to see some of the amazing Buddhist temples in the ancient city of Pagan (now Bagan) in the Mandalay region (still Mandalay) and to see the beautiful Inle Lake and its incredible leg-rowed boats. While crisscrossing the country I saw extremely basic conditions with no access to the outside world. Any television broadcasts were regime propaganda. But the people I met during the trip were very kind.

Figure 14.2
I spent tens of hours in the back of this covered pickup truck touring Burma in 1985.
Source: Author.

We stayed in a couple of old hotels that the British had built as resorts and that had maybe fifty rooms apiece but were literally empty—we were the only people there. These and other very beautiful colonial-era buildings were all in decay. What a striking example of the impact of bad economic policies: In the 1960s medical students from Singapore would come to study in Rangoon because it had a better medical school than Singapore did—and of course we see now what Singapore has become with good economic policies.

Recently things in Myanmar have started to improve, as the regime loosened its grip on the country, seeing the writing on the wall and changing course a few years ago to avoid total collapse. The military remained in power until constitutional reforms led to a nominally civilian government in 2011. After decades of isolation, Myanmar has begun instituting reforms with startling speed, from lifting restrictions on foreign ownership of businesses to easing media censorship. Reporters Without Borders' 2015 World Press Freedom Index ranks Myanmar 144 of 180 countries, up 25 places in just three years and surpassing Russia (152) and Singapore (153). The United States ranks 49.

The world has taken notice of this reform movement and has begun easing economic sanctions. If Myanmar can maintain its reform momentum (although it has stumbled in this regard, Myanmar held its first multiparty general election in November 2015), it is poised to reintegrate with the global economy. Myanmar is a country of 53 million people, the twenty-fourth most-populated country in the world (just behind the United Kingdom and Italy and just ahead of South Africa and Korea)—so it is potentially a big market. I see many Thai companies, for example, investing in neighboring Myanmar. What Thailand was thirty years ago, Myanmar could be soon: a manufacturing base with a large domestic market.

Myanmar is blessed with abundant natural resources (oil and gas, and precious gems, including the vast majority of the world's rubies), agriculture (rice and teak), and cheap labor. The McKinsey Global Institute predicts that Myanmar's economy could quadruple, and its urbanization rate could double, from 2013 to 2030. And while no stocks are available to trade in Myanmar right now (the Yangon Stock Exchange opened with great ceremony in December 2015, but with zero listed stocks), we have invested in companies with operations in the country but headquartered or listed in Asian markets outside Myanmar. I think more such opportunities will come, and I expect a handful of companies to list on the Yangon exchange in the near future.

* * *

This is what my experience investing in emerging markets for the past thirty-five years has taught me: Today's frontier markets—with their sheer size; fast growth; young, growing populations; strong macroeconomic foundations; accelerated integration into the global economy spurred by advances in technology; and attractive market fundamentals—make for a compelling long-term investment opportunity that I plan to pursue for the rest of my career.

I believe allocating a portion of your existing global or emerging markets portfolio to frontier markets can provide attractive and complementary investment returns. How large a portion? Certainly greater than their 0.5 percent allocation in the MSCI All Country World Index, or even their 4 percent share of global equity market capitalization. Given that frontier markets contribute 19 percent of the world's PPP-adjusted GDP and comprise most of the world's fastest-growing economies, I advocate a double-digit allocation to this asset class. The best way to take advantage of frontier markets' compelling growth story is to apply rigorous top-down thematic and bottom-up fundamental analysis to a universe of frontier market countries and companies selectively expanded beyond that of passive indices.

As an investment analyst, moreover, I believe extending the tools of financial analysis to the world's nascent equity markets invigorates and expands the horizons of our profession while benefiting the companies and markets on which we focus our efforts. The CFA Institute, which awards the highly respected Chartered Financial Analyst credential around the world to only the most qualified investment professionals, has granted thousands of charters in mainstream emerging markets over the past decade. It now reports a surge in charter holders across frontier markets as well: Twenty-six Nigerians earned the CFA designation in 2014, up from three in 2004; in Bangladesh, fourteen charters were awarded in 2014 versus just one in 2004; and over 100 charters were awarded in Vietnam from 2010 to 2014, five times more than in the previous five years. Nearly a hundred new charters are now awarded in the United Arab Emirates (UAE) annually.

Frontier market managements—and governments—held to a higher standard of scrutiny by both local and global finance professionals will be compelled to implement more open and equitable corporate and government policies. Their reward will be greater investment into their companies and economies by the global investment community, accelerated integration with the rest of the world, and ultimately, better lives for their citizens.

Happy investing!

Appendix

Below is a list of the 195 countries that make up the world (the 193 members of the United Nations plus Hong Kong and Taiwan). Thirty I classify as developed markets, fourteen I classify as mainstream emerging markets, and the remaining 151 I classify as frontier markets. The last column indicates whether a country is included in an MSCI index—the MSCI World Index (DM), the MSCI Emerging Markets Index, or the MSCI Frontier Markets Index.

Country	Author's Classification	MSCI Index
Andorra	Developed	—
Australia	Developed	DM
Austria	Developed	DM
Belgium	Developed	DM
Canada	Developed	DM
Denmark	Developed	DM
Finland	Developed	DM
France	Developed	DM
Germany	Developed	DM
Hong Kong	Developed	DM
Iceland	Developed	—
Ireland	Developed	DM
Israel	Developed	DM
Italy	Developed	DM
Japan	Developed	DM
Liechtenstein	Developed	—
Luxembourg	Developed	—
Malta	Developed	—
Monaco	Developed	—
Netherlands	Developed	DM
New Zealand	Developed	DM
Norway	Developed	DM

(*continued*)

Country	Author's Classification	MSCI Index
Portugal	Developed	DM
San Marino	Developed	—
Singapore	Developed	DM
Spain	Developed	DM
Sweden	Developed	DM
Switzerland	Developed	DM
United Kingdom	Developed	DM
United States of America	Developed	DM
Brazil	Mainstream Emerging	EM
Chile	Mainstream Emerging	EM
China	Mainstream Emerging	EM
India	Mainstream Emerging	EM
Indonesia	Mainstream Emerging	EM
Korea (South)	Mainstream Emerging	EM
Malaysia	Mainstream Emerging	EM
Mexico	Mainstream Emerging	EM
Poland	Mainstream Emerging	EM
Russia	Mainstream Emerging	EM
South Africa	Mainstream Emerging	EM
Taiwan	Mainstream Emerging	EM
Thailand	Mainstream Emerging	EM
Turkey	Mainstream Emerging	EM
Colombia	Frontier	EM
Czech Republic	Frontier	EM
Egypt	Frontier	EM
Greece	Frontier	EM
Hungary	Frontier	EM
Peru	Frontier	EM
Philippines	Frontier	EM
Qatar	Frontier	EM
United Arab Emirates	Frontier	EM
Argentina	Frontier	FM
Bahrain	Frontier	FM
Bangladesh	Frontier	FM
Bulgaria	Frontier	FM
Croatia	Frontier	FM
Estonia	Frontier	FM
Jordan	Frontier	FM
Kazakhstan	Frontier	FM
Kenya	Frontier	FM
Kuwait	Frontier	FM

Country	Author's Classification	MSCI Index
Lebanon	Frontier	FM
Lithuania	Frontier	FM
Mauritius	Frontier	FM
Morocco	Frontier	FM
Nigeria	Frontier	FM
Oman	Frontier	FM
Pakistan	Frontier	FM
Romania	Frontier	FM
Serbia	Frontier	FM
Slovenia	Frontier	FM
Sri Lanka	Frontier	FM
Tunisia	Frontier	FM
Ukraine	Frontier	FM
Vietnam	Frontier	FM
Afghanistan	Frontier	—
Albania	Frontier	—
Algeria	Frontier	—
Angola	Frontier	—
Antigua and Barbuda	Frontier	—
Armenia	Frontier	—
Azerbaijan	Frontier	—
Bahamas	Frontier	—
Barbados	Frontier	—
Belarus	Frontier	—
Belize	Frontier	—
Benin	Frontier	—
Bhutan	Frontier	—
Bolivia	Frontier	—
Bosnia and Herzegovina	Frontier	—
Botswana	Frontier	—
Brunei Darussalam	Frontier	—
Burkina Faso	Frontier	—
Burundi	Frontier	—
Cabo Verde	Frontier	—
Cambodia	Frontier	—
Cameroon	Frontier	—
Central African Republic	Frontier	—
Chad	Frontier	—
Comoros	Frontier	—
Congo (Republic of)	Frontier	—
Costa Rica	Frontier	—

(continued)

Country	Author's Classification	MSCI Index
Côte d'Ivoire	Frontier	—
Cuba	Frontier	—
Cyprus	Frontier	—
Democratic People's Republic of Korea (North)	Frontier	—
Democratic Republic of the Congo	Frontier	—
Djibouti	Frontier	—
Dominica	Frontier	—
Dominican Republic	Frontier	—
Ecuador	Frontier	—
El Salvador	Frontier	—
Equatorial Guinea	Frontier	—
Eritrea	Frontier	—
Ethiopia	Frontier	—
Fiji	Frontier	—
Gabon	Frontier	—
Gambia	Frontier	—
Georgia	Frontier	—
Ghana	Frontier	—
Grenada	Frontier	—
Guatemala	Frontier	—
Guinea	Frontier	—
Guinea Bissau	Frontier	—
Guyana	Frontier	—
Haiti	Frontier	—
Honduras	Frontier	—
Iran	Frontier	—
Iraq	Frontier	—
Jamaica	Frontier	—
Kiribati	Frontier	—
Kyrgyzstan	Frontier	—
Lao PDR (Laos)	Frontier	—
Latvia	Frontier	—
Lesotho	Frontier	—
Liberia	Frontier	—
Libya	Frontier	—
Macedonia	Frontier	—
Madagascar	Frontier	—
Malawi	Frontier	—

Country	Author's Classification	MSCI Index
Maldives	Frontier	—
Mali	Frontier	—
Marshall Islands	Frontier	—
Mauritania	Frontier	—
Micronesia	Frontier	—
Moldova	Frontier	—
Mongolia	Frontier	—
Montenegro	Frontier	—
Mozambique	Frontier	—
Myanmar	Frontier	—
Namibia	Frontier	—
Nauru	Frontier	—
Nepal	Frontier	—
Nicaragua	Frontier	—
Niger	Frontier	—
Palau	Frontier	—
Panama	Frontier	—
Papua New Guinea	Frontier	—
Paraguay	Frontier	—
Rwanda	Frontier	—
Saint Kitts and Nevis	Frontier	—
Saint Lucia	Frontier	—
Saint Vincent and the Grenadines	Frontier	—
Samoa	Frontier	—
São Tomé and Príncipe	Frontier	—
Saudi Arabia	Frontier	—
Senegal	Frontier	—
Seychelles	Frontier	—
Sierra Leone	Frontier	—
Slovakia	Frontier	—
Solomon Islands	Frontier	—
Somalia	Frontier	—
South Sudan	Frontier	—
Sudan	Frontier	—
Suriname	Frontier	—
Swaziland	Frontier	—
Syria	Frontier	—
Tajikistan	Frontier	—

(*continued*)

Country	Author's Classification	MSCI Index
Tanzania	Frontier	—
Timor-Leste	Frontier	—
Togo	Frontier	—
Tonga	Frontier	—
Trinidad and Tobago	Frontier	—
Turkmenistan	Frontier	—
Tuvalu	Frontier	—
Uganda	Frontier	—
Uruguay	Frontier	—
Uzbekistan	Frontier	—
Vanuatu	Frontier	—
Venezuela	Frontier	—
Yemen	Frontier	—
Zambia	Frontier	—
Zimbabwe	Frontier	—

NOTES

Introduction

1. All subsequent references to "I" or "we" taking actions regarding investments are generally intended to refer to actions taken by Everest Capital.

1. Emerging Markets Have Emerged

1. "Pittsburgh—OECD," accessed September 24, 2014, http://www.oecd.org/g20/meetings/pittsburgh/.

2. The members of the G-20 are Argentina, Australia, Brazil, Canada, China, France, Germany, India, Indonesia, Italy, Japan, Korea, Mexico, Russia, Saudi Arabia, South Africa, Turkey, United Kingdom, United States, and the European Union.

3. "The World's Most Valuable Brands," *Forbes*, accessed July 20, 2015, http://www.forbes.com/powerful-brands/list/.

4. "Facebook Statistics and Metrics by Country," *Socialbakers.com*, accessed September 24, 2014, http://www.socialbakers.com/facebook-statistics/.

5. "Short Statement by Philipp Hildebrand on 6 September 2011 with Regard to the Introduction of a Minimum Swiss Franc Exchange Rate Against the Euro," accessed December 8, 2015, http://www.snb.ch/en/mmr/speeches/id/ref_20110906_pmh/source/ref_20110906_pmh.en.pdf.

6. "Media News Conference, Introductory Remarks by Thomas Jordan," accessed December 8, 2015, http://www.snb.ch/en/mmr/speeches/id/ref_20141218_tjn/source /ref_20141218_tjn.en.pdf.

7. "SNB's Danthine Says Cap on Franc Remains Policy Cornerstone -RTS," *Reuters*, January 12, 2015, http://www.reuters.com/article/swiss-snb-idUSL6N0UR3LW20150112.

8. "Swiss Miss," accessed September 18, 2015, http://www.economist.com/news /finance-and-economics/21640305-fallout-swiss-francs-gyrations-only-just-beginning -swiss-miss.

2. Frontier Markets Are the New Emerging Markets

1. Airports Council International, "International Passenger Traffic for Past 12 Months Ending July 2014," accessed November 19, 2014, http://www.aci.aero /Data-Centre/Monthly-Traffic-Data/International-Passenger-Rankings/12-months.

2. Terry Miller, Anthony Kim, and Kim Holmes, "Highlights of the 2014 Index of Economic Freedom" (The Heritage Foundation, 2014), 2.

3. Peter Blair Henry, "Capital Account Liberalization, The Cost of Capital, and Economic Growth" (Cambridge, MA: National Bureau of Economic Research, February 2003); Dennis P. Quinn and A. Maria Toyoda, "Does Capital Account Liberalization Lead to Growth?" *Review of Financial Studies* 21, no. 3 (May 1, 2008): 1403–1449.

4. Geert Bekaert, Campbell R. Harvey, and Christian T. Lundblad, "Does Financial Liberalization Spur Growth?" (April 2001). NBER Working Paper No. w8245. Available at SSRN: http://ssrn.com/abstract=267430.

5. Horst Feldmann, "Economic Freedom and Unemployment Around the World," *Southern Economic Journal* 74, no. 1 (2007): 158–176.

6. Ari Aisen, *Does Political Instability Lead to Higher Inflation? A Panel Data Analysis*, 2005–2049 (International Monetary Fund, 2005); Jakob De Haan and Cle- mens L. J. Siermann, "Central Bank Independence, Inflation and Political Instability in Developing Countries," *Journal of Policy Reform* 1, no. 2 (January 1, 1996): 135–147, doi:10.1080/13841289608523360; Stephan Haggard and Robert R. Kaufman, *The Political Economy of Inflation and Stabilization in Middle-Income Countries* (World Bank Publi- cations, 1990).

7. "Urban World: Mapping the Economic Power of Cities," McKinsey & Company, accessed September 22, 2014, http://www.mckinsey.com/insights/urbanization /urban_world.

8. "World Urbanization Prospects, the 2014 Revision," accessed February 5, 2016, http://esa.un.org/unpd/wup/Publications/Files/WUP2014-Report.pdf.

9. Norman Loayza, Jamele Rigolini, and Gonzalo Llorente, "Do Middle Classes Bring About Institutional Reforms?" *Economics Letters* 116, no. 3 (September 2012): 440–444, doi:10.1016/j.econlet.2012.04.013; Augusto de la Torre and Jamele Rigolini, "MIC-Forum-Rise-of-the-Middle-Class-SM13.pdf" (The World Bank, n.d.), http:// www.worldbank.org/content/dam/Worldbank/document/MIC-Forum-Rise-of-the -Middle-Class-SM13.pdf.

10. Rafael La Porta, Florencio Lopez-de-Silanes, Andrei Shleifer, "Investor Protection and Corporate Governance," *Journal of Financial Economics* 58, no. 1–2 (2000): 4.

11. Organisation for Economic Co-operation and Development, *OECD Principles of Corporate Governance* (Paris: OECD, 2004).

12. Stijn Claessens and Burcin Yurtoglu, "Corporate Governance and Development—An Update" (International Finance Corporation, 2012), 67–68.

13. Jonathan Anderson, "Explaining the EM Equity-Growth Puzzle (Revisited)" (Emerging Advisors Group Limited, April 4, 2013).

14. Brazil, Chile, Hong Kong, India, Korea, Malaysia, Mexico, Singapore, South Africa, Taiwan, and Turkey.

15. Jonathan Anderson, "Yeah, But Strong Companies Don't Mean Strong Countries" (Emerging Advisors Group Limited, May 16, 2012).

16. Anderson, "Explaining the EM Equity-Growth Puzzle (Revisited)."

3. Frontier's Bright Economic Outlook

1. ERS, USDA calculations based on annual household expenditure data from Euromonitor International; World Bank Global Consumption Database.

2. Steven Globerman and Daniel Shapiro, "Global Foreign Direct Investment Flows: The Role of Governance Infrastructure," *World Development* 30, no. 11 (November 2002): 1899–1919.

4. The Young and the Restless: Frontier's Favorable Demographic

1. Robert D. Arnott and Denis B. Chaves, "Demographic Changes, Financial Markets, and the Economy," *Financial Analysts Journal* 68, no. 1 (2012): 42.

2. Based on World Bank PPP-adjusted GDP data.

3. This and following remittance data from World Bank, "News & Broadcast —Migration and Remittances," accessed April 28, 2014, http://go.worldbank.org /RR8SDPEHOo.

4. Ibid.

5. "Can You Hear Me Now?": Frontier's Integration with the Global Economy

1. World Bank, *Global Economic Prospects 2008: Technology Diffusion in the Developing World*, Global Economic Prospects (The World Bank, 2008).

2. Pun-Lee Lam and Alice Shiu, "Economic Growth, Telecommunications Development and Productivity Growth of the Telecommunications Sector: Evidence Around the World," *Telecommunications Policy* 34, no. 4 (May 2010): 185–199.

3. United Nations, *Information Economy Report 2013: The Cloud Economy and Developing Countries.* ([S.l.]: United Nations Pubns., 2014).

4. Donald Clark, "E-Learning Africa—7 New Narratives," *Donald Clark Plan B,* accessed September 24, 2014, http://donaldclarkplanb.blogspot.com/2013/06/e-learning -africa-7-new-narratives.html.

6. Frontier Equity Markets Offer Value and Diversification

1. Based on comparisons of MSCI Frontier Markets Index, MSCI Emerging Markets Index, and MSCI World Index.

2. Patricia Crisafulli and Andrea Redmond, *Rwanda, Inc.: How a Devastated Nation Became an Economic Model for the Developing World* (New York: Palgrave Macmillan, 2012), 167.

3. Squaring the correlation coefficient of two sets of values gives you the coefficient of determination, or the R^2 (R-squared), of the two streams, which is the percentage of the variation of one set of values described by the other set of values. Since $0.82^2 = 0.67$, this means that roughly two-thirds of emerging market equity returns can be described by developed market returns.

7. The Pitfalls of Passive Management and Advantages of Active Management in Frontier Markets

1. ADRs (American Depositary Receipts) and GDRs (Global Depositary Receipts) are certificates issued by international banks, and represent ownership of a foreign company's domestically listed shares. They are typically denominated in U.S. dollars (sometimes pounds sterling or euros) and traded on major U.S. and European stock exchanges. One often sees "Depository" used as a variant spelling of Depositary in this context.

2. According to MSCI, an index "designed for those facing various obstacles in replicating broader frontier markets indexes"—another disadvantage of passive investing.

3. B. S. Reporters, "Sebi May Move to T+1 Trade Settlement Cycle," *Business Standard India,* April 18, 2013, http://www.business-standard.com/article/markets/sebi-may-move-to-t-1-trade-settlement-cycle-113041801090_1.html.

8. Do-It-Yourself Investing in Frontier Markets

1. This table is illustrative only and does not represent my investment opinion of any of the names shown.

2. The S-curve is a growth curve characterized by shallow initial growth followed by accelerated growth over time.

3. According to an HSBC study of the 200 companies with frontier exposure in a broader sample of nearly 2,000 companies under coverage. Wietse Nijenhuis, "Frontier Markets Strategy" (HSBC Global Research, December 10, 2012).

4. "Triennial Central Bank Survey 2013, Foreign Exchange Turnover in April 2013: Preliminary Global Results" (Bank for International Settlements, September 2013).

9. Special Situations in Distressed Debt

1. Apu Sikri and Soma Biswas, "Brady Bonds Dying Out as Countries Replace Them with Cheaper Debt," *Wall Street Journal,* eastern edition, September 27, 1996.

10. Privatizations

1. "Banks Ordered to Fund French State Industries," *Financial Times,* May 13, 1982; also Paul Lewis, "France's New Industrial Policy," *New York Times,* November 28, 1982.

2. Sylvia Maxfield, "The International Political Economy of Bank Nationalization: Mexico in Comparative Perspective," *Latin American Research Review* 27, no. 1 (n.d.).

3. Michael Slackman, "Egypt Concedes to Resistance Against Privatization," *New York Times,* June 27, 2010, sec. World / Middle East, http://www.nytimes.com/2010/06/28/world/middleeast/28egypt.html.

4. William L. Megginson, *The Financial Economics of Privatization* (New York: Oxford University Press, 2004).

5. Oli Havrylyshyn and Donal McGettigan, *Privatization in Transition Countries—A Sampling of the Literature* (International Monetary Fund, 1999).

6. On September 23, 2014, Fondul shareholders approved a new two-year management term for Templeton.

11. Political Risks in Frontier Markets

1. Jutta Bolt and Jan Luiten van Zanden, "The First Update of the Maddison Project; Re-Estimating Growth Before 1820," January 2013, http://www.ggdc.net/maddison/maddison-project/home.htm.

2. "The World Factbook," accessed August 4, 2015, https://www.cia.gov/library/publications/the-world-factbook/geos/kn.html and https://www.cia.gov/library/publications/the-world-factbook/geos/ks.html.

3. Hisham Handal Abdelbaki, "The Impact of Arab Spring on Stock Market Performance," *British Journal of Management & Economics* 3, no. 3 (2013): 183.

4. MSCI added Russia to its Emerging Markets Index on December 1, 1997.

5. A mechanism to fix a country's exchange rate versus another currency or basket of currencies.

6. Paraphrased from an interview with the author published in Steven Drobny, *Inside the House of Money* (Hoboken, NJ: Wiley, 2006): 293–294.

7. Ari Aisen and Francisco José Veiga, "Does Political Instability Lead to Higher Inflation? A Panel Data Analysis," Working Paper 05/49 (International Monetary Fund, 2005): 3.

8. "The World Factbook," accessed August 4, 2015, https://www.cia.gov/library /publications/the-world-factbook/rankorder/2172rank.html.

9. "Helping Countries Combat Corruption: The Role of the World Bank," accessed October 5, 2015, http://www1.worldbank.org/publicsector/anticorrupt/corruptn/cor02.htm.

12. Other Risks in Frontier Markets

1. Choate, Hall & Stewart LLP, "Quantitative Tools of Asset Allocation: Inflation," accessed March 11, 2014, http://www.choateinvestmentadvisors.com/uploads/103/doc /Stochastic%20Determinants%20CPI0.pdf.

2. Steve H. Hanke and Alex KF Kwok, "On the Measurement of Zimbabwe's Hyper-inflation," *Cato J.* 29 (2009): 353.

3. "Stop playing games, and let's be reasonable about this."

4. Goldman Sachs Global Investment Research, "The World Cup and Economics," May 2014, 9.

5. "Garment Exports Show Resilience," *Daily Star*, April 23, 2014, http://www. thedailystar.net/garment-exports-show-resilience-21162.

6. "GW to Outsource Management of $1.375 Billion Endowment," *Washington Times*, March 13, 2014, http://www.washingtontimes.com/news/2014/mar/13/gw-to -outsource-management-of-1375-billion-endowme/.

7. "Merrill Lynch Report: Hedge Fund Replication Avoids Headline Risk," August 3, 2007, http://seekingalpha.com/article/43441-merrill-lynch-report-hedge-fund -replication-avoids-headline-risk.

13. Megatrends in Frontier Markets

1. Mthuli Ncube, Charles Leyeka Lufumpa, and Steve Kayizzi-Mugerwa, "The Middle of the Pyramid: Dynamics of the Middle Class in Africa" (African Development Bank, April 20, 2011), 1.

2. Knight Frank, The Wealth Report 2015, www.knightfrank.com/wealthreport.

3. Rwanda banking penetration data from Renaissance Capital.

4. "Mozambique Country Mining Guide" (KPMG International, 2013), 15; "Mozambique's Coal Sector Still Embattled, but Bottlenecks Should Soon Go," *Mining Weekly*,

accessed December 7, 2015, http://www.miningweekly.com/article/mozambiques-coal
-sector-still-embattled-but-bottlenecks-should-soon-go-2015-10-16-1.

5. Michael Alsford and David Byrne, "European E&P Highlights: Weathering the
Storm—Low Cost Curve Position Remains Key" (Citi Research, December 1, 2014), 9.

14. Frontiers of Frontier Markets Investing

1. "BP Statistical Review of World Energy June 2014," June 2014.

INDEX